Contents

Illustrations

Foreword

Bess of Hardwick, quite simply, was a remarkable person who lived in a most remarkable time and place. That place was England during the late Tudor period, principally the reign of Queen Elizabeth the First, and the opening years of the Jacobean period. Born a daughter of a relatively humble Midlands family with some modest claims to local gentry status, she was destined during her lifetime to marry and be widowed four times, on each occasion raising her social status until she ultimately became the Countess of Shrewsbury. An enthusiast of fine buildings, she inspired the creation of several of the greatest of the Elizabethan prodigy houses, including of course Hardwick Hall, to which her name and reputation are so prominently linked. However, as well as creations of wood, glass, lead, stone, bricks and mortar, she also left important genetic legacies in the form of her descendants. Bess is an ancestress of much of the British aristocracy for the last few hundred years (including members of the British Royal Family) and her descendants were eventually to lay claim to numerous dukedoms, including those of Devonshire, Portland, Rutland and Newcastle-upon-Tyne, as well as many other lesser titles in the peerage. Indeed, Bess herself might well have lived to see her granddaughter Arbella proclaimed Queen of England had not the Crown been successfully (and speedily) passed to King James the First (King James VI of Scotland) upon Queen Elizabeth's death. Arbella's hereditary claim to the English throne was in the eyes of many of her contemporaries nearly equal to that of King James, and she had the advantage of having been born English, which was an important consideration to many – though given Arbella's character, it seems safe to conclude that had she attained the throne, Arbella would have fallen short of proving to be another Gloriana.[1]

---

[1] Edmund Spenser gave Queen Elizabeth the name Gloriana in his work *The Faerie Queen*.

But there was far more to Bess than the simple building of dynasties and great houses. Though certainly not illiterate, she had relatively little formal schooling, was not descended from a particularly wealthy or influential family and much of the wealth that the family did possess was lost during her early childhood upon the death of her father. Nevertheless, whilst she lived at a time when the laws and customs of the land made it difficult for women to exercise any real form of economic or social independence beyond that dictated by fathers, husbands, brothers or other male relatives, Bess succeeded in acquiring a personal fortune which not only made her the second wealthiest woman in the kingdom after Queen Elizabeth herself, but for generations after her served as the financial bedrock upon which her descendants would continue to build, in some cases right up to the present day. Here, it is worth noting that popular myth ascribes the accumulation of Bess's wealth to the fact that she was widowed four times, with each husband in turn richer than his predecessor, and that she owed her fortune to the simple process of inheriting each husband's riches when he died. There is some truth to this, in that she did (eventually, and not without some troubles along the way) acquire what proved to be substantial wealth from each of her last three husbands. Bess did not however spend her long life passively waiting for a series of inheritances to enrich her. She was, or at least became, a shrewd businesswoman in her own right, steadily enriching herself (and other family members) through the careful husbanding of her financial resources and revenues and the reinvestment of her profits. Moreover, she was forced on several occasions to defend herself and her wealth in the courts against generally spurious claims brought not only by what we would today call her business rivals, but also by avaricious in-laws and other family members, including most notably her fourth husband, the Sixth Earl of Shrewsbury, from whom she was estranged for much of the second half of their marriage.

With the exception of Queen Elizabeth herself, no other woman of her time (indeed, few other people of any time) could lay claim to anything like the range of accomplishments that Bess could (and did) point to with legitimate pride as she approached the end of her life in 1608. The story of her life, if it were to be presented as a work of fiction, would for many people seem too far-fetched to be readily believable, and yet the tales of how her triumphs and achievements, and even occasional defeats, came about are firmly rooted in fact and hold a fascination for many of us today. And that story begins, as did Bess's life, in the wilds of the English county of Derbyshire, in the third decade of the sixteenth century.

Chapter 1

Beginnings

Bess's life story begins, for us, with a mystery, for we do not know exactly when she was born. Though there is some evidence that she may have been born as early as 1521, many (though not all) of her biographers incline to the view that it is likely she was born sometime between June and November in the year of 1527,[1] during the reign of King Henry VIII, but the exact date, for the moment at least, is lost to us. We do know that she was born into a Derbyshire farming family, the Hardwicks, originally perhaps of yeoman rank, a family which had been quietly and slowly prospering for a number of generations and which could, by the time of Bess's birth, probably claim to have gained at least a tenuous entry into the lower ranks of the lesser gentry. That was an important achievement at a time and place when social rules and distinctions between classes were taken seriously and when rank and perceived status could significantly dictate the opportunities available to a person as they passed through life. As members of the lesser gentry, albeit relatively poor and undistinguished, the Hardwicks were generally seen as ranking a step or so above those of their neighbours who only retained yeoman status (itself an important rank at the time). As a result, not only were they treated as having some importance within their immediate locality, but they also were able to establish, and crucially maintain links with other, more important but more distant families, such as the baronial la Zouche family, to whom the Hardwicks were distantly related. Such links were in time to prove to be of vital importance to Bess.

Bess's father John, born in 1495, inherited the family farm just outside Ault Hucknall in Derbyshire in 1507 when his father died at the early age of 37. Despite his youth (he could hardly have been more than

---

[1] An assumption made in this book. See Appendix 1.

1

twelve years old when his father died) and in an interesting contrast to the treatment meted out to his estate and heirs when he himself died young, John appears to have been able first to claim and then successfully work his inheritance. For a while, he even prospered after a fashion, ultimately farming around 600 acres of land and marrying Elizabeth Leake, who came from a respectable local family, sometime around 1520. Before long, they had children together, and he seems to have felt financially comfortable enough to begin making modest alterations to the family home, apparently intent on slowly changing what had originally been a simple farmhouse into a more substantial manor house.

Assuming she was born in 1527, Bess would have been the couple's sixth surviving child (and fifth daughter), being preceded by two elder sisters that we know of (Mary and Jane), two others about whom we know very little and presumably died young (one of them may have been called Dorothy), and a single brother James, born in June 1526 and who was heir to the family estate. For the first few months of Bess's life, all seemed well and by January 1528, Elizabeth was pregnant once again, this time with Bess's younger sister Alice. But then disaster struck the family – John was taken ill at the beginning of January 1528 and was forced to take to his bed. The exact nature of his illness is unknown, but it was serious enough for him to make plans for his funeral, and hurriedly to seek advice as regards the disposition of his estate. Such advice was vital because if John were to die whilst his heir was underage the financial future of the Hardwick family would suddenly be under threat.

The dangers facing the family because of John's prospective death (which happened on 24th January 1528) arose primarily due to the way the law at the time governed land ownership and the disposition of an estate when the principal heir was underage. Strictly speaking, an underage male heir (meaning under the age of 21[2]) could not legally inherit land absolutely, and a system known as "wardship" had developed over time. The original intention of this was to protect the interests of an underage heir until he came of age, whilst at the same time ensuring that the land remained productive and the Crown's rights in relation to the landholding (for example, the right to claim the services of a specified number of armed knights supported by the estate during times of conflict) were respected. This was usually done by making the heir a ward of the Crown, with the Crown assuming responsibility for the operation of the estate until the heir was old enough to shoulder the legal and practical burdens himself. Often the Crown assigned the estate to the temporary care of another wealthy local landowner for the duration of the wardship. Initially, during the early feudal period, although not universally loved, the system had at least worked reasonably well, but it began increasingly to be viewed as archaic as society generally started to evolve away from its feudal roots and particularly once it became clear that the invention and use of gunpowder on fields of battle meant that the days of the supremacy of traditionally mounted knights were numbered. Moreover, and unsurprisingly, the system of wardship was generally unpopular with the families of the underage heirs, and by the start of the Tudor period with the reign of Henry VII, enterprising lawyers had found various mechanisms involving what we would today term "trusts" which could at least sometimes fend off the powers of the Office of Wards,[3] and retain control of the family estates within the families themselves. It was through such a system of trusteeships that John Hardwick, whilst underage, had been able to claim ownership of the farm at Hardwick when his father died in 1507.

---

[2] The wardship system also applied to females under the age of sixteen, but even if a female was aged over sixteen, there were other restrictions on the ability of females, especially married females, to own land outright.

[3] In the early 1540s, the Office of Wards would be reorganised and become known as the Court of Wards and Liveries.

The Office of Wards may have become nearly moribund by the time Henry VII assumed the throne in 1485, but the laws of the land underpinning its existence remained in force. As part of his series of reforms of the machinery of government generally (which led to England and Wales developing one of the most efficient governments in Europe at the time) and with a particular eye to increasing the revenue of the Crown without needing to call upon Parliament, Henry VII revived and updated the Office of Wards, breathing new life into the antiquated wardship procedure. Henry VIII in turn made further changes to the system, requiring that all estates in cases where there was an underage male heir[4] should be subject to administration by the Office of Wards, and either run by that Office, or (and this was the more common option) auctioned to the highest bidder for the duration of the wardship, with the auction proceeds being passed directly to the Crown. Sometimes of course, it might be the bereaved family itself (or close friends) who offered the highest bid, and by doing so they essentially retained the right to continue to administer their own family land. More often than not though, the successful bidder was no more than an unprincipled speculator, with no connection or loyalty to the family, and eager only to extract as much value from the estate as he could before it reverted to the true heir once he became of age.

This was the fate that John Hardwick hoped to evade for his own lands as he lay dying during the cold days and nights of January 1528 – on 6th January he purported to give his lands as a gift to eight "feoffees" (as trustees were known in those days), whose number included his brother Roger and other close relatives and friends. The gift of his lands was to be for a term of 20 years, after which they were to revert to his son James. Three days later, he made his will, which made mention of the "gift" but did not attempt to dispose of the lands itself, not least because it was

---

[4] Or no male heir at all, for instance where there was only an underage daughter to inherit. When this happened, it was not unknown for a successful bidder for a wardship to find ways of compelling the female ward to marry a male member of his own family, thus ensuring the land subject to the wardship would eventually become the legal property of his family.

essential, if this plan was to have any chance of succeeding at all, for the lands to have passed to the eight feoffees before John had drawn his last breath so that they did not form part of his estate and thus prove vulnerable to the attentions of the Office of Wards.

And so John died, and matters rested for a few months as John's family and friends dealt with their grief and funeral duties whilst continuing as best they could to continue to administer the Hardwick lands. Then, on 2nd October 1528, as was customary upon the death of a substantial landowner, an official enquiry known as an Inquisition Post Mortem was held in relation to the death of John Hardwick, the purpose of the enquiry being to establish whether or not the lands held by the deceased had properly and legally been passed to legitimate new owners, and whether rights in relation to such lands, for example, a widow's rights to claim some of the income generated by such lands as dower payments, and any rights of the Crown, were being honoured as they should have been. In the case of the disposal of the Hardwick lands, after listening to the testimonies of relevant witnesses and examining pertinent documents, the Inquisition Post Mortem identified no issues to concern the authorities; the transfer of the Hardwick lands to the feoffees shortly before John's death was accepted as legitimate and the enquiry into the affairs of the Hardwick estate was concluded.

Or so everyone thought. Unfortunately, back in London, Henry VIII's wars and general extravagance were rapidly depleting the Royal Treasury, and the King's servants were being placed under even greater pressure to generate income for the Crown. One result of this was that the Feodary of the Office of Wards – essentially the Office's "watchdog" – took even greater pains to identify cases where it was suspected that evasions of the wardship system were being attempted, and the eye of one eager clerk working for the Feodary must have alighted on the papers relating to the case of John Hardwick and found them wanting. Exactly who that clerk was, and what first stirred his suspicions we do not know, but the result was that following further investigation, the Office of Wards called for a second enquiry which finally convened in early September 1530. The enquiry was to be led by three commissioners, two of whom, John Vernon (whose family held nearby Haddon Hall) and Anthony Babington (a local landowner who had become the MP for Nottingham the previous year[5]) were old family friends of the Hardwicks. The third commissioner was John Gyfford, a prominent Staffordshire landowner.

This time, even allowing for the ties of family friendships, there was little chance of the enquiry's commissioners accepting the fiction of the transfer of lands to feoffees for a period just long enough to allow the heir James to come of age. Key to this conclusion was the fact that it was discovered that when purportedly making the gift of his lands to his feoffees, John had omitted to do so by deed,[6] rendering (the commission of enquiry declared) the entire purported transfer of lands to the feoffees invalid. Consequently, the commissioners had no option but to declare that the lands had passed to the infant James when John Hardwick died, thus justifying the intervention of the Office of Wards.

Once again, we do not know the detailed machinations that must have occurred as a result of the Office of Wards taking control of the Hardwick lands. We do know that Elizabeth Hardwick managed to establish, to the satisfaction of the commissioners, that she had a lifetime interest in the income deriving from one-third of the lands – this being deemed to constitute her "widow's dower" - and thus (provided Elizabeth lived long enough) James's inheritance of this portion of the estate was, at least for the moment, secure. We also know that the Hardwick family appear not to have had the financial resources to allow

---

[5] His great grandson who had the same Christian name would in due course be executed for conspiring with Mary, Queen of Scots to murder Queen Elizabeth as part of the "Babington Plot".

[6] Probably because under the emotional stresses suffered by all the participants in the affair at that time, the need for a deed was not identified, and anyway, there was insufficient time to permit the family to gain sober legal advice on the point before John died. It also didn't help the Hardwicks' case that Roger Hardwick, John's brother, who as one of the leading feoffees might have been expected to be a principal witness in favour of the family, himself died in the spring of 1530, which complicated matters considerably.

them to purchase a wardship over the rest of the Hardwick estate themselves, or at least that they failed to do so. Instead (and this may be an example of the commissioners wishing to be kind to one of their neighbours during a time of trouble), a wardship was declared over only half of the remaining estate. This was promptly snapped up by a Chancery clerk called John Bugby, who held the court post of "Officer of the Pantry". He had been assisting with the day-to-day administration of the enquiry, and clearly recognised a bargain when he saw it. The remaining portion of the Hardwick lands was retained by the Crown itself and rented back to Elizabeth Hardwick. The Hardwick family thus effectively retained control of two-thirds of the lands that had been farmed by John; nevertheless, the result was that the net family income had been substantially reduced, and Elizabeth, like many other widows before her and since, had no choice but to reduce her household's expenditure whilst at the same time seeking alternative sources of income.

We can imagine Elizabeth took whatever steps she could to minimise the costs of running her farm and household. No doubt there was considerable emphasis on making do and repairing old but still potentially serviceable household items such as clothes, pots, plate and furniture, and the farm's produce could at least be relied upon to ensure that the Hardwick family and such servants as they could retain were adequately, if not very excitingly nourished. Seeking additional income however was easier said than done. With a young family depending on her, and the responsibility of running the portion of the Hardwick farm which the family had been permitted to retain, there was no question of Elizabeth going out to work, even if such a course of action had been socially acceptable. In practice, the only real option available to Elizabeth was to marry again, but given her family circumstances, there was little chance of her being swept away by a wealthy landowner, no matter how personable she herself might have been. She did in fact eventually marry (exactly when we do not know), but her second husband, Ralph Leche, was only a younger son of another local landowning family based at Chatsworth about 20 miles from Hardwick, with relatively little wealth of his own, and very little prospect of acquiring much more in the foreseeable future. Still, he was capable of taking on the management of the Hardwick farm and in this regard at least was able to provide Elizabeth with some respite from her exertions to support her family. They soon had three children together, Elizabeth, Jane and Margaret, who were thus half-sisters to Bess and James and their sisters.

The records are silent as to how Bess and her siblings and half-siblings spent the next few years; it is generally assumed they all lived on the family farm. Throughout her life, Bess remained on close friendly terms with her sisters and half-sisters, and by and large, allowing for occasional feelings of exasperation, also with her brother. Therefore, it seems likely that Bess's childhood family life, at least once her mother had remarried, was happy enough.[7] We know that both Bess and James (and presumably, the other children) received a reasonable education by the standards of the day; both Bess and James were literate although exactly where they received their education is unknown. Probably they received much of it at home from their mother, who we may speculate also taught the girls at least the rudiments of the household skills they would need when running their own family homes one day. Religious instruction would have been received both at home and in the local church from the incumbent. This was the time when at the behest of King Henry VIII, the Church in England was beginning to break free from the might of the Roman Catholic Church. The commencement of the dissolution of the monasteries was imminent, but while religious disputes and troubles were causing social and political convulsions across Europe, there is no real evidence that such matters troubled the

---

[7] Though it is unclear exactly how Bess regarded her stepfather - he seems to have been or became financially unreliable, being imprisoned for debt in 1538 and again in 1544, before dying that same year, and on at least one occasion, Elizabeth complained that he had deserted her and the children. This must have created at least some degree of financial unease over the whole family, and there has been speculation that this may have been a factor which led Bess to being unusually determined to secure her own financial future.

Hardwick family, who seem to have accepted the new religious order without difficulties. Indeed, throughout her life, Bess had no problem in accepting the basic principles of the reformed religion, and there was no question at all of her having any genuine sympathy for the "old" version.

In any event, practical household skills and a modern religious outlook were to be of more immediate importance to Bess. Many biographers of Bess recite (though with little documented evidence in support) that when Bess was twelve, it was decided that she should be sent "into service" in the household of the Hardwick's distant kinsmen, the la Zouche family. Assuming this is true,[8] it is important to stress at the outset that this does not mean that Bess would have been hired as a humble servant. Quite the contrary; it was common practice at the time (and would be for at least the next half century, and possibly longer) for the children of gentry and even some of the lesser noble families, both boys and girls, to be sent to live in the households of great noble families where they could become familiar with the social etiquette of the nobility, and learn at least some aspects of the courtly graces and the sound and practical household management skills which they would be

---

[8] The principal evidence in support of the argument that Bess spent time in service with the la Zouche household comes from a manuscript prepared by the Yorkshire antiquarian Nathaniel Johnson. The problem is that Johnson was writing 150 years or so after the event, and moreover, his account contains some known inaccuracies. For instance, he refers to the meeting of Bess with her first husband Robert Barlow and recites that when he died, he settled "… large inheritances of lands …" on Bess. He didn't. If Johnson is incorrect about Bess's service in the la Zouche household, it is unclear where Bess was during those years of her supposed service; presumably she remained at Hardwick. On the other hand, Bess clearly must have had some training in courtly etiquette, as she would demonstrate within a few years, most notably in relation to her marriage to Sir William Cavendish (he wouldn't have wished to marry a simple unpolished Derbyshire country girl) and of course her future dealings and friendship with Lady Frances Grey (né Brandon). It is difficult to see where Bess might have acquired knowledge of appropriate etiquette if she hadn't been in service with some noble family when young, and the most likely contender is the la Zouche family.

expected to have mastered by the time they grew up. Such children were often treated as members of the host household, and grew up alongside the children of their hosts, with whom they often formed strong friendships which could last lifetimes. (One follower of this practice was William Cecil, Lord Burghley who became Queen Elizabeth's Lord High Treasurer, and who over the years welcomed dozens of young noblemen under his roof for the sake of their educational development and the possible creation of future political alliances. Alas many of them, when they grew up, identified with anti-Cecil factions at Court and generally became quite a nuisance to Burghley and later to his son Robert, who in due course would succeed his father as the Queen's principal adviser.)

Such places in rich men's houses were eagerly sought, and Elizabeth and Ralph Leche would no doubt generally have been considered to have done well in securing a place for Bess in the la Zouche household (assuming of course that they indeed did so), even allowing for the kinship between the two families.

The la Zouche family was one of the more impressive noble families of the Midlands at that time. With an ancestry which they could trace back to early Norman times, the family, in various guises, held important lands and posts throughout the Midlands for much of the Medieval and Tudor periods, and the Lady Zouche of Bess's time (born Anne Gainsford) had herself served as lady-in-waiting to both Anne Boleyn (before and after she became Queen) and later to Jane Seymour, until Jane had died following the birth of the baby who would become King Edward VI. The family thus had important connections with the Court and with other powerful families throughout the land. Working in the la Zouche household during these early years would have involved Bess making occasional trips to London and elsewhere and these would have been the first real opportunities Bess had of observing true power and political pomp, and of interacting with influential people. She would have soaked up the lessons of what she saw and heard, and they would prove useful in later life, but her days as a member of the la Zouche household (assuming she was) were to be relatively few, for some time during the winter of 1542 or the early spring of 1543, Bess found herself betrothed and then married to her first husband, Robert Barlow[9] who was a son of yet another of the Hardwicks' landowning neighbours.

Again, we don't exactly know how Bess and Robert came to know each other, though they may have met when Robert was visiting the la Zouche family – Nathaniel Johnson recites a story of Bess nursing him through a brief illness whilst she was attending Lady Zouche in London. Alternatively, as the Hardwicks and Barlows were neighbours, even distantly related, they might have met back in Derbyshire. Nor do we know exactly how they came to be betrothed, though in court papers relating to a subsequent lawsuit brought by Bess to claim her dower rights after Robert's death, Bess says that Robert's father contacted Elizabeth and Ralph Leche in order to promote the marriage. That they were young we do know – assuming Bess was born sometime in 1527, she would have been in her sixteenth year (she was described in the later court papers as having been of "tender years" when she first married, which generally signified being under sixteen) and Robert a little younger, probably around thirteen and a half - and we also know that Robert's father, Arthur, may well have been sick when they married, for he died on 28th May 1543, seemingly only a few weeks after the wedding took place. It may be that the marriage represented both a means of strengthening relations between two local landowning families as well as between two young people who felt warmly for one another, and (given that if Arthur were to die whilst Robert was still a minor, the Office of Wards would intervene to seize the Barlow lands) a measure taken to avoid the possibility of a purchaser of the wardship somehow forcing Robert to marry someone to the benefit of his family rather than the Barlows.

In due course the Office of Wards did establish a wardship over the Barlow estate. Fortunately, a distant (but apparently kindly) relative of

---

[9] Some sources give the surname as "Barley" and certainly Robert's father Arthur was known by this surname.

the family, named Godfrey Boswell (who in due course would marry Bess's sister Jane and hence become Bess's brother-in-law), was able to buy the wardship, keep the lands intact and for a time protect them from being destroyed by greedy speculators.

Following Arthur's death, Bess and Robert enjoyed about 20 months or so of married life, presumably together, though where they spent that time is unclear - it may have been with Robert's widowed mother. Then tragedy once again struck, for Robert was taken ill in late 1544, and he died on 24th December 1544. For the first time in her life, at the age of seventeen, Bess was a widow, Godfrey Boswell's wardship over the Barlow lands terminated (Robert's heir to the lands being his younger brother George who was barely twelve years old) and the Office of Wards once again seized control of the estate and in due course sold it to another local landowner called Sir Peter Frencheville. On this occasion however, Bess, as Robert's widow, was entitled to one third of the land's income as her dower rights and she (almost certainly with assistance from her mother Elizabeth, for whom the process was no doubt horribly familiar, and whose own husband was then undergoing a period of imprisonment for debt) claimed those rights from Sir Peter. Sir Peter at first resisted, compelling Bess to launch a claim through the courts. Tudor legal cases could last for years, and Bess was still fighting for her dower rights in October 1546 when finally, she obtained a court ruling that she was entitled to a life interest over approximately one-third of the Barlow estate, though legal squabblings with Sir Peter over the exact nature of those rights would continue for several years more. With the estate being primarily based in rural Derbyshire, this was not as valuable an award as might be thought, but it did mean that Bess was now entitled to claim an annual income of approximately £30 a year from the Barlow lands for the rest of her life. £30 a year was not a significant sum even then (equal to about £18,000 today) but it was better than nothing, and meant that for the first time, Bess could claim money that was hers as of right, without having to depend ultimately upon the charity of others. It offered Bess therefore, at least a hint of financial independence, and that income, together with her new status as a widow, raised her social standing in Tudor society to a considerable extent. No one who now encountered her would consider her a child. Aged nineteen by the time she successfully claimed her dower rights, despite her youthfulness, she was now to all intents and purposes an adult, possessing of at least some means, and entitled to be treated accordingly. The question now facing Bess was what she would do next.

Chapter 2

Lady Cavendish

In truth, we are not sure what she did next; the historical record is not clear. Many accounts assume (though again with little hard evidence) that she once more entered the household of a noble family with whom the Hardwicks had links of kinship. This time the household is thought to have been that of Lady Frances Grey, the niece of Henry VIII, and wife of Henry Grey, then the Marquess of Dorset, which was again based in the English Midlands, at Bradgate Park in Leicestershire. Lady Frances was the daughter of Princess Mary, the King's younger (and favourite) sister who, for a short period, had been the Queen of France by virtue of her marriage to King Louis XII. Her father was Charles Brandon, the Duke of Suffolk. Lady Frances could also claim kinship to the Royal House of Scotland; her aunt Margaret Tudor (sister of Henry VIII and Princess Mary) had been married to King James IV of Scotland.

There are two main reasons why historians make the assumption that Bess joined the Grey household. First, Bess in the years to come would prove to be a close friend of Lady Frances[1] and indeed appears to have been popular with the entire Grey household, which included Lady Frances' daughters, Jane, Katherine and Mary. The friendship between Bess and Lady Frances must have started around this time, if not before, and it would seem logical that as a consequence of her first widowhood, Bess would have sought safety and position in the household of a family such as the Greys to whom she was distantly related. What is intriguing (assuming Bess did indeed spend her time following Robert Barlow's death with the Grey household) is the fact that the Greys were

---

[1] This was not necessarily an easy achievement. Lady Frances had a reputation, which grew worse as the years passed, of being acutely aware of her various royal connections and, as a consequence, of being difficult, sometimes to the point of explicit cruelty, to those she considered to be her inferiors. Some have suggested that this may have extended to her own daughters.

apparently willing to accept such a distant cousin into their household and family circle. After all, the Greys by virtue of their wealth and royal connections ranked at the pinnacle of Tudor society, considerably higher in fact than the la Zouche family had ever managed or would ever manage to achieve. In joining the Greys at Bradgate Park, Bess would indeed have been at least glimpsing the world of the true Tudor elite. Entering that world as an accepted member was not something that was easy to do, especially for someone without wealth or influence, and yet this is exactly what Bess would achieve, if not immediately following Robert Barlow's death, then shortly thereafter. And this brings us to the second reason why many historians accept the theory that Bess spent time with the Grey household, because at some time before the summer of 1547, Bess met and became engaged to Sir William Cavendish, a rising star of the Tudor Court. It is not easy to see how she might have met Sir William, except within the bounds of a household such as that of the Greys, to whom Sir William was a potentially useful political ally. Adding support to the theory is the fact that at least one other member of the Cavendish family – perhaps one of William's cousins - was also attached to the Grey household at around this time.

In any event, Bess and Sir William did meet, and they must soon have developed feelings for one another, for they became engaged and were married at Bradgate Park at two o'clock in the morning of 20th August 1547. Sir William recorded the event in a family notebook:

> *Memorandum: That I was marryed unto Elizabeth Hardwick, my third wyffe, in Lecestersheere, at Broadgat, my Lord Marquesse's House the 20th of August, in the first Yeare of Kinge Edward the 6. at 2 of the Clock after Midnight, the domynical Letter B.*

Exactly why the event took place at Bradgate Park and not the Hardwick's family home is not known; it may well have been that Bradgate Park was chosen to emphasise the links between the couple who were to be married and the Greys, and it may also be that the Hardwick home as it then stood was deemed to be insufficiently grand.

It was after all at this time little more than a large farmhouse. Nor is it obvious why the ceremony had to take place at two o'clock in the morning, which was no more a common time for a marriage ceremony in Tudor times than it would be today. Some biographers have tried to assert some astrological significance for the time and date of the wedding, but such arguments remain unconvincing; it may be that the answer is as simple as some important guests being delayed, but it is unlikely that we shall ever know for sure. Contrary to the assertions of some biographers, the reference to a "domynical letter" was not of astrological significance; rather the dominical letter system was (and is) an archaic dating system developed by the Church (which in turn had acquired it from the Romans) and used as a mathematical device to assist in the calculation and construction of ecclesiastical calendars.

Upon her marriage to Sir William, Bess promptly became known by the courtesy title of Bess, Lady Cavendish and had thus taken a step which again significantly improved her social position as well as her financial security. To cynical eyes, it is harder at first to see similar worldly advantages for Sir William in a marriage to a relatively impoverished and obscure Midlands widow such as Bess.[2] We have no details of their courtship which might shed light upon the matter. What we do know is that events were to prove that not only were Bess and Sir William personally compatible (there is no suggestion that they were anything other than happily devoted to each other and the family they established during their marriage) but also that they functioned well together in the wider social, financial and political worlds that lay outside the family bounds. In particular, Sir William was a well-established servant of the Crown and well placed to significantly increase his family's financial and social standing. Experienced in the ways of the Tudor world, he had important skills he could teach, and in Bess, he in turn had a most apt

---

[2] Save for the obvious point that in marrying Bess, he had married a woman considerably younger than himself; at the time of their marriage Bess was nineteen (or possibly 20) and Sir William was 42 with three surviving daughters from his first marriage.

pupil, eager, willing and probably needing to learn what he had to offer. The results of such lessons were not slow to become apparent. Within a few years of her marriage to Sir William, and notwithstanding her assumption of the role of stepmother to Sir William's daughters by his first wife, and the arrival of children of their own, thanks to Sir William's training and example, Bess began to transform herself from being the wife of a Tudor gentleman, albeit an increasingly important and powerful one, to becoming over time effectively Sir William's informal business partner, upon whose shrewd views and advice he in turn discovered he could depend.

But who was Sir William Cavendish, without whom the story of Bess of Hardwick might very well have been significantly different, and indeed might hardly be worth recounting at all?

He was born (probably) in 1505, in the village of Cavendish in Suffolk, the second son of Thomas Cavendish and his first wife Alice. Thomas too had been a courtier, in due course holding the post of Clerk of the Pipe (effectively clerk to the treasurer of the King's Exchequer) during the earlier portion of the reign of King Henry VIII. This was an important position in the Tudor civil service, but his family also had long enjoyed connections with Suffolk as the name of his home village shows. An important ancestor had been Sir John Cavendish, a lawyer who had risen to become Chief Justice of the King's Bench (and Chancellor of Cambridge University) before becoming embroiled in the suppression of the Peasants' Revolt of 1381; he was murdered during the course of the Revolt by followers of Wat Tyler.

By the time of William's birth, the Cavendishes were well-established as members of the Suffolk gentry with a tradition of Court service. William's elder brother George (who married a niece of Sir Thomas More) typified this service by becoming gentleman usher to Cardinal Wolseley when the Cardinal was at the height of his power. George must have been a man of honour (or perhaps he had just had enough of the dangers and machinations of life at King Henry VIII's Court) for when Wolseley fell from power in 1529, and despite an offer of continued employment from the King himself, George elected to stay with his disgraced former master until the Cardinal's end in 1530. After that, George went home to his estates in Suffolk (his father had died in 1524 and George as his principal heir was now a wealthy man) and he remained there in quiet obscurity for the rest of his life. He is today best remembered as the author of a biography of Cardinal Wolseley, though the biography was only fully published in its original and final form in 1810.

It seems likely that George arranged for his brother William to start his career as a gentleman servant in the household of Cardinal Wolseley when he was in his late teens. Unlike George however, William showed no predilection for loyalty to Wolseley; when that statesman fell from power, William promptly switched his allegiance to Thomas Cromwell, Wolseley's successor, who before long was effectively the second most powerful man in the kingdom after the King himself, and at the centre of affairs of that most turbulent of reigns. It was Thomas Cromwell who found the practical (if not necessarily completely legal, at least to the eyes of the Roman Catholic Church) solution whereby King Henry was able to annul his marriage to Queen Catherine of Aragon, and in her place wed Anne Boleyn, and then later it was Cromwell again (acting on the King's orders) who instigated the Commission that led to Anne Boleyn's downfall and execution. And crucially, from the perspective of William Cavendish at least, it was Cromwell who initiated and masterminded the plan to restore the financial solvency of the Crown by dissolving monasteries and seizing their assets.

The dissolution of the monasteries represented a major opportunity for William, for he was one of the men tasked by Cromwell to travel round the country investigating various monasteries and other religious institutions, making recommendations as to how they should be treated, and in some cases, supervising their seizures. As early as 1530, he supervised the surrender to the Crown of various important properties and other land owned by the Priory of Sheen, near Richmond, which was a precursor to its dissolution in 1539. Then in 1532, William Cavendish was ordered to turn his attentions to the Abbey of St Albans.

During the Medieval centuries preceding the Tudor era, the Benedictine Abbey at St Albans had been one of the country's leading religious institutions, dominating the town of St Albans itself and the surrounding countryside. For much of the Medieval period, it had been wealthy, possessing major properties not only in Hertfordshire but also throughout the country, but as the sixteenth century dawned, the Abbey began to suffer a decline, as exemplified by the fact that St Albans town began to break free of the Abbey's dominance, with the townsfolk gaining control of important civic posts, such as those of the town bailiff and the clerk of the market, offices which had previously been at the disposal of the Abbot. At about the same time, principally due to a mismanagement of assets in the changing Tudor world, and despite the Abbey continuing to own significant amounts of land, the Abbey's income began to fall, so that by 1519, the Abbey had slipped into debt. The appointment in succession of three weak Abbots after 1521[3] further hastened the Abbey's decline. By the early 1530s, St Albans Abbey was little more than a shadow of its former self so far as its worldly power was concerned (the nearby nunnery of Sopwell was similarly afflicted) and unsurprisingly, the Abbey caught the eye of Thomas Cromwell. In 1532, he despatched William Cavendish to visit the Abbey to assess the situation and to take an audit of its possessions. William, by all accounts, carried out a sterling job, at least so far as the interests of the King were concerned, though he apparently found at least some of the monks of the Abbey to be "very obstinate". Cromwell must have approved of his work for with his connivance, in 1534, William Cavendish was able to extract from the Abbot of St Albans for his personal benefit, and on (to him) extremely beneficial terms a long leasehold of lands in and around the village of Northaw situated near the Hertfordshire/Middlesex border, including the local manor house. He (and his first wife

---

[3] The first of whom was Cardinal Wolseley, who held the post until his fall from power. Apart from an overnight stay in 1529, he bothered himself little with the Abbey's day-to-day affairs save for what income could be extracted from his appointment. The Abbey suffered from his lack of leadership.

Margaret) later received as an outright grant the freeholds of those lands and the manor house.

William received a significant promotion in May 1536 when he was appointed one of the ten auditors of the newly established Court of Augmentations, which had been created on the recommendation of Thomas Cromwell to supervise the sale of properties seized from the Church. Significantly, William Cavendish's salary for carrying out his duties as auditor was to be £20 per year together with "the profits of office". For William Cavendish (and indeed, the other auditors) this was a golden opportunity to make a personal fortune, and unsurprisingly, William seized it with both hands. Working with a fellow auditor, Dr Thomas Leigh, William's areas of responsibility covered the counties of Bedfordshire, Berkshire, Buckinghamshire, Kent, Oxfordshire, Surrey and Sussex, and he and Leigh were soon roving back and forth across these counties (and sometimes even further afield) assessing the values of all sorts of religious establishments and accepting their "submissions" to the King's mercy. This generally meant pensioning off or otherwise bribing such monks or other religious persons who were still occupying the premises and then arranging for the properties to be transferred to the Crown, which then usually sold them off as rapidly and as profitably as possible. During these tours, William did not hesitate to snap up for himself bargains of land here and there, and in doing so, he was not generally considered to be doing anything wrong. His appointment, after all, had specified he was entitled to the profits of his office. The rate at which he was capable of dissolving religious establishments is astonishing; it has been estimated that in 1537, when the dissolution process was at its peak, he was responsible for supervising up to ten dissolutions a month.

By 1539, William Cavendish had, one way or another, acquired significant landholdings in Hertfordshire, Norfolk, Lincolnshire, Suffolk, Cardiganshire and elsewhere and was by the measures of the day a rich man. He was also a family man; he and his wife Margaret had by now three surviving children (all girls – Catherine, Mary and

Margaret,[4] and they were joined in 1540 by another daughter, Ann). However, Margaret Cavendish died in June 1540, and to compound William's troubles, Thomas Cromwell's political luck had finally run its course. Cromwell was blamed for the diplomatic farce that led to Henry VIII marrying Anne of Cleves, rapidly condemned to death, and beheaded on Tower Hill in July 1540. No doubt there was no shortage of people who considered Cromwell's fall from grace and execution to be no more than he deserved. William Cavendish's views on the matter are not known but given it was hardly a secret that he had worked closely with Cromwell for a number of years, he probably considered the wisest course of action right then was to keep a low profile. In fact, he seems to have escaped any form of censure following Cromwell's downfall; instead, later in 1540 he was ordered to Ireland as one of three Crown commissioners appointed to survey and value newly acquired Crown lands as well as to investigate reports of corruption and mismanagement in relation to the King's army stationed there. He ultimately stayed thirteen months in Ireland, and on his return was generally regarded by the King and the Privy Council as having done a good job.

Once back in England, William found time to court and, in November of 1542, to marry at Blackfriars in London, his second wife, Elizabeth Parris, who was a widow.[5] She and William had three children together, none of whom survived early infancy, and then Elizabeth herself died in 1546. William once more found himself a widower with dependent children.

Notwithstanding this personal tragedy, his career continued to prosper. A few months before Elizabeth's death, King Henry had appointed him Treasurer of the Chamber, an important office, and for William, an

---

[4] Though William's daughter Margaret died in the same year as her mother and Mary for reasons that are not entirely clear appears not to have lived with her family, at least not after William married Bess, and may well have died in her late teens.

[5] She had been widowed twice.

expensive one, for the King's price for consenting to his appointment was £1000, an immense sum at that time, equal to about £700,000 today. William "borrowed" the money to pay the King from the Treasury itself on the understanding that he would repay it from payments he would himself receive in return for favours granted to others following his appointment. Such were the standards of Tudor public life that this was generally accepted as perfectly proper behaviour. Certainly, the King appeared to think so, for shortly thereafter William was appointed to the Privy Council, and on Easter Sunday of 1546, he received a knighthood. He was now officially recognised as an important and influential man in the machinery of the Tudor Court and government, and when Henry VIII died in January 1547, to be succeeded by the young and frail Edward VI, it is unlikely that anyone was surprised that Sir William was speedily reappointed as Treasurer. For Sir William himself, now effectively at the pinnacle of his career, perhaps the only blemishes in his life that he could then see were the need to provide a caring stepmother for his daughters, and the need to have a son as his heir. And in his marriage to Bess, he found a most satisfactory solution to both of these problems.

Chapter 3

Buying Chatsworth

Bess rapidly settled into her new role as Lady Cavendish, assuming responsibility for the running of the family household, which was then largely centred on the manor house at Northaw, and a house on Newgate Street in London, which the Cavendishes rented from the Marquess of Northampton. This was almost certainly the first time that Bess had taken charge of her own establishment – there is no evidence that she did so during her brief marriage to Robert Barlow. Nevertheless, despite initial inexperience, Bess rose to the challenge of claiming and ordering her own establishment as if she had been doing so all her life. Now a lady of consequence, she had at least two "gentlewomen" to assist her in domestic matters, essentially acting as ladies-in-waiting, one of them being her own younger half-sister Jane Kniveton (born Jane Leche), who was paid a wage of £3 per annum.[1] There were also at least fifteen other servants of various descriptions. Domestic affairs would have kept Bess and her servants busy; there were the usual housekeeping duties, which would have involved not only the making of a steady stream of purchases of various items, but also where and when possible, the gathering, preserving and dispensing of all types of produce from the various Cavendish estates scattered across the country, and ensuring that they were available as needed wherever the family was gathered.

The importance of such duties would have been exacerbated by the fact that the Cavendishes entertained regularly, and moreover at least when in London were frequently entertaining people of consequence such as the Greys and other members of the Tudor elite. With much of Sir William's time taken up by the duties of his office, ensuring such

---

[1] The employment of indigent or otherwise unattached or unoccupied family members (especially female family members) in this fashion in the households of the wealthy was not unusual at this time.

occasions proceeded smoothly and in a way that gave credit to the Cavendish family fell squarely on Bess's shoulders, but she appears to have borne the responsibility easily.

Before long, Bess was also assisting Sir William in the completion of the household accounts, which included not only keeping track of and collecting rents due on the various properties William had contrived to acquire over the previous ten years or so, but also where possible seeking to increase the family income. Sometimes these activities caused controversy and even legal actions; Northaw Manor for instance was being poorly run when it was first acquired by Sir William, and when time permitted, he was now attempting to improve the estate by various means, such as reclaiming wasteland for farm use. Unfortunately for the local tenantry, Sir William was also attempting to enclose for his own use common land at Northaw, to the detriment of the villagers who traditionally had enjoyed free grazing rights over that land. Enclosure of common land was to prove a problem in rural areas across the country for centuries, and Sir William was not unique in his efforts in seeking to implement it. What was relatively unusual in this case was that the local villagers banded together in an attempt to resist Sir William's depredations, initially ripping down newly erected fences and then at Pentecost of 1548, assaulting several of Sir William's servants, including his surveyor and his chaplain. The law intervened, and several of the villagers were brought before the courts and fined; significantly however, the planned enclosure on this occasion at least did not proceed. Bess assumed responsibility for ensuring the payment of her husband's legal costs in relation to the court action (23 shillings and four pennies), and presumably drew her own conclusions from the affair. Though she was certainly not averse to enclosing common lands, and would do so several times in the future,[2] she learned to approach such matters with at least some degree of delicacy and caution, and was never herself responsible for causing local riots.

---

[2] She once ordered an entire village be moved.

24

The family income at this time was substantial, more than £650 a year, about half a million pounds or so a year today. It primarily took the form of rents and annuities, though there were presumably also sums received for "favours rendered" by Sir William in the course of his office which would not necessarily have appeared in the account books. The annual household expenditure of the Cavendishes at that time has been estimated to be of the order of £340, so in that happy time of no income tax, they were in a position to build up rapidly their family's capital reserves. A significant portion of the household expenditure, incidentally, at least whilst the family was in London, took the form of gambling, a popular form of entertainment at the time, and one in which both Sir William and Bess indulged, though he to a considerably greater extent than her. Such expenditure was expected from those who moved in Court circles, but at no time during the years of their marriage did such gambling losses, as they did incur from time to time, (typically of the order of a few pounds a sitting in the case of Sir William, and a few pennies and occasionally shillings in the case of Bess) jeopardise their solvency or their steadily increasing level of wealth.

By all accounts, Bess was a loving stepmother to Sir William's surviving children Catherine and Ann, and the happy family was soon to be expanded for within a few weeks of her marriage, Bess found herself pregnant. The child, a girl whom Sir William and Bess named Frances, was born on 18th June 1548 and Sir William naturally noted the event in his records:

> *Frances, my ninth child, and the first by the said woman was born on Monday between the hours of 3 and 4 at afternoon, viz the 18th June, Anno 2 RE 6. The domynical letter the G.*

The new baby was vigorous and healthy, and her arrival gave Sir William and Bess an opportunity to emphasise the new eminence of the Cavendish family in Tudor society by a careful selection of godparents. Lady Frances Grey (after whom the child was named) agreed to assume the role of senior godmother, but given the close relationship between her and Bess, this was not surprising. What was more unexpected perhaps was that Catherine Brandon, the widowed Duchess of Suffolk (and Lady Frances' stepmother, as Catherine had become Lady Frances' father's fourth wife after the death of Mary Tudor[3]) also agreed to act as godmother. Catherine's son Henry, now the second Duke of Suffolk agreed to act as godfather. Henry himself died on 14th July 1551 of a "sweating fever"; he was succeeded (briefly) by his younger brother Charles who died one hour later of the same disease. The dukedom became extinct, but would subsequently be revived for Henry Grey (Lady Frances' husband – yes, it gets confusing) who became the first Duke of Suffolk of the third creation until he lost his titles (and his life) in 1554 following the attempt to place his daughter Lady Jane Grey on the throne.

Pleasant as it no doubt was to show the world that the Cavendishes were connected to some of the most powerful families in the land, the choice of baby Frances' godparents was not just a matter of pomp and show. At the time of Frances' birth, King Edward VI was in his eleventh year and halfway through the second year of his reign. The country itself was being ruled during Edward's years of minority by a Council of Regency. The Council was made up principally of the executors named in King Henry VIII's will, but at this time, it was dominated by Edward Seymour, uncle to the King, who contrived not only to get himself appointed as Edward's guardian and Lord Protector of the Realm but also had himself created Duke of Somerset. The Greys and the Brandons had links to various members of the Council, and others close to the King, including Seymour's brother Thomas, who had been appointed Lord High Admiral and was married to King Henry's widow Catherine Parr. Such connections helped to cement the social position of the

---

[3] Another example of the operation of the wardship system incidentally, as Catherine's father, Lord Willoughby de Eresby, one of the richest peers in the kingdom had died whilst Catherine was a child of seven. The Crown had claimed wardship over her, and Charles Brandon, Duke of Suffolk (Lady Frances' father) had purchased the wardship. He married Catherine when she was just fourteen in order to keep to keep control of the lands subject to the wardship. Charles Brandon died in August 1545.

Cavendishes as well as giving them important sources of information and influence. Before long, the Cavendishes were sufficiently friendly with the Lord High Admiral to entertain him socially, and in turn to be entertained by him.

Such proximity to real political power was dangerous (the Lord High Admiral for example would be executed for treason in 1549), but also vital for those who wished to prosper or even just survive in the turbulent society of the mid-Tudor period.

King Edward himself was not physically strong, and this was a concern not only to those who sincerely believed in the country's newly reformed religion, but also to all those who had prospered as a consequence of the reformation of the Church in England and Wales, and especially the dissolutions of the monasteries.[4] Amongst those concerned about the King's health was of course Sir William, whose duties of office kept him much in attendance around the King's person, and would have enabled him to gauge for himself the likelihood of King Edward long surviving into adulthood.

The principal concern of Sir William, and all those like him who had prospered from or otherwise had approved of the break from Rome, was what would happen to the succession to the English throne in the event of Edward dying early and without leaving a legitimate Protestant heir. According to Henry VIII's Act of Succession of 1543 his daughters Mary and Elizabeth (both of whom had been excluded from the succession at various times by earlier Acts) had now been reinstated in the line of succession and thus could assume the Crown (with Mary, and any heirs she might have, taking precedence over Elizabeth) in the event of Edward dying without any legitimate heir and without King

---

[4] Those two categories were of course not necessarily mutually exclusive, and many, probably most, of those who benefitted from the dissolution of the monasteries were also sincere supporters of the "new religion" though not necessarily calling themselves "Protestants", that term at this time being little used outside the German speaking areas of Europe).

Henry himself producing a further heir, which of course Henry never did. The prospect of Princess Mary, who had openly remained loyal to the Roman Catholic faith, succeeding to the throne worried many, but for the time being, all that could be done was to wait and see what events might transpire. There was certainly little appetite for seeking once again to remove her from the succession and there was, of course, still the prospect that Edward might yet produce a legitimate (and Protestant) heir.

Edward Seymour did not last very long as Lord Protector; he had too many rivals on or near the Council, and King Edward himself frankly feared and hated him. In 1548 and 1549, religious protests and complaints about the increasingly common practice of enclosing common land led to outbreaks of armed unrest in various parts of the country which were serious enough to require the authorities to order the intervention of military force. The revolts were suppressed, but the popularity of Seymour's government suffered badly, and Seymour's control of the Council began to slip away. By the beginning of October 1549, Seymour was feeling sufficiently unnerved to seize King Edward himself and transport him to Windsor Castle, from where Seymour hoped to gather sufficient military strength to overthrow the Council. Seymour's desperate plan did not work – the King so resented being kidnapped that Seymour lost whatever last vestiges of support he might have from him, and the Council gathered sufficient strength and nerve to have Seymour arrested. He was promptly sent to the Tower, and the King was moved to Richmond. Within a few weeks, John Dudley, Earl of Warwick (and later Duke of Northumberland) had assumed control of the Council, and whilst Seymour was set free a few months later (resuming his place on the Council though not as its head), his subsequent attempts to encompass Dudley's overthrow led to his own execution on 22nd January 1552 on Tower Hill.

Few mourned Seymour's passing, and most people hoped that the remainder of the King's minority would be a time of at least relative stability and calm for the country. Certainly, Bess and Sir William must have done so, for by now they had two further children, Henry, born on

17th December 1550 and William born on 27th December 1551, and Sir William had the satisfaction of knowing that at last he had two male heirs. There had also been another daughter Temperance, born on 10th June 1549, but she survived only a few months, dying early in 1550. Moreover, in addition to a busy family life, and to the obligations of Sir William's duties at Court, the couple had for the last few years been shrewdly improving their financial circumstances by a series of judicious acquisitions and disposals of lands throughout the country. These transactions included the acquisition of what would become the Cavendishes' Chatsworth estate in Derbyshire.

Chatsworth had originally belonged to the family of Bess's stepfather, Ralph Leche, but had been acquired by another local landowner, Thomas Agarde, in 1547. Thomas Agarde had died shortly after buying Chatsworth and had in turn left the property to his son Francis. The validity of the Agardes' acquisition of Chatsworth had however been challenged by some members of the Leche family, and word reached the ears of the Cavendishes that Francis Agarde, presumably in the hope of avoiding future protracted lawsuits with his neighbours, might be prepared to sell the estate (which comprised not only the manor of Chatsworth itself but other lands throughout the county) to the right buyer.

The acquisition of Chatsworth made a lot of sense from the perspective of Sir William and Bess. To begin with, they were close kinsmen of the Leche family, making it unlikely that any serious legal challenge for the possession of the estate would be mounted against them from that direction. Further, Bess would no doubt have known the Chatsworth estate fairly well in her youth and been aware of its attractions not only as a desirable country seat for an important courtier but also as a source of potential profit. A third factor was its remoteness from London. In those days (and for several centuries to come) Derbyshire would have a reputation of being a wild and isolated county, with few roads or major settlements and a difficult terrain (even as late as 1726, Daniel Defoe felt able to describe the county as being a "howling wilderness"[5]) and the difficult countryside meant it was unlikely that marauding bands would arrive to threaten the estate should civil unrest once more break out, as was quite possible given the political circumstances. Yet for all its remoteness, Chatsworth was not so far north that a determined traveller couldn't reach it from London with a mere four days or so of hard riding (though to make the same journey by coach and horses would take longer). The remoteness of Chatsworth contrasted favourably with the relatively exposed positions of many of Sir William's other properties (Northaw for instance was uncomfortably close to the Great North Road, the main road linking the north of England to London, and an obvious route for an army to travel). And of course, Chatsworth was near to Bess's childhood home and members of her family still lived close by.

Most biographers report that the initial impetus to buy Chatsworth came from Bess, and that may well be true, but it seems likely that Sir William was rapidly persuaded of the advantages of owning the estate, if indeed, he had any doubts in the first place. On the last day of 1550 (a few days after the birth of their son Henry), he and Bess acquired the estate from Agarde for £600 (a distinct bargain, as Agarde's father had paid £700 for it in 1547).

The manor house at Chatsworth was old, somewhat shabby and its estate relatively small, and the Cavendishes swiftly concluded that considerable work would be needed to bring it up to the standard that Sir William and Bess had by now come to expect. In December 1551, Sir William made a payment of 20 shillings to Roger Worde, a master mason of increasing renown at that time,[6] commissioning him not only to make various repairs to the existing manor house but also to design

---

[5] Though interestingly he excepted Chatsworth from this general description, describing it as a "wonder of art", and by that time, it well deserved that description.
[6] He would in due course work for Sir William Cecil on the construction of Burghley House.

a new house at Chatsworth. Work on the new house would continue in bursts of activity over the next few years, presumably as funds and circumstances permitted, and ultimately that version of the house would only be fully completed 30 years later. In the meantime, Sir William and Bess began to arrange for furniture and other domestic items such as candles, tapestries and plate to be shipped to Chatsworth from their various other properties across the country. There was so much that an inventory of property held in the (old) Chatsworth manor house which was taken as early as 1553 recorded the presence of 2124 ounces of gold and silver plate, 58 separate pieces of tapestries (often in demand in Tudor houses not only for their decorative qualities but also as a means of reducing draughts) and sufficient furniture to fully furnish thirteen bedchambers.

Whilst all this was going on, Sir William was quietly arranging for the disposal of various of his other properties around the country, though when he came across what he considered to be a suitable property for sale, he was not averse to acquiring more land, as evidenced by his acquisition in 1550 from the Earl of Westmorland of the manor of Ashford in Derbyshire; its 8000 acres of land represented a significant boost to the Cavendishes' landed presence in that county. The family's landholdings in Derbyshire were extended even more in 1552 when in June of that year, Sir William and Bess agreed with the Crown to exchange Northaw and other lands they held in Cardiganshire for lands at Doveridge, some 30 miles from Chatsworth as well as other properties elsewhere in the county and in Lincolnshire. All these acquisitions needed to be taken in hand and organised to ensure they were run with maximum possible financial efficiency, and with Sir William's hearty approval, Bess was fully involved in the planning and organising of the new properties. Now in her mid-twenties, she had become well experienced in giving orders to servants and advisers, and seeing to it that her commands were carried out promptly and with no fuss.

We can get a flavour of her firm determination to ensure that her wishes, and those of Sir William, were carried out exactly as she decreed from a letter she wrote from London on 14th November 1552 to the Cavendishes' steward at Chatsworth, Francis Whitfield.[7] After instructing Whitfield that he should himself make use only of such "cleats or boards" as were not needed by Master Neusante, a master carpenter who was then working on the Chatsworth rebuilding project, she ordered Whitfield to see that all things went well at Chatsworth, in particular emphasising the importance of ensuring that the house had adequate supplies of beer,[8] charcoal and wood, and leaving Whitfield in no doubt as to who Bess would blame if she identified any deficiencies when she next visited. She also stressed the importance of ensuring repairs were made to various rooms of the house, noting that she had heard that her sister Jane, almost certainly Bess's younger half-sister Jane Kniveton, who was then paying a visit to Chatsworth, could not obtain all the things that she needed. Bess emphasised that whilst she did not want wasteful extravagance, she did intend to ensure that Chatsworth had all things that were necessary.

Bess's somewhat imperious tone in several of her letters (and this one in particular) has been criticised by some biographers over the years as demonstrating a steely and unattractive determination on her part to manipulate others to her own advantage and to get her own way, not only with her various servants but also her successive husbands, and particularly her fourth, the Sixth Earl of Shrewsbury. That view has been challenged in more recent times, with some historians noting that this letter and others of similar tone need to be read having regard to the social context in which they were produced, and in particular the potentially delicate scenario of the mistress of a wealthy estate giving complex instructions on behalf of her husband as well as herself to senior male servants in their employ. When viewed in this light, Bess's tone in the letter of 1552 is not noticeably different from that used in

---

[7] One of the earliest letters of hers which has survived.

[8] An important command, as in most households, the drinking of light beer was considered to be (and often was) far safer than drinking local water from potentially unclean sources.

letters at that time by other persons in authority in similar situations. This was after all a time when people were expected to fully play the role that social rank bestowed upon them and it would probably have seemed odd if Bess's letters had not had at least some degree of a tone of command about them. In any event, Francis Whitfield himself appears not to have taken offence at Bess's letter; we know that he continued to be employed by Bess as steward at Chatsworth for several years to come, and that in October of 1561, Bess was still writing to him there about further improvements to be made to the house (and in that later letter, she addresses him cordially as "Francis").

In her letter of 14th November 1552, Bess made reference to her next return to Chatsworth, insinuating that it would not be too long delayed. In fact it was, for the Cavendishes were kept busy in London during the winter of 1552 and early 1553, not only because of extensive socialising, but also because of developments at Court. As had long been feared, the young King Edward fell ill in February of 1553 with what now seems certain to have been pulmonary tuberculosis, a sickness for which there was no cure in Tudor times. With the King's early demise now a distinct possibility, the atmosphere of the Court took on an even more ominous air, as the likelihood of Princess Mary's ascent to the throne and the forced re-imposition of the Roman Catholic faith on the country seemed increasingly certain with each passing week. Some awaited the accession of Mary passively with quiet dread, but unwilling or unable to countenance any challenge to the laws of succession; there were however those who were determined to act to prevent Mary's succession at all cost. Chief amongst these were Henry Grey, now the Duke of Suffolk, and of course John Dudley, Duke of Northumberland, and the latter had no hesitation in using his influence as Lord Protector to urge the dying King to alter Henry VIII's rules of succession in favour of a "legitimate" Protestant heir.[9] King Edward for his part was more than willing to agree to Dudley's proposals as the prospect of a Catholic

---

[9] The requirement for legitimacy excluded, to Edward's eyes at least, any right on the part of Princess Elizabeth to a claim to the throne.

successor filled him with horror, and he took an active role in preparing a document entitled "My Device for the Succession", which, in its final form, disinherited both Mary and Elizabeth and instead settled the Crown on his first cousin once removed, Lady Jane Grey. Lady Jane happened not only to be the daughter of Henry Grey, Duke of Suffolk, but also (as a consequence of having been forced into marriage on 21st May 1553 to Guildford Dudley, fourth surviving son of the Duke of Northumberland), Dudley's daughter-in-law. The Council were informed of the change to the succession in the middle of June. There was some initial opposition from some of the members, but after threats from Dudley and the personal intervention of the King himself, the majority of the Privy Council and senior judges of the land reluctantly agreed to accept the alteration to the rules of succession as valid. Princess Mary, having been warned of her proposed exclusion from the throne, had already fled to her estates in Kenninghall in Norfolk, and for the moment at least was safe from Dudley's clutches.

Edward VI died on 6th July 1553, and Dudley proclaimed Lady Jane as queen three days later. On the same day, 9th July, Mary wrote to the Privy Council from Kenninghall, demanding to be proclaimed as queen; to her delight, she had found there was much greater support for her throughout the country, even from those who did not share her religion, than she had feared. By 12th July, she was at Framlingham Castle in Suffolk, assembling a military force. Support for Dudley, and the proposed change to the succession, evaporated almost overnight. On 19th July, Lady Jane was deposed as queen, and Dudley and various supporters were conveyed to the Tower of London (Lady Jane and Guildford Dudley were already there). Mary, accompanied by her half-sister Princess Elizabeth, rode triumphantly into London on 3rd August to claim the throne in person; she was crowned at Westminster Abbey on 1st October. John Dudley did not live to see Mary's coronation; he was executed as a traitor on 22nd August 1553.

As for Lady Jane and Guildford, Queen Mary had initially been inclined to be merciful to them both. Although they were condemned to death for treason on 13th November (as were two of Guildford's brothers and the now deposed Protestant Archbishop of Canterbury, Thomas Cranmer), the sentences of death were not immediately carried out on the young couple, and they were allowed to live for several months under guard in the Tower. Their fates were sealed by the rebellion of Sir Thomas Wyatt the Younger in January 1554 in protest over Mary's proposed marriage to King Philip II of Spain, a rebellion in which Lady Jane's father, Henry Grey, the Duke of Suffolk, took part – Lady Jane and Guildford were deemed too dangerous to be allowed to live in light of the rebellion, and even as its last vestiges were being stamped out, they were beheaded on 12th February, Guildford in public on Tower Hill, and Lady Jane privately within the Tower itself. Henry Grey (as he then was, his titles having been attainted), followed them to the block on 23rd February 1554.

While these dramas were unfolding, the Cavendishes were noticeable by their absence. Given their various links to the Greys, Sir William's prominent role at Court, and undoubted Protestant sympathies, as well as the various properties Sir William had contrived to acquire during the Dissolution process, it would not have been surprising to find him identifying strongly with the cause of Lady Jane. He seems however (not for the first time) to have been too wily a politician to have been caught in that trap; certainly, we know that he had taken pains to stay in polite if distant contact with Princess Mary in the years before her accession, and he made sure that he and Bess and the Cavendish household were safely settled at Chatsworth before the King's death. During the tumultuous weeks that followed, they remained there; Sir William would later claim to have raised a fighting force in support of Mary at the personal cost of £660, though it is a matter for debate as to whether he actually did so. In any event, he succeeded in holding onto his position at Court following Mary's accession, and neither he nor Bess appear to have had any qualms in seeming to accede to the restoration of Roman Catholicism as the national religion.[10] Moreover, as the fateful year of 1553 progressed, the Cavendishes had domestic matters of their own to concern themselves. Bess was pregnant once again, and gave birth to her third son Charles, in November, and it is surely a mark of Sir William's political survival skills that he persuaded not only Bishop Stephen Gardiner (one of Queen Mary's most ardent supporters, and now following the restoration of Catholicism one of the most powerful men in the land) to act as godfather to the new infant, but also the Queen herself to act as godmother. The choice of the Queen and the Bishop as godparents suggests a determination on Sir William's part (and probably of Bess as well) to continue to cling close to the founts of power under the new regime. Yet, before we simply conclude that the Cavendishes were motivated solely by cynical reasons, we should note their choice of third godparent for Charles, none other than Henry Grey, Duke of Suffolk (not yet implicated in Wyatt's rebellion), who had only just been released from the Tower and pardoned for his part in attempting to place Lady Jane on the throne. Was the choice of Henry Grey an attempt by the Cavendishes to signal to the Protestant factions at Court and throughout the country (still potentially powerful at this stage) that they had not completely transferred their allegiance to the Catholic cause? Or was it (as some biographers have suggested) an attempt to bring about the rehabilitation of the Grey family in the eyes of England's new rulers? Was it perhaps even done at the request of the new Queen herself, at this time still trying to reconcile her Protestant subjects to the national change of religion by means of persuasion rather

---

[10] They were hardly alone in this; many former supporters of Protestantism had little moral problem with the thought of publicly attending Catholic services regardless of their own private beliefs – this was a time when many thought the ruling prince had the right to determine the national religion for his realm and people. Of course, once Queen Elizabeth assumed the throne and the cause of Protestantism was once more in the ascendance in England and Wales, there were relatively few who had any problems in switching back again.

than (as would soon become the case) force?[11] For now, at least, we cannot know of course, but in any event, once the repercussions of Queen Mary's accession and Wyatt's rebellion had dissipated, Sir William and Bess could comfort themselves that they had survived the political turbulence with their positions of influence and wealth (as well as their heads, and other portions of their anatomies) intact. They could now seek to prosper further under the new reign.

---

[11] In this regard, it is interesting to note that Queen Mary allowed Lady Frances, the widow of Henry Grey, to remain at Court, where she was treated with some distinction (though never fully trusted) even after her husband's final downfall and execution.

Chapter 4

"Our Great Misery"

For the next few years, the Cavendishes lived fairly quietly as the reign of Queen Mary turned more and more bloody. Bess spent much of her time at Chatsworth, which was slowly being transformed into one of the finest houses in the Midlands, and Sir William joined her there whenever his duties permitted. He continued to extend his landholdings in Derbyshire, and having surrendered the lease on the Newgate house in London, in 1555 he rented a house at Brentford owned by their Derbyshire neighbour Sir John Thynne. This became the Cavendishes' principal residence when visiting London. The Brentford house was convenient, large enough to house the Cavendish household in some comfort, close enough to London to allow easy access to the capital and Court and yet hopefully far enough away for them to avoid any civil unrest that might break out as a result of the increasingly tyrannical policies of Queen Mary and her advisers. Both Bess and Sir William liked the house, and Bess gave birth to her second surviving daughter, Elizabeth, there on 31st March 1555. Bess must have become pregnant again within weeks of Elizabeth's birth, for in January 1556 (this time at Chatsworth) Bess produced another daughter Mary who was destined to play an important role in much of the family history which was to unfold. Mary was followed (on 2nd March 1557) by Sir William's and Bess's last child, Lucres (a variant name for Lucretia). Lucres, however, was a sickly infant and she died in the same year.

Terrible as this was, Bess had other concerns on her mind. Sir William had been taken ill at around the time of Mary's birth, and although it seemed for a while that he had recovered, so much so that he was able to return to his duties in London for a time, the fact was that his health continued to deteriorate throughout the remainder of 1556. By July of that year his condition[1] was so bad that he was writing to Sir John Thynne to say that he was unable to ride a horse. To make matters worse, he had attracted the suspicions of the authorities, who were beginning to ask awkward questions such as exactly how had Sir William been able to pay for all the land and other properties he had been acquiring over recent years? In March 1557, an audit was ordered of his Privy Chamber accounts, and the auditors swiftly found that Sir William had been failing to keep proper records of his official finances since at least 1546; moreover, such records as there were suggested Sir William had been having some difficulty in distinguishing between public funds and his own purse.

The result was that the Lord High Treasurer, William Paulet, the Marquess of Winchester, called upon his old friend Sir William Cavendish (Paulet was godfather to Sir William's son William) to inform him that the audit had identified a deficiency in his official accounts amounting to more than £5000 (more than £2 million today) which would have to be repaid.[2]

One of the key questions at that time, and indeed ever since, was whether Sir William (possibly with the assistance of Bess) was simply an embezzler of public funds? The question is easier to pose than it is to answer; investigations of the household accounts maintained by Bess during the relevant period have failed to reveal any conclusive evidence of the misuse of public funds in the daily expenditure of the Cavendish household. Moreover, as previously noted, it was the custom of the day that public servants were allowed – indeed expected – to claim some of the proceeds of their office as a form of remuneration. It was essentially

---

[1] It is unclear exactly what his illness was.

[2] The audit of Sir William's department was part of a wider drive on the part of Queen Mary and her advisers to increase the revenues of the Crown. Queen Mary's husband, Philip II of Spain, notwithstanding that he had virtually deserted her, had succeeded in embroiling England in Spain's war against France, and the resulting cost was having a dire effect on the finances of both Crown and country. Sir William's expenditures at Chatsworth and elsewhere must have made him one of the prime targets to be investigated.

one of the perks of the job, and if challenged, it was supposedly justified by the fact that official salaries for public posts were low. It would have been impossible for an official like Sir William to have fulfilled his duties without claiming at least some of the monies that flowed through his fingers in his official capacity. The key point is that there was an unwritten rule that officials were supposed to maintain a sense of proportion when diverting public funds for their private use. A deficit of over £5000 suggests Sir William had forgotten this rule, and that this was the simple answer as to how he could afford to make all those land purchases and to rebuild and furnish Chatsworth so sumptuously.

Sir William for his part tried to defend himself on a number of grounds, arguing that his department's accounts had been in arrears when he first assumed responsibility, that there were some official expenditures that he had met out of his own pocket, and even that some of his assistants must have been involved in fraud or at best been grossly negligent. His pleas to the Queen fell on deaf ears; and he was ordered in August of 1557 to appear before the Star Chamber the following October to answer the charges against him. The Star Chamber was a court, originally set up in the fourteenth century, comprised of both Privy Council members and common law judges; the original intention was that it would be a court tasked with ensuring the fair application of law in respect of powerful people who might find ways of evading justice if tried in more "usual" courts. It initially fulfilled this role fairly well, but over time became more of a political instrument of control and repression. Given Sir William's prominence, it is not surprising that he was ordered to appear before it to answer the charges levied against him.

Bess was at Chatsworth at the time Sir William was summoned, but hastened to join him in London, arriving there around the 24th of August. She found Sir William ill once more and drinking far more than was good for him. As the late summer turned into autumn, his condition deteriorated; he was due to appear before the Star Chamber on 10th October, but when it convened, he was absent, having previously sent a message that he was too ill to attend. The court may have thought he was shamming, and in any event rapidly concluded that Sir William did indeed owe the Crown more than £5000. It then politely asked Sir William to acknowledge the debt from his sickbed and to provide a power of attorney to one or more of his clerks so they could take the necessary steps to secure the debt's repayment. He instead sent clerks before the court on 13th October to again protest his innocence and sought to advance further reasons why he should not be held liable. His appeals included a letter addressed to the Star Chamber judges in which he referred to himself as a "right humble, meek and poor sick man", and asking for mercy in the name of "… my poor wife, my miserable and innocent children and family …" Once again, his appeals fell on deaf ears, but before the Star Chamber could take further action, Sir William Cavendish died. Taking up Sir William's notebook in which he had recorded so many family events, Bess made a final entry:

> *Sir William Cavendish, Knight, my most deare and well beloved husband, departed this present life on Mondaie being the 25th daie of October, betwixt the Howers of 8 and 9 of the same day, at night, in the yeare of our Lord God 1557 the domunicall Letter then C. On whose Soule I most humbly beseech the Lord to have Mercy and Ridd me and his poore Children out of our greate Misserie.*
>
> *Elizabeth Cevendyshe*

Sir William was buried at the Church of St Botulph-without-Aldersgate in London, but the issue of the debt remained. For the time being at least it looked like Bess's pleas for mercy and relief from the debt would, like those of her now late husband, fail to have any effect – the Star Chamber remained adamant that the Sir William's debt would have to be repaid. Ruin and disgrace for Bess and her children seemed inevitable.[3]

Bess's response to this crisis gives us one of the clearest indications of her steely determination to survive, and if possible, to flourish even in the face of extreme adversity. It would have been so easy for her to

---

[3] Bess was now responsible for six surviving children of her own (Lucres must have died at about the same time as Sir William) and two stepdaughters.

surrender to the forces of the Crown and to acquiesce to the sale of Chatsworth and the majority of the other lands and possessions she and Sir William had acquired over the previous decade – with luck there might just have been enough left over for her and her children to survive in a modest way, perhaps amongst her family and neighbours back in Derbyshire. But having lived the grand life of a lady of a wealthy Tudor family for more than ten years, she would have found it difficult to retreat to the relatively simple life of a Derbyshire villager once more, not merely because of the loss of power and material comfort, but also because of the social scandal and gossip that such a fall would inevitably entail. Bess refused to countenance such a course and instead she began to fight for her rights and properties.[4] Even as a bill was being introduced into Parliament authorising the confiscation of land to pay debts owed to the Crown (which would include the debt that Bess had now seemingly inherited), she began to contact lawyers and other men of influence and power, seeking ways to challenge the debt and especially the passage of the bill. Bess was not the only opponent of the bill, of course, and it is unclear how much of the credit she could subsequently and legitimately claim when its passage was effectively stalled in Parliament for several years. Nevertheless, she must have been at least partly responsible for that result, which meant that the danger of the imminent confiscation of her lands receded; the debt however remained outstanding.

With the bill stalled, Bess spent much of the spring and early summer of 1558 at Chatsworth, ordering the affairs of the estate which had become disorganised in the wake of Sir William's illness and death. During that time, rumours began to circulate that the Queen, who initially had been thought to be pregnant, was in fact suffering from an incurable disease. The rumours proved to be true. Queen Mary was dying, probably of stomach cancer, and Bess, like the rest of the nation realised that the Queen's early death would bring a Protestant heir to the throne, in the form of Princess Elizabeth. In that succession, Bess saw

---

[4] Sir William had left most of his property to Bess for life.

a glimmer of hope of a solution to her debt problems, for the sovereign could waive the debt. There was no possibility of Queen Mary doing so, of course, but Elizabeth (who was godmother to Bess's eldest son Henry, and shared Bess's Protestant faith) just might be prepared to be more generous. In the middle of June, Bess quit Chatsworth once more and returned to Sir John Thynne's house at Brentford which she had arranged to rent for a year; she was joined a few days later by her children. Through the summer and early autumn months of 1558, as she continued to wrestle with bringing order to Sir William's affairs, she, like many others, must have watched with more than a little self-interest as Queen Mary's health steadily declined. As Bess waited, she would have been conscious that Princess Elizabeth was then living at Hatfield, not too far from Brentford, and whilst we cannot be certain, it seems likely that Bess would have found an excuse to visit Princess Elizabeth, probably assuring the Princess of her loyalty, and no doubt hinting gently for a measure of debt forgiveness.

Bess left Brentford to return to Chatsworth with her children on 25th September 1558 and she remained there until early November, when she once more moved back to London. She was certainly there on 13th November. Whether she was there on 17th November, when news of Queen Mary's death was announced is unclear – she may well have been visiting Hatfield once again, one of the many Elizabethans (as we should now call them) who felt it advisable and appropriate to cluster near the new Queen at the start of her reign. By 26th November, Bess was back at Brentford, and her household accounts show that she was now busy making purchases for the furnishing and provisioning of the house, and arranging for her children, her half-sister Elizabeth and an aunt to join her there for the Christmas season.

Queen Elizabeth was crowned on 15th January 1559 (the date was set after consulting astrologer Dr John Dee, who had told her that a coronation on that date would mean a glorious and prosperous reign) and Bess may have been at Westminster Abbey to watch the ceremony. During the weeks preceding and immediately following the crowning, the new Queen and her closest advisers were busy establishing the new government, which required the removal of many (not all) of Queen Mary's councillors and other Court officials and appointing in their place others more in accord with the new regime. Queen Elizabeth's first Privy Council was noticeably smaller than Mary's had been – the new Queen wanted the Council to focus on advising her and she feared (no doubt rightly) that too many Councillors "would make rather discord and confusion than good counsel". One of the appointments made was to be of great significance for Bess and her descendants. Sir William St Loe, a wealthy soldier and courtier who had shown impeccable loyalty to the cause of Queen Elizabeth during the darkest days of Queen Mary[5] was appointed Captain of the Queen's Guard and Chief Butler of England, positions of important distinction in the new Court.

Whether or not Sir William St Loe was already acquainted with Bess at the start of the new reign is not entirely clear, but he could have been, as St Loe would almost certainly have known Sir William Cavendish. In any event, if they hadn't met before, they soon did, and the first few months of the new reign saw them becoming very close. With the full approval of the Queen (and the Queen did not give such approval lightly), Bess and St Loe, who was a widower, became betrothed sometime during July 1559.

One of the questions that repeatedly arises to challenge students of the life of Bess of Hardwick is why St Loe and Bess became engaged at all. Cynical observers may once more conclude that it is easy to see why Bess married him – after all, he was rich and well-connected with significant landholdings in the West Country, a widower with two

---

[5] He could boast of being committed to the Tower by Queen Mary on suspicion of involvement in the rebellion of Sir Thomas Wyatt in 1554 and of having survived the experience, which Queen Elizabeth no doubt regarded as significant credentials of respectability, though as a general rule the Queen did not approve of plots against anointed monarchs. Elizabeth herself had been arrested and held in the Tower for a time in the aftermath of Wyatt's rebellion, also suspected of involvement in the plot, and this common experience they shared may well have been one of the factors which caused her to look with approval on St Loe when she finally attained the throne.

grown daughters and a favourite of the Queen, perhaps even more so than Bess. Crucially he offered potential salvation from the problem of the debts that still plagued her life. It might be argued that it is less easy to see why he married her – why would a wealthy man, so well-connected and seemingly at the beginning of a glittering new career at Court at the start of a new reign choose to marry a widow with several young children and whose financial difficulties would hardly have been a secret? To pose the question in this way is to miss several important points. To begin with, Bess herself was a person of intelligence and great strength of character – there was no hint of personal scandal about her life and the more acute of her contemporaries would also have given her great credit for her ability to manage her family responsibilities and especially her household and financial affairs, notwithstanding the difficulties that the Cavendish debts posed for her. Moreover, she too was now well-connected, known to be looked on fondly by the Queen herself no less, and it was by no means impossible that the Queen might eventually agree to remit some, or even all of the debt owed to the Crown. Even more importantly, Bess was still relatively young, a woman whom men seem to have instinctively liked and found physically attractive; at this stage in her life, she had curling red hair, and she had a striking face, with sharp blue eyes. Men respected her too, and she was capable of great personal charm when she chose to show it. And presumably she chose to show it to St Loe, and it was reciprocated by him to her in return – both before the marriage, and during it - surviving correspondence between the two of them during the course of their marriage suggests nothing other than deep mutual attraction and respect.

In any event, whatever the reason or reasons, they were married, on 27th August 1559, a date suggested by the Queen herself and (sensibly) adopted. It was the start of a new chapter for them both.

Chapter 5
Lady of the Privy Chamber

By marrying William St Loe, Bess had married into a distinguished Somerset knightly family of Norman ancestry, with a long history of service to the Crown, usually military in nature. The earliest references to the family in Court records date back to the early twelfth century, and each century which had passed since then had seen them generally prosper, so that by the time of St Loe's father, Sir John St Loe, the family had built up significant landholdings throughout much of the West Country, particularly in Somerset and Gloucestershire.[1] By the time William St Loe was born (in 1518), the family had for several generations been using the manor house of Sutton Court in Chew Magna, Somerset as their main residence, and it was principally there that William spent his first few years.

The family may have been distinguished, but it had also had its share of dramas and tensions. Sir John and his wife Dame Margaret produced four sons (of whom William was the eldest) and a daughter. William St Loe was raised with the expectation of being his father's heir, and indeed he followed in his father's footsteps (and family tradition) by serving as a soldier in Ireland (as his father and uncle had done before him) during the 1540s. He was generally considered to have been a good soldier, popular with his men and superiors alike, and in 1549 his service earned him a knighthood. By then he had married Jane Baynton, the daughter of Sir Edward Baynton, a wealthy courtier, and together they had two daughters but no sons.

Jane died in the autumn of 1549. Thus, unless William St Loe remarried and had a son by a later wife, or he deliberately acted to make

---

[1] They significantly extended their landholdings following the dissolution of the monasteries.

alternative testamentary arrangements by means of a will, the apparent heir to William's landed property would be William's brother, Sir John's second son Edward.

Unfortunately, Edward was generally regarded, with cause, as the black sheep of the family. Irresponsible with money, he had been involved in various physical brawls, legal disputes and scandals which had threatened the good name of the St Loe family, including having an affair with the wife of a man called John Scutt, a local landowner, and then marrying her promptly after the death of her husband (while she was three months pregnant with what was presumably Edward's child). The fact that the wife died only a few months after marrying Edward in somewhat mysterious circumstances merely added to the scandal and there were suggestions that Edward was a poisoner. He then proceeded to marry his now deceased wife's daughter Margaret, notwithstanding that he had become her stepfather. He was also criticised for indulging in dubious property transactions to the detriment of others which also did nothing to enhance his reputation, had sought to ferment discord between various family members and was generally regarded as a man to avoid. Even his own mother would at a later date refer to him in correspondence with Bess as being a "devil".[2]

Sir John viewed his second son's activities with mounting anger, and eventually took the step of rewriting his will, so that William was to remain his principal heir, his two youngest sons and daughter were reasonably provided for, as was Dame Margaret, but Edward was to receive nothing. We do not know if Edward was made aware of the

---

[2] Edward was also suspected of poisoning John Scutt, who had died suspiciously quickly, yet conveniently from Edward's point of view. Interestingly, for all Edward's bad reputation, he was elected as the MP for Bath for the Parliament which assembled on 23rd January 1559, the first Parliament of Queen Elizabeth's reign. Edward was presumably elected because of the local influence of the St Loe family, but had the elections been held a year or so later, it is debateable whether the family would have supported Edward's candidacy. It is worth adding that Sir John and Sir William also gained seats in the House of Commons at this time.

terms of his father's will whilst Sir John was still alive (perhaps not given Edward's volatile, sometimes violent nature), but he certainly would have learned of his disinheritance when Sir John died on 20th March 1559. Even then though, he could comfort himself that he was still the apparent male heir to his elder brother, whose wealth of course had just increased significantly thanks to his inheritance from Sir John. Edward seems to have decided to keep a low profile during the months immediately following his father's death, perhaps to avoid giving William any excuse to alter *his* will.

Edward must therefore have been dismayed to learn in July 1559 that his brother had become betrothed to marry a young woman who already had healthy children, including several sons, and might be expected to have more during the course of her third marriage. It was at this point when matters became, potentially at least, dangerous indeed both for Bess and for William. Perhaps William, for all his military prowess, did not at this time fully appreciate the potential danger posed by his brother, and almost certainly Bess did not, but Edward had already shown himself to be a thoroughly unscrupulous individual, quite possibly capable of murder, even if he had never actually been charged with that particular crime. Although the newly betrothed couple may not have known it, or at least fully appreciated it, the next year or so was to prove one of the most dangerous periods in William's life, notwithstanding his years spent on active military service, and probably, for Bess, the most dangerous period of her entire life.

In the meantime, the marriage of William and Bess in August 1559 proceeded smoothly and happily, although it is not entirely clear where the actual ceremony took place, it may have been at Sutton Court in Somerset. William and Bess (now, of course, Lady St Loe) were certainly there a few weeks later in September, as Bess (with her new husband's approval) placed instructions for some alterations and improvements to be made to the old manor house. William St Loe seems to have recognised, and appreciated, Bess's skill and judgment when it came to building works.

We also do not know whether Bess's children (or William's two daughters, for that matter) attended the wedding, or joined them afterwards on what was effectively their honeymoon, but we do know that William St Loe appears to have had considerable affection for his new stepchildren (as indeed Bess did for hers) so some or all of them may have done so. Certainly, at various times over the next few years, St Loe would show his affection for Bess's children by providing them with financial support in various matters, including the meeting of school fees. He also was willing to provide funds to allow Bess to order the resumption of the building work at Chatsworth, which had been in abeyance since the discovery of Sir William Cavendish's financial irregularities. Insofar as he could, St Loe also tried to assist with the resolution of the problems caused by the debt resulting from those irregularities, on occasions attending various legal meetings at which the matter was to be discussed when Bess could not. The issue of the debt however remained unresolved.

William and Bess were back in London by the beginning of October and William resumed his Court duties. Around this time too, Bess's position at Court was strengthened by Queen Elizabeth making her a Lady of the Privy Chamber, a singular honour from the Queen who was very particular about such appointments, not least because the duties associated with the post often involved personal service to and attendance upon the sovereign herself. Having such close access to the Queen had its disadvantages, particularly as Queen Elizabeth could be a very demanding and at times intolerant mistress, but for any Court lady who had the sense to be careful, competent and measured in their dealings with the Queen, as Bess most certainly was, holding such a post offered at least the possibility of a degree of private access to the Queen that was almost impossible to achieve by any other means. This was a simple fact of life which was appreciated by every Court family having any form of political ambition, or indeed, in some cases, sense of self-preservation, and many families went to considerable efforts to try to secure any vacancy that might arise for a member of their own family.

By accepting the role of a Lady of the Privy Chamber, Bess had raised the political and social status of the St Loe family to a noticeable extent.

Acceptance of her new duties coupled with the simple desire to stay close to her newly-wedded husband kept Bess in London through the remainder of the year and the first three months of 1560. It was while she was there, in February 1560 that she seems to have first met Edward as he arrived around that time at William's and Bess's London home, officially with the announced intention of paying his respects to Bess and welcoming her into the family. He also used the occasion to complain about his exclusion from any form of family inheritance, and to inform William that Sir John had told him that he had intended that a life interest in Sutton Court and its estate be granted to his wife Margaret. Consequently, he claimed, he and Margaret should be permitted to take up residence there forthwith and even more importantly, the income of the estate should be regarded as his.

It would have been fascinating to witness how William and Bess responded to this quite brash and astonishing claim for which there was exactly no evidence whatsoever and which was completely contradicted by such evidence as there was, not least the terms of Sir John's last will. So far as Bess is concerned, it seems likely that Edward's demands caused the prompt falling away of scales from her eyes as regards the true nature of her new brother-in-law, that is if she had been under any illusion about his character in the first place. Furthermore, if she had allowed herself, her probable immediate reaction after recovering from the incredulity that Edward's spurious claims must have generated would surely have been the summary dismissal of Edward's demands, and probably of Edward himself from her house. Wisely she seems to have allowed William to deal with the matter.

As for William, Edward may have failed to take into account that he was now dealing with an experienced soldier as well as a man used to life at the Court of Queen Elizabeth, which was not exactly an environment in which weak-willed individuals thrived. If he had expected William to meekly acquiesce to his demands, Edward was to be disappointed, for

William who now also was under no illusion as to his brother's character, had no intention of doing so, not least because to William's eyes it would have seemed a shameful betrayal of his father's wishes. Having said that, William St Loe was not an unkind or unjust man; indeed, the available evidence suggests that when allowed to be, he was kindly and generous, and he may well have thought that Edward's exclusion from any form of inheritance was severe. This probably explains why, although he was unwilling in any way to agree to Edward's demands, he was willing to offer him the role of steward at Sutton Court, with a suitable salary, which would at least have given Edward and Margaret somewhere to live and hopefully allow them to improve their lives with time.

Edward accepted the post, probably with very little grace, and departed. Shortly afterwards, Bess fell ill. It was immediately thought that she had been poisoned. Bess's condition was serious, but this was an age when the threat of poisoning was taken seriously by wealthy and powerful people, and it seems that a supply of various antidotes to common poisons was available. These were promptly administered to Bess, perhaps by William's mother, the Dowager Dame Margaret, who was paying a visit at the time and might well have had the knowledge of how to apply antidotes effectively. In any event, one of the antidotes at least seems to have worked, for Bess recovered, but her life had been in serious danger for a while. Dame Margaret alluded to this in a later letter addressed to Bess, adding that she was sure that Bess's illness had been the result of poison and that it would have been fatal if an antidote had not been readily available.

As for who was responsible for poisoning Bess, the finger of suspicion was of course promptly pointed at Edward although no actual evidence of his guilt could immediately be found.[3] Once Bess was clearly seen to have recovered, William set about initiating a thorough investigation of

---

[3] William himself seems to have escaped being poisoned, if that is what happened.

the whole business, reasoning that Edward could not have acted alone and a friend of his, John Mann, helped him to identify a possible suspect. This was Hugh Draper, who owned a tavern in Bristol, not too far from Sutton Court, a man reputed to be interested in astrology and mysticism generally and who might well have known Edward and been willing to cooperate with him in nefarious dealings. Draper was arrested and charged, interestingly not for attempting to poison Bess, but on suspicion of being "… a conjuror or sorcerer …" and having "… thereby to practice matter against Sir William Sentlo and my Ladie". Draper loudly protested that he no longer had any interest in his "science" and had burned all his books on the subject, but he was committed to the Tower anyway. He was soon joined by several suspected accomplices, namely a man called Francis Cox, who was accused of conspiring with Draper to commit sorcery, and a man called Ralph Davie who, together with his daughter (who was also sent to the Tower) was accused of practising "… with the said daughter, for the poisoning of my lady Sentlo".

William had not yet finished with his accusations. Shortly after Davie was charged, William accused his own sister (or possibly his cousin), also confusingly known as Mistress Elizabeth St Loe, of being in league with Draper. Elizabeth had drawn suspicion on herself by asking too many questions, particularly of Dame Margaret, about Bess's health and whether she had in fact been poisoned and was likely to recover. She was known to consort with Edward and according to some biographers, as a result of William's accusation, she too was despatched to the Tower for a time.[4]

---

[4] Elizabeth's reported incarceration at this time has been the cause of some confusion for several of Bess's biographers in the past. Misidentifying Elizabeth with Bess, several recorded that it was Bess who was imprisoned in the Tower, though the exact reason for this supposed imprisonment perplexed many. Others speculated that it may have been linked to the scandal involving the marriage of Lady Katherine Grey which erupted into public knowledge in August 1561, and may have led to Bess being interrogated in the Tower, though

Cox, Davie and his daughter were kept in the Tower for many months before they were released, one by one, on the promise of good behaviour and the provision of sureties. As for Draper, the first of the group to be arrested, it is not entirely clear when he was released, and on what terms, or indeed if he was ever released at all but he left a permanent record of his time in the Tower, in the form of graffiti carved into the walls of his cell in the Salt Tower. The graffiti, which can still be seen today, depicts a circular astrological calendar, which would seem to contradict Draper's declaration that he no longer had an interest in astrology. Above the calendar itself is an inscription which states that "Hew Draper of Brystow made thys spheer the 30 daye of Maye anno 1561", Bristow being a common spelling of "Bristol" in Tudor England. The calendar and its inscription are inscribed low upon the wall, and it is thought Draper was lying sick on the floor when he carved them. In any event, the inscription suggests that Draper must have remained imprisoned for over a year, as he was committed to the Tower on 21st March 1560.

As for Edward, he escaped any charges at this time, and he and Margaret were free to make their way to Sutton Court where Edward was supposed to assume his duties as his brother's steward. So matters rested for a while, and whilst William and other members of the family seem to have been certain in their own minds of his guilt, they had other affairs to attend to which occupied much of their time. For Bess, in addition to her duties to the Queen, there were also the affairs of Chatsworth to deal with, both the house and the estate, and in the summer of 1560, when Queen Elizabeth set out on one of the first of her several Progresses[5] she would make travelling around the country, Bess

---

not imprisoned. In fact, as more recent research has shown, Bess was not imprisoned or otherwise in trouble with the authorities in 1560 or the first half of 1561, and once she recovered from her poisoning, continued to serve at Court and to build at Chatsworth. To add to the confusion, Sir William St Loe had both a sister and a cousin named Elizabeth St Loe.

[5] A tour of their kingdom, or at least parts of it, by a monarch and his or her retinue and entourage.

obtained leave to depart for Derbyshire in order to spend the next few months at Chatsworth. Sir William's presence, however, was required by the Queen, and so he and Bess were largely parted for several months that summer and early autumn, only very occasionally being able to meet for a snatched two or three days before William was obliged to hurry back to his sovereign. That they missed each other badly whilst they were parted is shown by some of the correspondence between them that survives from this period in their lives, with one letter from William to Bess written early in September 1560 referring to Bess as being "more dearer" to him than he was to himself, adding a plea that "... as thou doth love me, let me shortly hear from thee, for the quieting of my unquiet mind ..."

Nevertheless, they both understood the importance of William's attendance upon the Queen, and accepted it, though they looked forward to William being able to make a long visit to Chatsworth, and Bess, in September once the Progress had ended and the Court had settled at Windsor once more. At that time too, William would be able to consider what, if any, steps he should take to deal with Edward.

Events elsewhere served to disrupt their plans. Queen Elizabeth had succeeded in keeping the watching world enthralled with the questions of whether she would marry, and if so to whom, important questions given the perceived need at the time to ensure a clear line of succession. The Queen was adept at keeping potential suitors, both within the Court and from abroad, at bay whilst at the same time giving them just enough encouragement to lead them and others to believe, at least for a time, that marriage was a possibility. She behaved this way partly for political reasons, and partly because whilst she did have concerns about marriage – the examples of her mother and half-sister had taught her well the dangers of being anything other than her own mistress - she did have a flirtatious, even affectionate side, and did think fondly of several of her suitors, at least most of the time. The one man at her Court she probably felt closest to however, she could not have as a husband, even if she wanted to, for he was already married.

That man was Lord Robert Dudley, the fifth son of the late and largely unlamented John Dudley, Duke of Northumberland who had been attainted for treason and executed by Queen Mary in 1553 following the attempt to place Lady Jane Grey on the throne. His father's downfall had led to Robert Dudley and his surviving brothers losing their honours and positions and being imprisoned in the Tower for a while but he and his brothers had eventually been released. Following military service on behalf of Queen Mary, they had been restored to the station of Duke's sons, though neither Queen Mary nor subsequently Queen Elizabeth were foolish enough to authorise the restoration of the Dukedom of Northumberland itself.

Lord Robert was one of those who had quietly supported Elizabeth both financially and morally in the difficult days before her accession, and once she ascended the throne, the two of them established a close, openly affectionate relationship which was widely noted and caused considerable concern for several of Queen Elizabeth's other advisers, particularly Sir William Cecil, later Lord Burghley, who at that time was Elizabeth's Secretary of State and who feared Lord Robert's influence over the Queen (as he saw it) might jeopardise his own position and political power.

In fact, history was to show that Cecil (in the long run) had little to fear from Robert Dudley, primarily for two reasons. First, the Queen was certainly fond of Lord Robert, willing to listen to him (for the most part and most of the time) and even to an extent indulge him. In the final analysis however, she simply trusted Cecil's political and legal judgment (and possibly that of one or two other advisers, such as Francis Walsingham who in time would effectively act as Queen Elizabeth's spy master, though he only became one of her principal advisers in the 1570s) more than she trusted that of Dudley.

Secondly, there was also the simple fact that at this time, Robert Dudley was married, as he had wed a woman called Amy Robsart on 4th June 1550. Amy Robsart was the daughter and heiress of a wealthy Norfolk gentry farmer, well-educated by the standards of the day, and she had stood by Lord Robert during his time of troubles following the downfall of his father. Although the accession of Queen Elizabeth brought at least a partial restoration of Robert Dudley's fortunes (Elizabeth made him her Master of the Horse), Amy herself was not permitted to enjoy the perquisites of being the wife of an influential courtier for the simple reason that the Queen made it clear she had no wish for Amy to show her face at Court. Amy was to stay secluded in the country, out of sight and preferably out of mind, so that Lord Robert could focus solely on Queen Elizabeth.

Out of sight she may have been, but the fact that Robert Dudley was married was common knowledge, and as the close relationship between Queen and courtier developed following the accession, there were some, including the Spanish ambassador, who began to speculate that it would be remarkably convenient for Elizabeth and Dudley if some form of misadventure, preferably terminal, were to befall Amy. There were rumours to the effect that Lord Robert was actively trying to poison Amy, with the Queen's knowledge and approval.

This was precisely the sort of gossip that Queen Elizabeth could ill-afford to have spread, and she knew it. Her grip on the throne was not so strong that she could allow it to be widely believed that she was prepared to countenance the murder of a woman simply to satisfy her own wishes and desires – there were already too many people, in England and abroad, who thought she had no right to the throne and that she was capable of committing any crime in order to retain it and achieve her ends. So long as Amy remained alive, the Queen could not have Robert Dudley as her husband even if she wanted him (and it is by no means certain that she would actually have married Dudley in say 1559 or 1560, even if he had been free to marry[6]). On the other hand, if

---

[6] Though she probably came closer to marrying Lord Robert than she did any other man. For his part Dudley certainly was attracted to the Queen, not just because of the worldly advantages that she could bestow but also because they had known each other for many years and through many tribulations and he

Amy were to die, the resulting rumours and suspicions might well have threatened her position on the throne itself. And so for the first couple of years or so following her accession, the relationship between the Queen and Robert Dudley was trapped in some form of romantic, possibly even near-sexual, no-man's land, with them unable to progress towards what might in other circumstances have been the natural goal of marriage, but at the same time, with neither of them for their own reasons being able to concede that the relationship was unable to progress any further. The presence of other suitors and rivals covetous of Dudley's position merely complicated matters even more.

It is difficult to speculate what might have happened if matters had continued on this basis – possibly Dudley would eventually have tired of waiting for the Queen and returned to his wife or sought female companionship elsewhere.[7] Fate however conspired so that matters did not so continue.

Amy had obeyed the Queen's instructions to stay well away from the Court and in early September 1560 was living at Cumnor Place, sometimes called Cumnor Hall, in the village of Cumnor in what is now Oxfordshire but then was part of Berkshire. She had been ill, suffering from what was called a malady of the breast, though the exact nature of her illness was a mystery to the doctors she had consulted. On the morning of Sunday, 8th September 1560, Amy's lifeless body was found in the Hall lying with a broken neck at the bottom of a flight of stairs. How long it had lain there is not entirely clear, as the household apart

---

was scarcely alone in feeling the attractive power of Elizabeth Tudor in her prime. On the other hand, though quite possibly his feelings of attraction to Amy may have diminished over time, there is no evidence that he actually wished to have his wife killed.

[7] In 1578, he did in fact marry Lettice Knollys, the Queen's cousin once removed, but kept the fact of the marriage secret from the Queen for several months. When the Queen found out, she was, as another much later Queen is reputed to have been, "not amused".

from Amy had been away at a local fair the previous day. Nor was it clear whether Amy had died in an accident, or been murdered.

News of the tragedy reached the Court at Windsor the following day, and scandal erupted. Robert Dudley loudly denied any involvement in the matter at all, but there were few who believed him. Queen Elizabeth promptly ordered him from the Court, directing that he should stay secluded at his house in Kew until an investigation as to what happened had been carried out, but this did not prevent rumours that Dudley had murdered his wife, as many had long predicted that he would, and that the Queen was involved. The rumours even were circulated abroad, and the Elizabeth's position on the throne was suddenly perceived to be under threat. Security measures protecting the Queen were enhanced at once, and Sir William St Loe's permission to leave the Court was inevitably revoked. He and Bess had to accept that their separation would continue for longer than they had anticipated.

The investigation into Amy's death was carried out swiftly. There was no evidence advanced that Lord Robert had murdered his wife, or indeed that she was murdered at all, and a verdict of accidental death was recorded. With that verdict, Dudley was permitted to return to the Court, but his relationship with the Queen thereafter, though still close, had subtly changed. The rumours of Dudley's guilt, and of the Queen's connivance with Amy's death, continued to circulate despite the verdict, no doubt spread in part by those who were eager to see the blackening of both their names, and the whispered allegations would continue for the rest of their lives, and indeed after their deaths. It is now believed[8] that the verdict of accidental death was in fact correct, as Amy's symptoms were consistent with breast cancer, and it is now understood that breast cancer can in certain circumstances lead to a weakened spine, meaning even a simple fall might indeed break the

---

[8] But not universally – there are still occasional suggestions that Amy might have been murdered, though not necessarily by Robert Dudley. Suicide has also been suggested on occasion.

spine of someone suffering from the condition. This of course was not appreciated in Tudor times.

In any event, from Sir William St Loe's perspective, a formal verdict of accidental death meant that he could at last gain permission to quit the Court and travel to Chatsworth to join Bess, and he did so in late October 1560, arriving on 21st October. He arrived however with the news that he would be unable to stay as long as he had hoped, for he had received information to the effect that Edward was once again causing trouble at Sutton Court. It was time, William decided, to challenge him.

Chapter 6
Lady St Loe

Shortly after Edward and Margaret made their way to Sutton Court, supposedly so Edward could assume the post of steward, William began to receive complaints from his servants, tenants and neighbours that his brother was once again causing trouble and threatening the good name of St Loe with scandal. Not only was he demanding that rents and other payments due to Sir William be paid directly to him, and then failing to account for them, but he had also attempted to usurp William's position as Lord of the Manor, going so far as to declare himself entitled to dispense justice by means of a baronial court which he established in the hall of the manor house itself. This was a clear and brazen affront to William's rights, and also threatened to attract the attentions of the Elizabethan authorities, who were increasingly eager to see that England's judicial system operated openly, efficiently and within the bounds of the law. William had no choice but to investigate the matter of Edward's behaviour as a matter of urgency, and so at the beginning of November 1560, accompanied by his younger brother Clement and a group of supporters, he set off for Somerset.

They travelled first to visit their mother, Dame Margaret, who was now living in one of the family properties in Somerset, for whom they carried jewellery and cloth as presents, and with whom they no doubt discussed Edward's latest antics and how he might best be dealt with, Dame Margaret having a reputation for shrewdness and common sense. William then set off for Sutton Court, possibly accompanied by Clement though this is not clear. On his arrival at his ancestral home, William soon discovered that the reports he had been receiving concerning Edward, were, essentially, true in every respect, and he promptly dismissed Edward as his steward and ordered him and presumably Margaret to leave Sutton Court as soon as possible. Unfortunately, the Queen was by now demanding his immediate return to the Court and was by all accounts (as he later reported to Bess by letter) less than happy with what she perceived as William's long absence. William had no choice but to immediately set off back for London once more and he did so before Edward had departed. Bess, still at Chatsworth, set off for London herself a few weeks later with the intention of spending Christmas there with Sir William.

Without William being present to supervise Edward's ejection from the house and estate, Edward simply ignored the fact of his dismissal and continued to reside at Sutton Court as if he were the Lord of the Manor. As a consequence, with his patience more than exhausted, William issued legal proceedings against Edward in January 1561, essentially arguing that Edward was illegally occupying Sutton Court, withholding monies due to William, usurping his rights of the Lord of the Manor, had made false financial claims, stolen and falsified documents and in summary was acting in breach of the duties he had owed William as his steward. Interestingly, it would appear that no mention was made in the initial charges brought against Edward of his alleged attempt to procure the poisoning of Bess. It may be that William (and Bess) thought they had sufficient evidence to justify the charges which were brought and concluded that it might weaken their case generally if they were to make a claim for which no evidence against Edward himself could yet be found, even though they themselves were certain as to his guilt.

The court hearing, once it convened, soon degenerated into a series of claims and counterclaims, with Edward for his part seeking to respond to the charges brought against him by claiming once again that his wife Margaret had been given a life interest in Sutton Court and that his brother owed him considerable sums for payments he himself had made as steward on William's behalf. Evidence was advanced as regards Edward's poor character; Edward responded by alleging that Bess was using "unnatural devices and practices" (meaning sorcery and witchcraft) to undermine Edward's position as William's heir and to benefit herself in his place.

William responded to this (through his lawyer) by declaring that Bess had never indulged in unnatural activities of any kind, and that in any event, prior to the poisoning attempt (which had by now been raised in the proceedings as an issue, albeit one of many), Bess had shown nothing but good will towards Edward, both before the marriage and after. Moreover, she:

> ... *prswaded the same Sr Willm Stlowe to entaile the Remaynder of all his Lande for faulte of issue of theyre Bodyes to the sayd Edwarde Stlowe and ever refused the joynt fee simple thereof wt the said Sr Willm until prceyving his Brothere to moche unaturalnes and unseamley speaches of hym and his wife did of verye good will towarde her convey the same unto her ...*

Which seems clear enough.

Considering the weight of evidence against him, Edward (or more likely, his lawyer) did a very effective job of raising counter-challenges, confusions and complications to the point where what had seemed to be a fairly straightforward set of facts began to be seen by the presiding judge as being nothing of the sort. Eventually, perhaps if only to bring the whole proceedings to some sort of conclusion, under the judge's guidance, a compromise of sorts was reached whereby Edward and Margaret were permitted to continue to live at Sutton Court in exchange for the payment of rent to William. All rents and other payments arising from the estate were to be paid to William, with some being remitted back to Edward, presumably as a form of remuneration for him essentially continuing to act as William's steward, although this last point is not entirely certain. Exactly what William and Bess thought of this compromise, which to a significant extent appears to have left Edward in much the sort of position he would have been in if he had carried out his duties properly in the first place is unclear, but it seems unlikely that they would have looked upon it with any great enthusiasm. Still, it had the merit of drawing a line under the matter at least for the moment, and William now had a court ruling specifying how Edward should behave in the future, and which could be referred to in the event of further delinquency.

All the troubles surrounding the court case, the poisoning and the possibility of Edward causing further mischief in the future did galvanise William St Loe in one important respect, and in a way that would prove to be of immense significance to Bess and the Cavendish family. In default of William producing a son, Edward was still his primary heir and as matters stood, it was not impossible that Edward might still inherit the bulk of the St Loe fortune that had been so slowly and carefully accumulated over the preceding centuries. William was determined to make sure that this would not happen. One possibility for William might have been for him to make a new will leaving his property, or a significant portion of it at any rate, to Clement or his other younger brother John, which would have had the merit of keeping the St Loe lands within the St Loe family, but for whatever reason, William chose not to do this.

Instead, he arranged matters so his estate would pass to Bess and thereafter to her heirs and confirmed this by making a deed of gift which passed the titles to his lands to her. Whether Bess had urged him to do this is unclear, but it seems out of character, particularly bearing in mind how William during the trial had vehemently denied Bess had tried to influence him to Edward's disadvantage. Moreover, his actions in this regard would be consistent with what we know of the depth of feeling William St Loe clearly had for Bess. That said, when news of the will was finally made public, following Sir William's death, there were not lacking those (including, inevitably Edward) who loudly proclaimed Bess had exerted what we would today call undue influence and sought to challenge William's actions accordingly. For the time being, however, William kept the knowledge of the change to his testamentary arrangements a secret. After all, he and Bess might yet have a son of their own, in which case (assuming this hypothetical son survived), any question as to who might inherit the St Loe lands would become largely academic. And it may also have been that neither William nor Bess saw any reason to antagonise Edward any more than necessary if that could reasonably be avoided.

In the meantime, life continued much as before, with William often busy with his Court duties, and Bess dividing her time between her responsibilities as a Lady of the Privy Chamber, her obligations as a wife, a mother and stepmother (her two eldest sons were now away much of the year being taught at Eton) and as always supervising either by letter or in person the building works at Chatsworth and the operations of the estate.[1] Then, in August 1561, and through no fault of her own, Bess found herself being drawn into the latest of the scandals to befall Queen Elizabeth's Court and, potentially into serious trouble with the sovereign herself.

The origins of the problem lay with Bess's friendship with Lady Frances, the mother of Lady Jane Grey. In 1555, having been widowed after the execution of her first husband Henry Grey, she had married her Master of the Horse, Adrian Stokes, an act which had caused her a certain degree of notoriety at the time as she was generally considered to have remarried considerably below her station. It may well though have afforded her some modicum of protection from the ongoing suspicions of Queen Mary who understandably remained acutely aware of the potential threat to her throne posed by any children Lady Frances might have. Queen Mary might have had suspicions about Lady Frances' ambitions for her surviving children by Henry Grey, but even she would have had to concede that any threat posed by a child produced by Lady Frances with Adrian Stokes was unlikely to be significant. Lady Frances and Stokes went on to have three children, but they were either stillborn or died in infancy, a sad fact that nevertheless did not preclude Lady Frances and Stokes enjoying what was generally considered to be a happy marriage until Lady Frances died in 1559.

This left Lady Frances' two surviving children by Henry Grey, Lady Katherine Grey and Lady Mary Grey. Perhaps because the eldest, Lady

---

[1] It is rather surprising that the Queen appears to have been far more tolerant of Bess attending to personal matters than she was of Sir William, or indeed her other ladies-in-waiting. Perhaps she felt that the presence of one St Loe at Court was enough.

Katherine, technically became the heir-presumptive to the English throne when Queen Mary died, Queen Elizabeth was known to dislike her, although she did eventually appoint Lady Katherine as one of her Ladies of the Bedchamber, probably to keep a close eye on what she was up to. Like her half-sister, Queen Elizabeth had her suspicions about the extent to which the surviving members of the Grey family harboured ambitions for the Crown.

Being an object of dislike for the Queen would have been a serious problem for anyone, particularly someone who held a position in close proximity to the throne, but the situation was exacerbated at some point in 1558 or thereabouts when Lady Katherine met Edward Seymour, Earl of Hertford, the son of the Duke of Somerset who had been the Lord Protector in King Edward VI's reign until his fall from power and subsequent execution. Before too long, Edward Seymour and Lady Katherine decided they wished to marry, and having informed their respective and redoubtable mothers, received their tentative blessings and consents. Unfortunately, the Succession to the Crown: Marriage Act of 1536 (commonly referred to as the Royal Marriage Act of 1536) forbade the marriage of anyone having royal blood without the consent of the monarch. Lady Katherine was certainly subject to its provisions, and so arguably, was Edward Seymour. This meant of course that it would be necessary to obtain the Queen's consent to the marriage before it took place, but no one seems to have been willing to take upon themselves the task of actually asking her, and she might well have refused permission in any event.

For a little while therefore, the romance was halted in its tracks, with Lady Katherine fully occupied at Court under the watchful eye of her sovereign, and Edward Seymour unable to procure a way to spend any meaningful time with her. At this point, fate intervened in the form of Lady Jane Seymour, Edward's sister, and a friend of Lady Katherine, who offered the courting couple the opportunity to meet in her rooms at Court. There, the two decided to marry as soon as possible, or at least as soon as the Queen left London, and to do so without the Queen's permission.

In late November 1560, the Queen and most of her courtiers departed from Westminster, where the Court was then resident, to go hunting near Eltham. Somehow, by feigning illness, Lady Katherine and Lady Jane secured permission to remain behind, but shortly after the Queen and the rest of the Court had left, they crept out of the palace and made their way to Seymour's house in Canon Row where the Earl was waiting for them. A clergyman was supposed to join them to perform the marriage service but was nowhere to be found – he may have realised the proposed marriage had not been sanctioned by the Queen and wanted nothing to do with the proceedings – and so Lady Jane went out into the streets in search of another one, returning about fifteen minutes later with a priest who was willing to perform the service. That took place in Edward Seymour's bedchamber, after which Lady Jane gave the priest ten pounds (about £5000 today) and then ushered him out, leaving the newly married couple to consummate their marriage. Consummation complete, Lady Katherine and Lady Jane took their leave of Seymour and made their way back to the Palace of Westminster, with nobody there being aware that they had been absent.

Lady Katherine and her new husband contrived to meet secretly a few times over the next two or three months, usually with the amiable assistance of Lady Jane, but on 19th March 1561 Lady Jane died, probably of tuberculosis, and meetings thereafter became much harder for the couple to arrange. Then the Queen ordered Seymour to accompany Thomas Cecil, Sir William Cecil's eldest son, on a tour of Europe which was supposed to widen Thomas' education and appreciation of the wider world beyond England (and quite possibly Seymour's as well).[2]

---

[2] One of the primary reasons for this tour was William Cecil's concern that Thomas was lazy and growing up without the self-discipline and knowledge that Cecil believed would be vital if Thomas was to thrive in the harsh world of Tudor politics as his heir, and which Cecil himself had demonstrated so ably. Cecil no doubt meant well (and Thomas in fact went on to enjoy a successful life, becoming in time the First Earl of Exeter and a stout supporter of his far more able half-brother Robert Cecil), but the trip from an educational standpoint

Just before they departed, Lady Katherine managed to snatch a few furtive moments with Seymour, and confided she might be pregnant. She promised to write to him when she had more definite news and he promised to return to stand with her if it transpired she was pregnant. A little while later, she wrote to tell him she was indeed expecting a child, and asked him to return but, whether because he thought it advisable to loiter a little longer on the continent, or because he genuinely could not return, he failed to do so.

Lady Katherine contrived to keep her pregnancy secret until the summer of 1561, when she suddenly seems to have realised that she could do so no longer. Seymour being absent, she desperately needed someone in whom she could confide, and perhaps unsurprisingly, given the close and longstanding friendship that had existed between Bess and her late mother, she chose Bess as the person best placed to help her. Conveniently, Bess was now once more at Court, carrying out her duties as a Lady of the Privy Chamber. On the evening of 9th August 1561, Lady Katherine managed to speak with Bess alone,[3] and hurriedly explained her circumstances and troubles. Perhaps she expected Bess to respond with expressions of sympathy and support if not hearty approval of the situation, but what actually happened was that on hearing the news, Bess (according to later testimony given by Lady Katherine):

---

was a small disaster. Not only did Thomas fail to improve his foreign language skills, but Cecil was disturbed to receive reports that his son had stolen money from his own tutor (who had joined the tour) and was in the process of seeking to seduce the daughter of a French aristocrat. "I see in the end my son will come home like a spending sot and meet to keep a tennis court" Cecil complained bitterly. Exactly where Seymour was whilst all this was going on is unclear.

[3] It should be noted that some biographers assert that Lady Katherine in fact spoke with Mistress Elizabeth St Loe (well, one of them anyway), rather than Bess. The available evidence is such that the possibility cannot be discounted; on balance however, it seems more likely that in the circumstances, Lady Katherine would have spoken to an old family friend, that is, Bess, and that is the assumption made in this book.

"… fell into great weeping and saying that shee was very sorrie that she had so done without the consent and knowledge of the Queen …"

Bess was all too aware of the implications of the Royal Marriage Act and how any breach of it might easily be regarded as an act of treason, causing the suspicious eyes of the Queen to fall not only on Edward Seymour and Lady Katherine, but upon anyone else with even a tenuous connection with the matter, now potentially including herself. Bess wisely refused to give any immediate advice or express any views, other than saying that she would consider the matter overnight and with that, she directed Lady Katherine to retire to bed.

The next morning, observing the behaviour of other courtiers and believing they were gossiping about her, Lady Katherine convinced herself that Bess must have spread the story of her pregnancy around the Court, though there is no evidence at all that Bess did so. Concluding that any further approach to Bess would be worse than useless, Lady Katherine approached the one other person who she thought might be able to help, Robert Dudley, who had been a friend of her father's and to whom she was distantly related by marriage. Dudley no doubt heard Lady Katherine's tale with the same amount of horror and trepidation as had Bess, but unlike Bess (who at least had simply sent Lady Katherine to bed and herself retired to give the matter careful consideration before deciding how to act), Dudley was not prepared to run any risk of being accused of being part of a conspiracy that potentially threatened the Queen. After hearing the story, Dudley curtly dismissed Lady Katherine from his presence and as soon as he could presented himself before the Queen to report all that he knew.

To say that the Queen's reaction to the news was explosive is, if anything, to understate matters; she was furious with Lady Katherine and Edward Seymour and desperate to be satisfied that this was not part of yet another plot to oust her from the throne. Lady Katherine was promptly arrested and sent to the Tower; Edward Seymour was ordered home from the continent at once, himself destined for the Tower the moment he returned. Sir Edward Warner, the Lieutenant of the Tower, was given strict instructions from Elizabeth to carry out a thorough investigation and report whether there was any evidence of a plot against the Queen, and those orders included specific reference to discovering the extent, if any, of Bess's involvement in the matter. Sir Edward took his duties seriously and Bess was summoned for interrogation, almost certainly in the Tower itself, although there is no evidence that she was actually imprisoned there. She no doubt spent several uncomfortable hours being questioned by Sir Edward and other investigators but seems to have managed to convince them of the extremely peripheral nature of her involvement in the matter and of her loyalty to the Queen. In any event, when her questioning was over, she was released and no charges were brought against her. It must have been an extremely harrowing experience, and no doubt the whole matter confirmed for Bess what she already knew, namely the dangers of becoming too closely associated with the political machinations of the Court, but in truth, in this instance, there was probably little Bess could have done to avoid becoming involved in the scandal to the extent she did.

As for Lady Katherine, she was held in the Tower in pretty atrocious conditions, perhaps in the hope that she might miscarry. In the event, she did not, and on 21st September 1561 she gave birth to a boy, Edward, who became known by the courtesy title of Lord Beauchamp (of Hache), this being a lesser title held by his father, the Earl. By now, Seymour had arrived back in England and had also been sent to the Tower, where he and Lady Katherine were both vigorously questioned; Sir William Cecil in particular had convinced himself the marriage was part of a plot against the Queen and emphasised the need for intensive questioning.

Despite this, no evidence of a plot was uncovered, though thanks to the death of Seymour's sister (and the apparent disappearance of the priest who supposedly carried out the marriage ceremony) no evidence that a legal marriage had taken place was uncovered either. The inquisitors seized on this, declaring the marriage void. This meant that Edward,

Lord Beauchamp was illegitimate, at least in the eyes of the law,[4] and thus could claim no place in the line of succession (and he never did so, at least explicitly). Upon this finding being formalised, the Queen relaxed a little and Seymour was fined £15,000 (about £6.8 million today) for seducing a virgin of the blood royal, though he ultimately only paid a fraction of this. In addition to the fine, it was declared that for the time being at least Lady Katherine and Seymour should continue to be held in the Tower pending a decision as to what was to be done with them. They were supposed to be kept separately, but somehow, they managed to evade this limitation with the result that Lady Katherine fell pregnant again.

This news prompted another royal explosion and the dismissal of Sir Edward Warner from his post. As for Seymour, together with his son he was sent in disgrace to live with his widowed mother, whilst Lady Katherine remained in the Tower and gave birth to another son, who was named Thomas, sometime in early January 1562. Eventually, perhaps prompted by a plague outbreak, she was sent to live under house arrest with one of her uncles, Lord John Grey and then, in fairly swift succession, two aging Tudor politicians called Sir William Petre and Sir John Wentworth respectively. She eventually died in 1568 from what may have been consumption or some other form of wasting disease, at the age of 27. Edward Seymour, slowly reinstating himself into the Queen's good graces, does not seem to have been notably distressed.[5]

---

[4] Presumably if he was illegitimate, strictly speaking he was not entitled to use the title of Lord Beauchamp, though he did so throughout his life. Moreover, *his* son Edward assumed the courtesy title of Lord Beauchamp when Edward, Lord Beauchamp died, and the title was inherited in turn by his younger brother William (who also succeeded his grandfather as Earl of Hertford in 1621 and eventually became the Second Duke of Somerset). The Barony of Beauchamp (of this creation anyway) became extinct in 1750.

[5] Given the Queen's known sensitivity towards the marriages of those in or close to the line of succession (and the legal position as laid down under the Royal

As for Bess, once she had effectively been cleared of any wrongdoing by Sir Edward Warner, she remained for the next few months in London, continuing to supervise the affairs of Chatsworth and its seemingly ever ongoing building works at a distance. In this she was assisted by two stewards, James Crompe and William Marchington, who apparently carried out their duties by and large to Bess's satisfaction, though not without a degree of hectoring from her from time to time. Bess's mother and her aunt (her mother's sister, Marcella Linnacre, sometimes referred to in the family as "Aunt Linnacre") were also then living at Chatsworth, together with Bess's younger children, and Bess could be reasonably sure that they would keep an eye on events at Chatsworth and let her know if they identified potential problems. She usually made it a point to try to visit Chatsworth for at least part of the summer each year, but in this year of 1561 she did not do so. Part of the reason for this may have been a feeling that having been subject to investigation by the authorities, albeit an investigation which had effectively exonerated her from any wrongdoing, being clearly seen to live soberly, openly and above all lawfully in London for a few months would do no harm.

Another reason for remaining in London at that time may have been that she had become involved with what would become a significant

---

Marriage Act) and the clear example demonstrated by the treatment of Lady Katherine and himself, Seymour's subsequent approach to marriage in the years that followed, as well as that of Lady Katherine's sister, Lady Mary, is surprising. Seymour married twice more, and on each occasion attempted, unsuccessfully as events transpired, to keep the fact of the marriages secret from the Queen. As for Lady Mary, she too married in secret on 16th July 1565, choosing as her husband the Queen's serjeant porter, Thomas Keyes. Like her mother, when the marriage eventually became public knowledge, as it did within a few weeks, Lady Mary too was judged to have married significantly beneath her station. More importantly, she had married without the Queen's permission (though unlike her sister, she could at least demonstrate that there had been a marriage service) and the couple were immediately separated. Keyes was despatched to the Fleet Prison and Lady Mary held under house arrest at Chequers in Buckinghamshire. They were never permitted to meet again, and Keyes died in 1571, having been held in Fleet Prison for three years before being released in 1569.

preoccupation of hers, namely the negotiation and encouragement of marriages for her children and stepchildren, an activity which when complete would see the Cavendish family linked matrimonially one way or another with some of the most powerful families in the realm (or families which would become powerful), and in time would lead to Bess becoming the ancestress of a significant portion of the British aristocracy. It may be that she felt that this was a task which could better be performed based in London with easy access to the Court rather than from Chatsworth. In any event, the late autumn of 1561 saw Bess still in London negotiating the marriage of her eldest daughter Frances, who was then thirteen.[6] The chosen spouse was Henry Pierrepont, then aged fifteen, the son of Sir George Pierrepont who owned a significant estate at Holme Pierrepont not too far from Nottingham. The Pierreponts had been a rich and influential Nottinghamshire family for generations and both Bess and Sir George saw significant advantages for both families in the union. Bess however probably had the upper hand in the negotiations that took place between herself and Sir George as regards matters such as the bride's dowry as Sir George was ill (he died in 1564) and almost certainly had concerns about his estate falling into the grasp of the Office of Wards. In any event, Bess and Sir George seemed to have reached an agreement fairly easily, for in November 1561, Sir George wrote to Bess confirming the terms of the marriage agreement, though he noted that it was subject to them seeing if the prospective bride and

----

[6] Marriage where the wife-to-be was only thirteen was not unknown in Tudor times, though it was perhaps generally perceived as being a little on the young side, and in fact Frances only married in 1562 when she would have been about fourteen. Broadly speaking the accepted minimum age for marriage then was twelve for females and fourteen for males, but often where the female was very young, and yet it was felt advisable that the marriage should still proceed, for example for property inheritance considerations, the parents might well agree that consumption of the marriage should be delayed until the female was somewhat older, though this did not always happen. Many Tudor couples did however only marry in their later teens or even early twenties. As already noted, Bess herself was in her sixteenth year when she married Robert Barlow. He was probably under the age of fourteen when he married Bess, but nobody seems to have worried about that.

groom actually liked each other. Apparently they did, for it was decided that the marriage should take place the following year, and in anticipation of that, it was agreed that Frances would spend a few months as a gentlewoman in the Pierrepont household, which seems to have been a successful arrangement. The marriage was by and large successful too, and Frances and Henry went on to become the antecedents of a number of significant noble families, including two dukedoms.

Securing the marriage of Frances and Henry was not the only matchmaking-related activity undertaken by Bess at this time. She was also diligently working on behalf of her stepdaughter Ann, one of Sir William Cavendish's daughters for whom Bess had assumed responsibility. Ann, now 21, was unmarried (Catherine, her sister, had married Thomas Brooke, a younger son of Lord Cobham) and Bess was keen to ensure Ann married wisely and to the greatest advantage. Unfortunately, as Ann had little money of her own, she was finding it difficult to find suitable suitors. To solve this problem, in the autumn of 1561 (it was a busy autumn), Bess arranged for an indenture to be drawn up, essentially a legally binding agreement, under which Sir William St Loe agreed to support Ann after Bess's death until she married. Moreover, he also agreed that he would identify a potential candidate as Ann's husband within a year (the candidate was to be approved by Bess, presumably assuming she was still alive). If Ann agreed to marry the candidate, Sir William would provide a dowry of 1000 marks (about £300,000 today), which seems astonishingly generous considering Sir William was barely related to Ann by marriage. His willingness to agree to this idea (almost certainly one suggested by Bess) is a testament to his kindness. If no candidate was identified within the one-year period, Ann would receive the money for her own use; however, if a candidate was proposed and Ann refused him, the sum she would be given was to be reduced to 600 marks.[7]

---

[7] A mark was about two-thirds of a pound sterling,

The indenture was duly executed and as a means of attracting potential suitors for Ann, it was extremely successful; with the full approval of Sir William and Bess, within a year Ann had agreed to marry Sir Henry Baynton, the younger brother of Sir William's first wife and presumably someone well known to Sir William and Bess. This marriage too proved to be a success, and Bess could comfort herself she had fulfilled her duties as a stepmother.

Chapter 7

Widowed Again

By early 1563, Bess and Sir William had surmounted a number of difficulties and dangers together and could reasonably begin to hope for calmer days in the future. Their positions at Court were at least for the time being secure, their financial resources (particularly those of Sir William) were continuing to grow and although not yet complete, the rebuilding work at Chatsworth had now reached a stage where it might be possible even for Bess to envisage its completion in the next year or two. Importantly, they enjoyed good health, as did their children. True, Edward and his wife Margaret continued to reside at Sutton Court, and neither William nor Bess had any doubt that Edward's resentment of them, and of Bess in particular, continued to fester, but at least for now he seemed to be behaving himself and adequately carrying out his duties of stewardship.

There were perhaps only two clouds that threatened the otherwise potentially blue skies of the future. The first of these was Sir William's lack of a male heir. When they married, William and Bess had probably anticipated that children, and quite possibly sons, would follow fairly swiftly; after all Bess had already produced several healthy children, and three of them had been boys. Bess herself seems to have had no objection to having William's children; she liked her children and stepchildren, and understood how important it would be for her husband to have a male heir of his own to inherit the ancestral St Loe lands. The fact that a male heir would be yet further assurance that Edward would not in due course inherit those lands was perhaps an additional incentive – Edward as yet knew nothing of the steps William had taken to seek to ensure the lands would pass to Bess in the event he died without an heir but there was always the possibility that William's actions in this regard might be successfully challenged and the birth of a healthy son would be the best insurance Sir William and Bess could have against this.

Unfortunately, although they had now been married for three and a half years or so, and when together enjoyed a close intimate relationship, Bess had shown no sign of falling pregnant. Exactly why this should be so is unclear; Bess was still only in her mid-thirties and had successfully given birth to her daughter Mary only six years earlier. She had of course also given birth to her daughter Lucres in 1557 who had died when less than a year old, and some biographers have speculated that difficulties with Lucres' birth may somehow have rendered Bess incapable of having further children. Whatever the reason, Bess and Sir William were destined not to have children of their own, although of course in 1563, they had no way of knowing this, and no doubt, though perhaps with increasing uneasiness, continued to hope that they might.

The second cloud that threatened their domestic harmony was the matter of the still outstanding debt that Bess had inherited from Sir William Cavendish. As a Lady of the Privy Chamber, Bess was in a position to raise the matter discreetly with the Queen at an appropriate moment in the hope that some sort of settlement might be reached, but if Bess ever did this (and there is no evidence that she did), the Queen must initially have been unwilling to sanction any compromise, or indeed perhaps discuss the matter at all, for during the first few years of Bess's marriage to Sir William St Loe, the debt remained outstanding and officially at least, the Queen's Exchequer continued to demand payment in full. The most that Bess had managed to achieve to date, with the assistance of her lawyers, was to initiate legal challenges through the courts which had served to delay matters and fend off the immediate attentions of royal debt collectors.

Matters finally came to a head in the summer of 1563 when Bess's challenge to the claims of the Exchequer were finally considered in full by the law courts. The exact reason for what happened next is not entirely clear – it may be that prior to the case coming to court, Sir William added his voice to that of Bess in petitioning the Queen for some sort of compromise - but for whatever reason, the hearing led to a settlement being agreed with the Exchequer. Under the settlement, Sir William agreed to pay £1000 on behalf of his wife, and his eldest stepson

Henry, who as heir to Chatsworth had become embroiled in the case, in order to settle the matter of the debt once and for all. Sir William seems to have paid the money willingly, or at least as willingly as anyone could who was expected to pay £1000 on behalf of someone else, and it may be that he was just pleased that he and Bess could now at last put the entire matter behind them and be free of the uncertainty that the debt must have been causing.[1] Bess too must have been relieved, and she celebrated by making a visit to Chatsworth, a trip which she had delayed making so far that summer pending resolution of the court case.

Sir William remained in London busy with his duties, but there is no reason to doubt that they were as close a couple as ever. Indeed, events over the next year or so show that Sir William was willing, perhaps even eager, to become more involved in the local affairs of Chatsworth, and of Derbyshire generally, for in the autumn of 1563 he became MP for Derbyshire, and the following year was appointed a Commissioner for the Peace in Derbyshire and Gloucestershire (effectively what we would today call a Justice of the Peace), signs that he increasingly regarded Chatsworth as his home.

Bess's rebuilding works at Chatsworth finally came to an end (at least temporarily) sometime in the early autumn of 1564. Sir William was visiting at the time, perhaps to see the completion of the final phase of the construction work for himself, and reference to the work having finished is preserved in the text of a letter dated 22nd October 1564 sent to Bess by an unknown friend. In the letter, the writer after commenting that he (or she) was glad that Bess was in good health, added that they hoped that Bess's sight of her "finished building" would continue it. Bess's good health did continue, and perhaps the sight of the finished

---

[1] The settlement must have had the prior approval of Queen Elizabeth, who was not known for being overly generous when it came to financial matters. The fact that she was willing to agree to compromise the debt at all, and on such relatively generous terms given the size of the original sum outstanding, must be a testament to the affection that the Queen privately had for Bess, or Sir William, or possibly both.

building did help, for Chatsworth as it then stood had the appearance of a fine new Elizabethan house, indeed state of the art for its time. It was perhaps not a prodigy house in the same class as for instance Longleat or Wollaton Hall would become, neither of which had yet been built, though work on Longleat would commence in 1567 following the loss through fire of the house which preceded it, but Chatsworth was fine enough, especially by the standards of Elizabethan Derbyshire. Then comprised of two storeys, it functioned well, both as a principal family home and as a testament to the power and influence that Bess wished to portray and she had good reason for being pleased with herself. For the moment at least, it seems that her building ambitions were satiated, though this would not last for very long.

Sir William was soon back at Court but Bess, presumably with the Queen's permission, stayed on at Chatsworth until early December when she headed south once again to spend Christmas with her husband in London. She remained with him there until sometime in early February of 1565 when once again she returned to Chatsworth, leaving Sir William behind. She appears to have left him on the best of terms and in the best of health, and so the shock must have been great when a few days after arriving at Chatsworth, she received an urgent message summoning her back to London as soon as possible. Sir William, she was informed, was gravely ill and possibly dying. This was a bad enough message to receive at any time, but what must have made matters even worse was her learning that shortly after she had departed for Derbyshire, her brother-in-law Edward had arrived unexpectedly to visit Sir William and had been staying with her husband when he had been taken ill. Bess must have immediately suspected Edward had poisoned his brother and she set off for London as rapidly as she could. She was however too late; by the time she reached London, Sir William was dead and Bess was a widow for the third time.[2]

---

[2] The exact date of Sir William's death is uncertain, but it must have been some time in the early second half of February 1565 because he was buried that month.

It is not known whether Edward was still staying in what was now Bess's London house when Bess arrived back in London but given that Bess (and no doubt others) must have openly suspected him of murder, it seems unlikely. Suspicion of Edward's guilt was however not sufficient by itself to support a charge of murder, and Bess had to accept that Edward would remain free (and, potentially, more dangerous than ever) as, whilst still in the depths of her own grief, she set about organising Sir William's funeral and sought to claim her rights to the ancestral St Loe lands. The funeral proved relatively simple to organise, and Sir William was buried at Great St Helen's Church in Bishopsgate, in a grave next to that of his father. Claiming the ancestral lands of her late husband proved more of a challenge.

It is fair to say that the news that Sir William had left his entire estate to Bess, and thereafter to her descendants, was not greeted with glee by many of her St Loe in-laws, and there were some at Court and elsewhere who had some sympathy with those family members who complained they had been improperly disinherited, though not every member of the family did so complain. Bess was soon being portrayed by some people as having exerted some form of improper influence over Sir William, causing him to favour her above all others, and inevitably it was not long before lawyers were being consulted and legal writs from various members of the St Loe family began to be issued.

One of the earliest claims, probably inevitably, came from Edward, who revived the old idea that his wife Margaret was entitled to a life interest in Sutton Court, a claim he had first asserted when his father had died but which had been dismissed. Now, within days of his brother's death, he was alleging that without telling Bess beforehand, Sir William had relented and secretly signed an agreement on the day of his death giving Margaret the life interest. Moreover, Edward asserted that he conveniently had a copy of the agreement to hand. If that had been true, one would have expected Sir William to have had his own copy of the agreement, but none could be found. Bess of course, through her lawyers denied that Sir William had entered into any such agreement and alleged that the document in Edward's possession was a forgery but Edward continued to press Margaret's claim and insisted the matter be resolved by a court of law.

This claim was shortly followed by one launched by Sir William's youngest daughter, confusingly also called Margaret, who called for her father's will to be entirely set aside, largely on the grounds that it was "unnatural" for a father to disinherit his own children without cause. Her claim was promptly dismissed by the Probate Court which found Sir William's will to be valid, but this seems only to have galvanised Edward into launching another attack upon Bess. He began once again to withhold rent monies which under the previous court settlement had been payable to Sir William and which now by right should have been paid to his widow. Bess immediately commenced legal proceedings against him, but when the court assembled in Somerset a mere two months after Sir William's death, Edward claimed as part of his defence that he had only been forced to enter into the previous compromise settlement as a result of Bess's malice towards him and effectively argued that the earlier settlement should be regarded as being void. He also alleged that many of the St Loe lands had been entailed[3] "since antiquity", so that they should have automatically passed to him when his brother died without a male heir, that Bess had known this and yet had still improperly induced Sir William to bestow all his property on her, resulting in the illegal disinheritance of his sister and himself.

Bess's lawyers countered by seeking to demonstrate that none of the St Loe lands were subject to an historic entail, that Bess had behaved perfectly properly in her dealings with Edward and that as the Probate Court had already ruled, Sir William's will was valid but as in the case

---

[3] The entailment of land involves the restriction of the succession of such land to a specific class of potential beneficiaries, so that the land cannot simply be disposed of, for example by sale or under a will at the discretion of the current landowner, but rather must pass to whoever has the benefit of the entail when the current landowner dies. If the St Loe lands had been entailed when William St Loe died and Edward had the benefit of the entail, Sir William could not legally have left the lands to Bess and her descendants.

of the hearings in 1561, an avalanche of claims and counterclaims between the parties only succeeded in obscuring the true facts and delaying matters. The case dragged on for two years, but finally, again as in 1561, the judge issued what to outsiders might have seemed as good a compromise judgment as could be achieved in the circumstances.

Broadly speaking, the judge confirmed the validity of the will, and that the bulk of the St Loe lands should be considered to have passed to Bess and her heirs. To the surprise of some observers, and no doubt to the private fury of Bess, although she seems to have had the sense to keep that fury to herself, the judge ruled that Sir William had indeed on his death bed signed an agreement granting a life interest in Sutton Court to Edward's wife; apparently the signature on the document purportedly made by Sir William was very convincing. The judge stressed however that Margaret only had a life interest in the property, and that after her death, Sutton Court and its estate would pass to Bess or her heirs, and not to Edward or other members of the St Loe family. It was a not inconsiderable but only partial victory for Edward and Margaret, and Bess did not seek to challenge it, presumably taking at least some comfort from the knowledge that the Sutton Court estate would one day pass into the full ownership of the Cavendish family,[4] and that her interest in the rest of the St Loe lands had been recognised. She may also have been anxious to draw a line under all her dealings with Edward and the claims of the St Loe family generally because by the spring of 1567, new matters were arising to occupy her attentions. Edward too appears to have accepted that he had won all he was likely to win from Bess, and after the conclusion of the court case, seems to have bothered her no more.[5]

---

[4] In fact, Bess and her fourth husband the Sixth Earl of Shrewsbury would buy the life interest in Sutton Court from Edward and Margaret early in 1568.

[5] Edward also had his distractions during the period of the court hearings and after. Perhaps to his own surprise, he had found himself ordered to Ireland on

Bess had moved back to Chatsworth following Sir William's funeral, no doubt partly to give herself some time to grieve for her late husband and wanting to do so in the place where she felt most at home, and in the company of her two as yet unmarried daughters (Elizabeth and Mary) and other family members, her three sons then being away at school for much of the year. Perhaps inevitably, it was not long before her need to indulge in further building works began to assert itself once more, and later in the year she ordered the commencement of the construction of a third floor to Chatsworth, including the creation of new and grand reception rooms. Fortunately, with the issue of Sir William Cavendish's debt now behind her, and no doubt anticipating that she was likely to have her interests in the St Loe lands confirmed, funds were now not lacking to meet the cost of this new work. This new project probably also served to distract her not only from her grief but also from the stresses of the St Loe court case.[6]

Bess almost certainly spent the remaining months of 1565 at Chatsworth there is no record of her being elsewhere. She no doubt would have been eager to see the new construction work well underway, and we might surmise that following Sir William's death, in the absence of a direct command from the Queen to return to Court (and no such command seems to have been issued), she preferred to spend Christmas in

---

military service, so he was outside England whilst many of deliberations of the court case were heard. By 1572, he was back in England, having contrived to get himself elected to Parliament as the MP for Downton in Wiltshire, perhaps with the aid of the Second Earl of Pembroke who occasionally employed him on various matters of a semi-official nature. Edward died in 1578, intestate, and seemingly not particularly missed by many.

[6] Even if Bess had lost the case, and she never seems to have doubted that she would win, she would still presumably have been entitled to her "dower's third" from the St Loe lands, though whether she would have been able to extract that income from a victorious Edward without yet another court battle is a different question. Even in that scenario however, that dower income coupled with that produced by her interests in the property bequeathed by Sir William Cavendish (and not forgetting her dower's third from the estate of her first husband, Robert Barlow) would have meant Bess was richer and more secure in her finances than ever before.

Derbyshire surrounded by friends and family rather than in London as had been her practice in previous years. She seems, however, to have returned to London sometime in early 1566, leaving the construction of the third storey at Chatsworth still ongoing, for it is referred to in detail in a letter dated 26th February 1566 addressed to Bess from one of her servants at Chatsworth, James Crompe. Bess clearly was keeping a close eye on all the details of the construction work, as of course she always had and would.

Some biographers have speculated that Bess returned to London, and the Court, in early 1566 for the primary purpose of acquiring a fourth husband but there is no evidence to support this. In fact, given that she was now well on the way to becoming independently wealthy (the court case against Edward had at least another twelve months to run), she may well have been wary about potential suitors pursuing her solely or primarily for her wealth and seeking to gain control of it, for at this time upon marriage a husband generally assumed a life interest in all his wife's property. Given the impecunious condition of many of the Elizabethan nobles of the time, most of whom would die in debt, this would have been a legitimate concern.

Bess was in the fortunate position, rare for a woman, even a noblewoman, of that time of having genuine financial independence – one estimate puts her income for 1566 at £1600, or about £773,000 today - and thus she had no need of a husband to support her. With this in mind, it would be understandable if, to the extent that she thought of it at all, she determined that if she were to consider marrying again (and aside from the need to fend off potential fortune hunters, she had no objection in principle to yet another marriage), she would only marry someone whose social position and fortune were at least equal to her own. Marrying below her newly acquired social station would not have been a viable option for Bess. If she did make such a private determination, this would have had the effect of removing most of her potential suitors from consideration, for those few noblemen she might encounter who might meet her criteria as regards social position and fortune would generally already have been married and thus unavailable to her even if she had been interested. In any event, she spent the rest of 1566 either attending to her duties to the Queen or at Chatsworth overseeing the ongoing construction work, supervising her various estates and properties and generally attending to family matters and for the time being at least, seems to have been contented to live a quiet life.

Such a state of affairs might have continued indefinitely, save for the fact that in early January 1567, Gertrude, the wife of George Talbot, Sixth Earl of Shrewsbury died. Shrewsbury, who had been born in 1528, was one of the richest peers in the land, far richer than Bess, and with an ancestry which could be traced back to the decades immediately following the Norman Conquest. The Talbot family had attained baronial status as early as 1331, and had prospered ever since, gaining numerous other titles and honours in the process, including the Earldom of Shrewsbury, which was created in 1442. The Talbot family therefore had a legitimate claim to noble status dating from the time of the Plantagenets and indeed before, something which thanks primarily to the bloodletting of the Wars of the Roses of the previous century had become increasingly rare. At a time when social status and ancestry was taken seriously, as it was in Elizabethan England, having Talbot blood in his veins gave the Sixth Earl of Shrewsbury a social cachet that very few other prominent men could match.

The effect of that social cachet was augmented by the Talbot wealth; by the start of the second half of the sixteenth century, the Earl of Shrewsbury not only owned or otherwise controlled a significant number of properties in London but also vast estates and houses across the country, particularly in the Midlands and the North of England including Derbyshire, Nottinghamshire, Yorkshire and Staffordshire. Those estates were not just farmed or rented out, as they might have been in the past; by the 1560s the Elizabethans were beginning to exploit England's mineral reserves, especially coal, lead and iron on a scale never seen before and the Talbot family, for all their noble status, had a significant involvement in that activity. Already important mines and iron smelting works had been established on Talbot lands which were producing substantial amounts of revenue for the Earl and he was eager to acquire more. In many ways, Shrewsbury was in the process of creating a prototypical industrial empire, albeit using Elizabethan technologies and approaches to business, one which in some ways anticipated the industrial concerns that would begin to emerge during the Industrial Revolution two hundred years or so thereafter.

Much like Bess, Shrewsbury would have gone through a period of mourning for his dead wife and then, (we do not know exactly when) again like Bess, formally appeared at Court once more, probably sometime in the spring of 1567. Unlike Bess however, he had less need to be worried about potential suitors seeking to wrest control of his fortune away from him, though he was worldly-wise enough to identify financially avaricious but otherwise insincere females and knew how to deal with them. In fact, after a suitable period of mourning, he was open to marrying again if he met the right woman, and it was in this frame of mind that he seems to have encountered Bess, presumably at Court.

They almost certainly already knew each other, both through their respective attendances at Court and as a result of them both being significant landowners in Derbyshire. In the past though, they had each been married; now they were widow and widower and could see each other in a new light. Details of their courtship are unknown to us, but at some point, perhaps in the summer of 1567, Shrewsbury must have proposed to her. Perhaps unsurprisingly given the financial interests of both families, Bess could not simply give an unequivocal answer of yes before various important matters concerning money and family had been clarified and agreed. This would not have distressed Shrewsbury; indeed, he would have expected it and probably have been surprised and even wary if Bess hadn't had concerns she felt she had to address before accepting his proposal.

Bess and Shrewsbury could each see obvious advantages to their union, both personally and for their respective families. Indeed, in many ways so far as their respective fortunes were concerned, it rather resembled a corporate merger of later years. From Bess's perspective however, given that Shrewsbury was so much richer than she was, the danger was that it might become not so much a merger but rather an actual takeover of the Cavendish fortune. The interests of her children, and especially her sons, had to be protected and then of course, there was the special place that Chatsworth held in her heart; she simply could not run the risk that for whatever reason, at some time in the future Shrewsbury, exercising his rights as her husband, might order its sale. Then too, she was conscious that marrying into the Talbot family could be of great advantage to the Cavendishes. She personally was not at all averse to rising still higher in the social hierarchy to become the Countess of Shrewsbury, and she would not have been the woman she was if she had not given some thought as to how she might secure some benefit from the union for her children, in particular her eldest son Henry and youngest surviving daughter Mary.

Shrewsbury appears to have understood Bess's point of view, and quite apart from his own feelings for her, which at this time were strong and sincere, he no doubt was conscious not only that Bess was highly thought of by Queen Elizabeth (and having another family member at Court upon whom the Queen looked favourably would do the Talbots no harm at all) but also that there were valuable coal and lead deposits under Cavendish lands. Both he and Bess therefore approached what we might call the pre-marital negotiations in constructive frames of mind, and they seem to have swiftly reached an accord as regards the form of their marriage settlement.

Broadly speaking, the two of them agreed that whilst Shrewsbury would gain control of the bulk of the Cavendish lands (including the former St Loe lands once Bess's claim over them had been confirmed by the courts) as would normally be expected of an Elizabethan husband, Bess would retain control of Chatsworth (it was entailed to her son Henry) and several other properties, and moreover be granted lifetime interests in several minor properties owned by Shrewsbury, presumably to give her a sense of security and a reliable and adequate independent income of her own. That much might have been expected, although to some contemporaries it might have seemed a little overgenerous to Bess. What was perhaps more surprising, although the practice was not unknown at that time, was the agreement Bess and Shrewsbury reached for the union not only of themselves but also of four of their children. Essentially it was agreed that Bess's eldest son Henry, aged about sixteen when the agreement was made in the summer of 1567, should marry the Earl's daughter Grace (then aged about eight). At the same time, Shrewsbury's son Gilbert (then aged fourteen) would marry Bess's youngest daughter Mary, then aged eleven. Both Bess and Shrewsbury (who agreed to the marriage proposals for the children wholeheartedly) seemed determined to ensure a close binding of the two families over several generations, both financially and emotionally.

The marriages of the four children took place on the same day, 9th February 1568, in Sheffield, at the Church of Saint Peter and Saint Paul,[7] although presumably given the ages of the brides, especially Grace, some time was to pass before the marriages were actually consummated. The date of the two marriages is well-established; what is surprising, given the social prominence of Bess and especially that of Shrewsbury, is that we don't know when they themselves married, or indeed where, though it was presumably somewhere with connections to them both, possibly Sheffield.

As to when it took place, some biographers have suggested it may have been as late as February or March 1568, possibly a few days or weeks after the marriages of the four children. This however is contradicted by a letter written by Bess from Sheffield to her old friend Sir John Thynne and dated 27th August 1567. The letter is short, and in it, Bess refers to a "suit" of Sir John's, perhaps a request of some sort, although the details are unclear. In the letter she writes that she herself could not "obtain" the suit but assures Sir John that she has earnestly moved her "Lord" to grant it. The Lord in question is presumably Shrewsbury; it is difficult

---

[7] Eventually, after some alterations and a few centuries, it became Sheffield Cathedral, the oldest intact building in the city.

to imagine anyone else at that time to whom Bess would refer to as being "her Lord", though Elizabethan rules of etiquette and courtesy mean that we cannot completely rule out the possibility that she is referring to some other peer of her acquaintance. More tellingly though, Bess signs the letter "E Shrousebury", something she presumably would not have done if she was still Bess, Lady St Loe. Unless the letter is misdated (and there appears to be no reason to suppose that it is), based on the evidence of that letter it seems that Bess and Shrewsbury must have married some time before 27th August 1567, and that by that date, she was the Countess of Shrewsbury.

That said, and having just boldly declared that Bess and Shrewsbury must have been married before 27th August 1567, it must be admitted that there is other evidence which suggests this cannot be true, not least a letter from Queen Elizabeth herself dated 29th September 1567, addressed to the Archbishop of Canterbury, in which she refers to Bess as "Lady St Loo". That letter concerns slander about Bess which had been spread by Henry Jackson, who had been a tutor to her sons, but who had fallen out with Bess, possibly with regard to his remuneration. His services promptly dispensed with (Bess's sons were in any event now approaching an age when University beckoned, at least by Elizabethan standards, and William for example would enter what was then Clare Hall, Cambridge in the autumn of 1567), Jackson had proceeded to spread slanders about Bess's private life, although the details are tantalisingly unclear. Slandering a friend of the Queen was a foolish thing to do, and upon hearing of the matter, the Queen wrote to the Archbishop (under whose jurisdiction Jackson now fell, as a result of Jackson having accepted a minor ecclesiastical office attached to St Paul's Cathedral) stating that she understood that the Archbishop had investigated the matter of Jackson's slander "against Lady St Loo" and that she required Jackson to suffer "extreme punishment", by corporal means or otherwise, which presumably happened, though yet again, the details are unclear. This reference in September 1567 to Bess still being Lady St Loe obviously contradicts the 27th August 1567 letter, but the apparent contradiction might of course have arisen simply as a result of much of the slander having been inflicted while Bess still bore her earlier title.

Alternatively, and even at a distance of more than 450 years, there is a certain hesitation in suggesting this, it might simply be that the Queen herself made a mistake; after all, if Bess had married before 27th August 1567, she might only have been married a matter of weeks by the time the Queen wrote to the Archbishop, and it may be that the habit of referring to Bess as Lady St Loe led the Queen astray. On balance, one might expect Bess to have known her proper name when signing the letter of 27th August 1567. Nevertheless, the contradictory evidence (and there are other examples, on both sides of the debate) means that there must in the final analysis, at least for the time being, still be a question mark over when the marriage of Bess and Shrewsbury actually took place. What is certain from other records, is that Bess and Shrewsbury must have been married no later than 25th March 1568, for she is referred to as being the wife of the Earl of Shrewsbury, and thus the Countess of Shrewsbury in documents from that date relating to a property transaction.[8] This was a title which she would retain for the rest of her life.

---

[8] It was around this time that Bess became a grandmother for the first time. Her eldest daughter Frances, married to Henry Pierrepont, gave birth to a daughter in 1568 who was named Elizabeth after her grandmother. Elizabeth Pierrepont spent part of her childhood and young adulthood in the household of Mary, Queen of Scots, which she joined at the age of four.

Chapter 8

Countess of Shrewsbury

Bess's marriage to Shrewsbury did more than simply raise her social status to pretty much the highest pinnacle of Tudor society, always of course excepting the Queen herself.[1] It also brought her much closer to the heart of Tudor politics and governance than she had ever been before, since her new husband's status inevitably meant he would be involved intimately in the great events of the day, and therefore, once she became his Countess, so would Bess. There were numerous issues and dangers challenging the country at that time, many of which might have embroiled them, but fate (and the firm direction of Queen Elizabeth) meant that a few months after their marriage, Shrewsbury and Bess were to be handed a task which, although apparently

---

[1] In terms of formal precedence, earls were and are outranked in the peerage only by marquesses and dukes, though there are of course hierarchies of precedence within any particular rank of nobility, generally determined by the date of the creation of the title in question. When Bess married Shrewsbury, regardless of whether it was in 1567 or 1568, there were only two marquessates in existence (those of Northampton and Winchester), and neither of the incumbent marquesses were then legally married. There was a single duke, the Duke of Norfolk (though not for much longer), but his wife Elizabeth whom he had married only in January 1567 died on 4th September that same year. This meant that when Bess married, there were no noblewomen ranking above her as marchionesses or (if Bess married after 4th September 1567) as duchesses. There were (arguably) four existing earldoms which had earlier dates of creation than that of Shrewsbury, those of Arundel, Oxford, Northumberland and Westmorland (though owing to the regrettable tendency of the Percy family to lose their titles and then subsequently having to have them restored, there is an argument that Shrewsbury should rank ahead of Northumberland). The first two incumbent earls listed were unmarried. Consequently, when Bess married, only the Countesses of Northumberland (if Northumberland took precedence over Shrewsbury) and Westmorland could claim precedence as countesses over Bess at times when this really mattered and in practice it rarely did. To all intents and purposes, aside from the Queen, Bess was now the highest-ranking lady of the realm so far as the rules of precedence and formal social status were concerned.

honourable and of supreme importance, would ultimately prove to be onerous (and indeed, expensive), and would be a significant factor leading to the destruction of their marriage. That task, passed to them on the direct instructions of Queen Elizabeth, was to act simultaneously as hosts and gaolers to the only other anointed sovereign queen on the island of Great Britain, namely Mary Stuart, Queen of Scots.

To explain how Mary Stuart was transformed from being Scotland's reigning monarch to Queen Elizabeth's guest captive (which, at least as regards the beginning of Mary's sojourn in England seems an appropriate description of her status) requires us to cast our minds back a few years before the time of Bess's and Shrewsbury's marriage. Mary Stuart had been born in Linlithgow Palace, in Scotland, on 8th December 1542. She was the only surviving legitimate child of King James V of Scotland (she had illegitimate half-siblings) but she also had Tudor blood in her veins, as her paternal grandmother, the wife of King James IV had been Margaret Tudor, the sister of King Henry VIII of England. Possession of that Tudor blood, coupled with her Catholic faith was ultimately to prove fatal to Princess Mary, as she then was.

Scotland, allied to France, had been at war with England when Mary was born, and it can be argued that the war impinged directly on Mary's life almost immediately as her father died six days after she was born. The exact cause of his death is unclear, but popular myth ascribes it to the despair he felt following the defeat of Scottish forces by the English at the battle of Solway Moss on 24th November 1542. News that his queen, Mary of Guise, had produced a daughter seems to have exacerbated his despair and perhaps hastened his death; of Mary's birth he is reputed to have declared that the Stuart dynasty "... cam' wi' a lass, it will pass wi' a lass ...", or at least words to that effect – there are several versions of what the King is supposed to have said.[2]

---

[2] The first half of this pronouncement was accurate enough for it is generally assumed to refer to the death of Marjorie Bruce, daughter of Robert the Bruce,

As Mary was a minor when she succeeded to the Scottish throne, it was agreed that during her minority, the government of Scotland would be headed by a regent, initially the Earl of Arran, though he was later replaced as regent by Mary's mother, Mary of Guise. Mary's first five years passed fairly uneventfully, at least so far as she herself was concerned, but then in early 1548, the French King Henri II, anxious to extend French influence to the north of England's border with Scotland, and aware that Mary, through her Tudor blood, had a potential claim to the English throne, proposed that Mary should marry his son, the Dauphin Francis, then aged four. The proposal was accepted by the Scottish Regent and Parliament, and at the age of five years and eight months, Mary was despatched to live at the French Court. She went on to spend her next thirteen years in France and seems to have thoroughly enjoyed the experience, culturally at least becoming a French noblewoman, but well aware of her royal links to Scotland. As planned, on 24th April 1558, she and the Dauphin married.[3] A little over six months later, on 17th November, Queen Elizabeth succeeded to the English throne, but her right to claim the Crown was not recognised by many Catholic rulers in Europe, including Henri II, who proclaimed that Mary and Francis were now the rightful English monarchs. To emphasise the point, he ordered that the English royal arms should be quartered with those of the Dauphin and Dauphine. These acts were seen by many in England, especially Queen Elizabeth and her principal

---

King of Scots and who was married to Walter Stuart, Sixth High Steward of Scotland. She was thrown from a horse, and died shortly thereafter, but not before producing a son who ultimately became King Robert II, the first Stuart monarch. The second half of the pronouncement was inaccurate as far as Mary herself was concerned; representatives of the House of Stuart continued to occupy thrones long after her death. In fact, the House as a ruling dynasty only came to an end with the death of Queen Anne in 1714, and so James V's prediction proved true after all.

[3] Just before the marriage, Mary secretly signed a document agreeing that if she were to die childless, her rights to the Scottish and English thrones would pass to the French crown. The English and Welsh of course might have had something to say about that had they known.

counsellors, not only as insults but as direct threats to the Queen herself, and would not be forgotten.

Then, on 10th July 1559, Henri II died from a jousting accident he had sustained a few days earlier. He was succeeded by Francis, then aged fifteen, who was crowned King as Francis II on 21st September 1559 with Mary as his Queen. Francis however was a sickly youth, and he delegated much of the day-to-day administration of the country to two of Mary's uncles, namely the Duke of Lorraine and the Cardinal of Lorraine who were members of the House of Guise. That done, Francis and Mary settled down to enjoy living as the French King and Queen.

Meanwhile, events were unfolding elsewhere. Following the death of the English Queen Mary, Queen Elizabeth of England and her Council had inherited a range of significant problems, including a depleted Treasury, a debased coinage, inflation, religious conflict and the problems of seemingly interminable war against both France and Scotland, which had led to the stationing of French troops in Scotland threatening the northern borders. Sir William Cecil in particular was anxious to bring an end to the wars – "A reign gaineth more by one year of peace than by ten years of war" was one of his favourite maxims – and both he and Queen Elizabeth saw the making of peace as an essential precondition to enable them to tackle the other serious problems facing the country. Peace overtures were therefore carefully launched, and in this, Cecil and the Queen were aided by the fact that in the years of Mary's absence from Scotland, a significant proportion of the population had begun to adopt Protestantism, and especially Presbyterianism which essentially developed from Calvinism, a strict form of Protestantism popularised by the legendary preacher John Knox. This swing towards Protestantism was by no means universal, but it paved the way for the making of peace with England. Peace became even more certain when Mary of Guise, who by now was the Scottish Regent, died on 11th June 1560, weakening the Catholic anti-English influence in the Scottish government, and placing effective control of the country in the hands of a group of powerful Protestant noblemen called the Lords of the Congregation. They responded favourably to peace overtures from south of the border.

So too, perhaps surprisingly, did the French government, now effectively under the control of Mary's uncles. The French were facing difficulties of their own, in particular conspiracy and rebellion on the part of some French Huguenots, and as a consequence, the need to recall French troops from Scotland was growing acute. The result of all this newly discovered desire for peace was the Treaty of Edinburgh, signed on 6th July 1560, under which both the French and the English agreed to withdraw troops from Scottish soil, and the French recognised Queen Elizabeth as the legitimate English monarch. Queen Mary however refused to ratify the Treaty, and continued to assert her claim to the English throne.

For the moment, that mattered little, and the arrival of peace was welcomed generally. Queen Elizabeth and Cecil in particular had reason to be pleased with the outcome of the peace negotiations, since the result was not only that the threat to England's northern borders had been diminished, but also that Scotland now had a Protestant-controlled government firmly in place and there was the hope of improved Anglo-Scottish relations in the years ahead.

This state of affairs might well have continued indefinitely, but for Francis II contracting an infection, almost certainly a mastoid abscess, in the late autumn of 1560. His health, never strong, rapidly deteriorated and on 5th December, he died, leaving Mary a widow. As Francis and Mary had been childless, the French crown passed to Francis' younger brother who succeeded as King Charles IX. He was ten years old and Catherine de Medici, the mother of Francis II and Charles IX, was rapidly appointed to act as his regent. For the young widow Mary, the changes brought about by her husband's death meant that there was no further place for her in France, and it was decided that she should return to Scotland.

On 19th August 1561, still only aged eighteen, Mary landed at Leith, and set about claiming such of the reins of power that she could lay her hands on, which was no easy task given the dominance of the Lords of the Congregation. Her Catholic faith was at best tolerated by many of her Protestant subjects, and while she succeeded in establishing a privy council of her own, there was criticism of her (to Scottish eyes) foreign manners and style of dress, with the preacher John Knox in particular being critical of her attendance at the Mass. Mary, for her part, demonstrated a willingness to accept as a reality of life the power of the Lords of the Congregation, and a majority of the seats on her privy council were occupied by Protestants, including her illegitimate half-brother, the Earl of Moray. Nevertheless, relations between the Protestant and Catholic factions both at her court and across the country generally remained tense and problematic.

Mary's Catholic faith, and her staunch refusal to renounce her claim to the English throne also raised concerns south of the border and threatened to jeopardise the slowly improving relations between England and Scotland which had been underway since the signing of the Treaty of Edinburgh. The proximity of Mary to the English throne under the laws of succession laid down by King Henry VIII, and the unwed state of Queen Elizabeth, meant that the English government kept a close eye out for hints as to whether Mary might be inclined to marry again, and if so, to whom. Her future choice of husband, and the possible production of heirs, were anticipated to be key factors in deciding whether England would enjoy peaceful relations with her northern neighbour, or whether the prospect of war would once again arise to trouble the northern lands.

The question of who Mary should marry also vexed the minds of many in the Scottish government, as well as Mary herself, much as the same question arose time and again in England in respect of Queen Elizabeth during the early years of that queen's reign. Elizabeth however, for all that she was adept at seeming to be enthusiastic about the prospect of marriage (to the right man, in the right circumstances, both of which she skilfully managed never to define), was ultimately too aware of the advantages of remaining unwed to seriously consider changing that state. Mary on the other hand made no secret of the fact that she would marry again if she found the right man and indeed actively set about searching for one. In the course of doing so, she appears to have given little or no consideration as to what would be in the best interests of her kingdom.

Despite these difficulties and suspicions, the first few years of Queen Mary's reign, once she had returned to Scotland, passed by relatively uneventfully. This satisfactory state of affairs came to an abrupt end in 1565, when Mary decided that she would marry her first cousin, Henry Stuart, Lord Darnley, the son of the Fourth Earl of Lennox. Darnley, who had been born in England, and whose family had connections both north and south of the border,[4] was descended from both King James II of Scotland and Henry VII of England (he and Mary could both claim Margaret Tudor, Henry VII's daughter, as their grandmother) and thus he too had a place in the lines of succession to both the English and the Scottish thrones. Nominally Catholic, on paper Darnley was a suitable husband for Mary and, not unnaturally, he was eager to become King-Consort of Scotland. He and Mary were married on 29th July 1565 at Holyrood Palace, something that infuriated Queen Elizabeth when she came to hear of it, as she took the view that Darnley, being an English subject, should have asked her permission first. She was of course, also conscious that merely by marrying each other, Mary and Darnley had strengthened their respective claims to the English throne. There was, however, little she could do about the marriage other than send missives of her displeasure through diplomatic channels. Anglo-Scottish relations began to become strained once more.

Queen Elizabeth was not the only person who was unhappy with Mary's choice of husband. Mary's half-brother, the Earl of Moray, together with several Protestant supporters, fearing that Mary's next step would be to seek to reimpose Catholicism on the country, rose in rebellion shortly after the marriage took place. However, despite briefly

---

[4] Though Lennox had spent 20 years in exile in England, having supported Henry VIII in his wars against Scotland, and his Scottish lands had been confiscated as a result.

seizing Edinburgh, Moray achieved very little other than wandering around the country being pursued by Mary's forces and without any definitive engagement between the two sides taking place. The rebellion, such as it was, soon became known as the "Chase-about Raid". Eventually, Moray and some of his closest supporters escaped over the border to Carlisle, seeking sanctuary in England, where, despite Queen Elizabeth not being exactly overjoyed to see them, they were allowed to stay in exile pending developments in Scotland. As for Mary, she could and did claim Moray's departure from her kingdom as a victory, but as part of the preparations taken to counter Moray, she had recalled from exile in France the Earl of Bothwell, a controversial Border noble who had been a firm supporter of Mary of Guise during the days of her regency and was known for his opposition to the Lords of the Congregation. She also appointed as her private secretary an Italian named David Rizzio, who had arrived in Scotland in the service of the ambassador to Mary sent by the Duke of Savoy, but who had somehow managed to inveigle his way into becoming one of the musicians at Mary's court. These two actions by Queen Mary would soon have consequences far beyond anything that she might have imagined.

Though Mary became pregnant by Darnley in October 1565, it did not take long for relations between the two of them to turn sour. Mary soon discovered that Darnley was weak, arrogant, vain, ambitious, generally unpopular and frequently drunk. Though treated as the king of Scotland alongside Mary as queen, and having been made the Duke of Albany just before his marriage, he was soon demanding to be made king in his own right, meaning that he would retain the title even if Mary predeceased him. Mary refused his demand, causing even greater estrangement between the two of them. Making matters worse, Mary had discovered in Rizzio a companion who reminded her of the brightness, erudition and sophistication of the French court of her youth, aspects of Renaissance life which were sadly lacking in the bleak and cold Scottish palaces of the 1560s, and which she understandably missed in her daily life. They became close and despite there being no actual evidence of any impropriety taking place between them, popular gossip began to assert that Mary and Rizzio were having an affair. These rumours caused significant damage to Mary's reputation, both within the court and elsewhere, and caused Rizzio to be despised by many Protestants.

By now, Darnley had begun to identify with some of the more extreme Protestants at Mary's court and elsewhere, including a faction led by Lord Ruthven, and he rapidly came to believe that Mary was having an affair with Rizzio. He began to plot with his new-found allies to seize power from Mary. On 9th March 1566 at Holyrood Palace, whilst the now heavily pregnant Mary, some of her ladies-in-waiting and Rizzio were dining, Darnley, Ruthven and a group of supporters broke into the Queen's dining chamber and seized Rizzio. Despite the protests of Mary, Rizzio was stabbed and then dragged into another room where according to later reports, he was stabbed a further 56 times.

Mary, naturally horrified by what had occurred, nevertheless kept a cool head. Kept under guard whilst chaos and disorder reigned about her, she managed to speak with Darnley and somehow convinced him that regardless of what had transpired between them, their lives were now in danger and it was vital that they escape as soon as possible. Darnley, perhaps discovering that his influence over the rebel lords was less than he had imagined, agreed, and in the late evening of 11th March, he and Mary and a small group of supporters succeeded in slipping out of the Palace and headed for the relative safety of Dunbar Castle, where they were joined by the Earl of Bothwell who brought with him several thousand mounted spearmen. Now with a substantial military force at her disposal, Mary returned to Edinburgh a few days later and re-established her control over her capital city and her privy council. Her half-brother Moray and other lords who had been in exile in England returned, and Moray, once more in favour, was re-appointed to the council. As for Lord Ruthven, he and many of his faction, seeing that they had failed to bend Queen Mary to their will, concluded it was now their turn to seek sanctuary in England and promptly headed there. Ruthven died in exile a few months later.

Darnley, who had certainly been involved with Ruthven and his fellow rebels and present at Rizzio's murder, now asserted that he was innocent of the crime and Mary, at least for the time being, appeared to accept that assertion. Relative calm was restored, though Mary's marriage to Darnley was now doomed, and Mary, safe in Edinburgh Castle, could focus on preparing to give birth. After a difficult labour, her son James was born in the castle on 19th June 1566. After he was born, Mary presciently declared: "This is the son who I hope shall first unite the two kingdoms of Scotland and England."

The months that followed saw Mary becoming closer to the Earl of Bothwell, who since the expulsion of Ruthven and his followers had been principally occupied in fighting skirmishes with border raiders. In October 1566, he was wounded, and taken to Hermitage Castle to recover; while there, he was visited by the Queen, who herself was taken ill on her return journey, possibly suffering from some form of internal bleeding. She eventually recovered and seems to have spent at least part of her period of recuperation deciding what she must do about her marriage, which had to all intents and purposes come to an end. Darnley had retreated to the environs of Glasgow, staying on an estate owned by his father[5] and Mary decided she had no choice but to seek a formal legal divorce. Before matters could proceed however, in early January 1567, Darnley was taken seriously ill with what was suspected to be smallpox. Mary herself had suffered from the disease when she had been living at the French court (she had recovered without facial or other scarring), and not withstanding her plans for divorce, travelled to Glasgow apparently intent on nursing her husband. Arriving at Glasgow on 22nd January, she remained five days with Darnley, before returning to Edinburgh, bringing her sick husband with her lain on a horse-litter.[6] They returned however not to Edinburgh Castle or

---

[5] By now, many of the confiscated Lennox estates in Scotland had been returned to the family.

[6] A carriage hung on poles, and borne by and between two horses; the most comfortable way of travelling on land before carriage suspension was invented.

Holyrood Palace, but to a house just within the city walls known as the Provost's House at Kirk o' Field, where it was decided Darnley should stay until he recovered from his illness. The house belonged to the brother of Sir James Balfour, a man who had served for a time as one of Mary's secretaries. Balfour, a skilled lawyer, was an ardent supporter of Bothwell but not averse to betraying his political allies when he found it expedient to do so. He was no fan of Darnley, and detested John Knox. To be fair, the detestation was reciprocated whole heartedly by Knox.

For the next few weeks, Mary divided her time between attending to her duties at Holyrood Palace and supervising the nursing of Darnley at Kirk o' Field. On 9th February 1567, she attended a wedding of a servant of hers at Holyrood in the morning and a banquet in honour of visiting diplomats in the afternoon, before paying a visit to Darnley in the early evening. Together with Bothwell and three other noblemen, she stayed with Darnley (who was now well on the road to recovery) for a couple of hours before departing with Bothwell to return to the wedding party at Holyrood, claiming that she had promised to do so. Darnley, grumbling, was still in quarantine and had to stay in the house, accompanied by his valet.

Then in the early hours of the following morning, two large explosions shattered the peace of the Edinburgh night air. They originated from the Provost's House, which was destroyed, and later investigations suggested they had been caused by two barrels of gunpowder concealed in a small room under Darnley's sleeping chamber. Those first on the scene must have feared that all the inhabitants of the house had been killed in the explosions and at least one of Darnley's servants was so killed, but then Darnley's body, and that of his valet were found lying against a pear tree in a nearby orchard. They were partially clothed (Darnley was only in his nightshirt), suggesting that they had either fled or been forcibly removed from the house with some haste. Moreover, they hadn't been killed by the explosions, but rather had been smothered to death. There seemed to be no doubt at all that they had been murdered.

For many there was no doubt as to who was guilty either; Bothwell was popularly supposed to have instigated Darnley's murder so that he himself could marry Mary, and there were a considerable number of people who believed that Queen Mary herself might have been involved in the plot, or at least have been aware of it and given it her tacit approval. Darnley's father, the Earl of Lennox, now returned from England, openly denounced Bothwell as a murderer and demanded that he be tried by Mary's privy council. With popular feeling about the murders growing ever more agitated, Queen Mary had little choice but to give her consent to a hearing being held, and it was scheduled for 12th April 1567. On the appointed day, the trial was held, but a lack of hard evidence led to Bothwell's acquittal on all charges after only a few hours. Popular opinion, and especially popular Protestant opinion, still considered him to be guilty.[7]

In the face of faction, scandal and unrest, Queen Mary's power to control her government and country now began to ebb away. A few days after Bothwell's trial, on 20th April, a group of noblemen and senior clergy, including the Earl of Moray and the Earl of Argyll, assembled in an Edinburgh tavern and signed what has been described as a "bond" approving of Bothwell's acquittal, declaring that the Queen should marry again, preferably to a Scotsman, and indicating that Bothwell would have their support if he should marry the Queen. The fact that Bothwell was at that time already married to someone else did not seem to be regarded as an impediment.

The next day, Mary set off to visit her son James, who was being cared for in Stirling Castle. It was to be the last time that she would see him. As she and her party returned on 24th April, they were intercepted by Bothwell and a large group of his armed supporters (some estimates put the size of the band at 800), and she was carried off by Bothwell to Dunbar Castle, supposedly for her protection, though it is not clear whether she went willingly or not. According to some reports, whilst at

---

[7] To this day the identities of Darnley's assassins remain unknown.

Dunbar Castle, Bothwell raped her, though this is not accepted by every biographer, and it has been suggested that the interception of Mary's party by Bothwell and her supposed abduction to Dunbar Castle may have been part of an elaborate plot concocted by Bothwell and the Queen. In any event, willingly or not, she remained at the castle for the next few weeks.

In the meantime, Bothwell busied himself securing a divorce, or rather an annulment of marriage, from his wife, who had been born Lady Jean Gordon, daughter of the Earl of Huntly, one of the most powerful noblemen in the Highlands. The annulment was granted on 7th May 1567, though it is by no means clear that legal grounds for an annulment, as opposed to divorce, existed. A little over a week later, on 15th May 1567, Mary and Bothwell were married at Holyrood Palace. There were those who believed that Mary had been forced into marriage with Bothwell, but this was not a view held by everyone, then or now.

The marriage, forced or otherwise, divided the Scottish people as even Mary's marriage to Darnley had failed to do, with many Protestants and Catholics alike appalled by the Queen marrying a man popularly supposed to have murdered her previous husband. Making matters worse, relations between Mary and Bothwell worsened rapidly after the wedding, even though Mary soon found herself to be pregnant once again. Popular rumour was reporting that notwithstanding the annulment of his marriage with Lady Jean (which many Catholics refused to recognise as legitimate), Bothwell was spending several days a week with his former wife. Before long, 26 Scottish noblemen (known as the "Confederate Lords") had risen in rebellion against Mary and had raised an army intending to challenge her authority. Mary and Bothwell raised a military force of their own, intending to confront the rebels, which they did at Carberry Hill near Musselburgh on 15th June 1567, but no fighting ensued, for the Queen's army made it clear they had no wish to fight on the Queen's behalf, and indeed many of her soldiers began to desert even as negotiations commenced between Mary, Bothwell and the Confederate Lords. Bothwell managed to secure safe passage for himself from the would-be battlefield on condition that he left the country, and promptly took advantage of this, leaving Mary to face the rebels alone.[8]

As for Queen Mary, she was taken into custody and transported back to Edinburgh, and then sent to Loch Levin Castle where she was imprisoned. Around 20th July 1567, she miscarried twins and then on 24th July, was forced to abdicate, the Scottish throne passing to her son James, who was then just one year old. The Earl of Moray was named as regent. The following year, on 2nd May 1568, with the assistance of a handful of supporters she managed to escape the castle in which she had been incarcerated for nearly eleven months. Even now, notwithstanding all that had happened, there were still Scots men willing to fight for her and she succeeded in raising an army to challenge Moray and his forces. The two sides engaged in battle at Langside, south of the River Clyde and just outside the then-boundaries of Glasgow; the result was that Moray's forces decisively defeated those of his half-sister. Mary fled again, this time heading for the English borders; though she still had supporters in Scotland (indeed her supporters would continue to fight what was essentially a civil war with Moray for the next five years), Mary now had no choice but to seek sanctuary, a temporary one she hoped, in the safety of England. Crossing the Solway Firth on 16th May 1568, she and 20 companions made their way to the small Cumberland port of Workington, where she met with Richard Lowther, the deputy of Lord Scrope, who held Carlisle Castle on behalf of Queen Elizabeth. Mary was courteously but firmly escorted to Carlisle Castle, and effectively kept there under lock and key whilst urgent messages were sent to the English Court asking for instructions as to what was to be done with her.

That was a question easier to pose than to answer, for by now Queen Mary was politically toxic (in different ways, to different people), both

---

[8] Bothwell made his way to Scandinavia, landing first in Norway where he was arrested, and then sent to Denmark where he was imprisoned by the Danish King. He died, still imprisoned in atrocious conditions in a Danish dungeon, in April 1578.

north and south of the border, and to Queen Elizabeth and her Council especially so, given that Mary's mere presence in the country might be sufficient to incite rebellion by English Catholics opposed to Elizabeth.[9] For her part, Queen Elizabeth's first instinct on hearing of Mary's presence in her realm had been to receive Mary at her Court, with all the honours due to a visiting monarch, but she had the sense to listen to her counsellors, who almost universally were opposed to that proposal, and it was soon dismissed from consideration. At the same time, there could be no question of Elizabeth supplying Queen Mary with soldiers and arms (as Mary was soon requesting) so that Mary could seek to regain her throne by force, not least because any such act would almost certainly lead to war with the Protestant Scottish government and quite possibly push Scotland into reviving its historic alliance with France. Simply allowing Queen Mary to leave England for France or Spain (which was another suggestion Mary made) was also not tenable, for once out of the country, and safe in one or other of the two great Catholic powers of the day, there would be little to prevent her from seeking to incite rebellion amongst Elizabeth's Catholic subjects; Elizabeth and her counsellors were acutely aware that Mary had still not relinquished her claim to the English throne. Indeed, assuming her abdication from the Scottish throne to be valid (and in practice at least, it was), the English Crown was now the only crown to which she had any remaining rights of succession.

Elizabeth and her Council soon decided that the only solution was for Queen Mary to be kept in honourable custody, at least until some other method of dealing with her had been identified. Mary protested vigorously when she heard the news, but to no avail. Keeping her at Carlisle Castle had the merit of keeping her far away from London, but

---

[9] Indeed, that such concerns of Elizabeth and her counsellors, especially Sir William Cecil, had merit was demonstrated little over a year after Mary's arrival in England when a number of northern English Catholic noblemen, intending to depose Elizabeth from the throne and place Mary there in her place, rose in a rebellion which became known as the Rising of the North. The rebellion was defeated, though not without some difficulty.

it was soon decided that it was too close to the Scottish border; there would always be the possibility either of Mary managing to escape or of raids from Scotland by her friends or enemies anxious to gain possession of her person. It was therefore decided in mid-July that she should be moved to Bolton Castle in Yorkshire, under the watchful care of Lord Scrope and Sir Francis Knollys. Several months later, it was decided that even Bolton Castle was insufficiently secure, and that Queen Mary should instead be held at Tutbury Castle in Staffordshire. It was reiterated by the Privy Council that whilst she was to be kept in confinement (she was technically still suspected of being complicit in the murder of Darnley, who after all had been an English subject as well as a kinsman of Queen Elizabeth), she should nevertheless be treated with respect and courtesy as befitted an anointed queen (Elizabeth was insistent upon this).[10] This meant that Mary's hosts and gaolers had to have the necessary social standing, as well as deep pockets, for Elizabeth had no intention of meeting the costs of Mary's incarceration herself if she could possibly avoid it. Most of the costs would have to be met by whoever was appointed to guard Mary. With these criteria in mind, the Earl and Countess of Shrewsbury seemed ideal choices for the task and were so appointed.

---

[10] Though Mary was not put on trial in England charged with the murder of Darnley, the matter was considered several months after her arrival in England during a conference initially held in York in October 1568, and then a month or so later transferred to Westminster, intended to negotiate details of an Anglo-Scottish treaty. Under the leadership of Thomas Howard, the Fourth Duke of Norfolk, the conference considered such evidence as was available (including the famous "Casket Letters" which supposedly demonstrated Mary had conspired with Bothwell to murder Darnley), but avoided reaching any definitive conclusions about Mary's guilt or innocence. It did however create sufficient confusion as to whether or not she had been a party to a murder plot so as to justify at least to many people the decision to keep Queen Mary in confinement, which may have been Queen Elizabeth's intention in the first place.

Chapter 9

"The Scotes Queen cumes to Tutbury ..."

Once Queen Elizabeth and her Council decided that Queen Mary should be put in the care and custody of Shrewsbury and Bess, matters progressed swiftly. On 13th December 1568, Shrewsbury, who was in London, wrote to Bess at Chatsworth, telling her that "the Scotes Queen cumes to Tutbury to my charge ..." and there seems little doubt that Bess was excited by the prospect, though she was realistic enough to understand that much of the task of entertaining Queen Mary and keeping her company would fall upon her. Shrewsbury too initially saw the appointment as an honour and a sign of trust from his sovereign. In early January 1569, he and Bess travelled to Tutbury to see for themselves the state of the castle, which, though substantial in size, had for many years been used as little more than a hunting lodge. Upon their arrival, they found Tutbury almost completely unfurnished, dark and damp, with a leaking roof and cracked walls, totally unsuited to house a queen or indeed anybody else. Appalled at the thought of the Scottish Queen being forced to stay there, Shrewsbury, at Bess's suggestion, on his return to London recommended to the Privy Council that Queen Mary be held at Sheffield Castle instead, which was also owned by Shrewsbury, at least until Tutbury could be restored to an acceptable condition.

Bess was at Chatsworth, and Shrewsbury still in London, when on 20th January 1569, a letter arrived from Robert Dudley (who had been created the Earl of Leicester in September 1564) confirming on behalf of the Privy Council that no matter the condition of Tutbury, that was where Queen Mary was to be held. With her husband still absent, and with Mary's arrival expected within two or three weeks at most, Bess had no choice but to try to repair and furnish Tutbury as best she could, pending the arrival of the royal guest. Writing to the Earl of Leicester, she confirmed that she had instructed local workmen to attend to the most urgent tasks of repair and restoration, and she also raided Sheffield

Castle for the best of its furnishings and had them shipped to Tutbury. Further items such as chairs, tapestries and gold plate were sent to Tutbury from the Tower of London and displayed as Bess thought best. By the time Queen Mary, her party and their escort arrived at Tutbury on 4th February 1569, the castle was as ready as Bess could make it.

Queen Mary greeted Bess and Shrewsbury with civility, but soon made it clear that she considered the domestic arrangements at Tutbury were far below the standards that an anointed queen should expect (and privately, both Bess and Shrewsbury agreed with her). Mary and her household were soon harassing Shrewsbury with complaints ranging from the quality and amount of food made available to them (local food suppliers were inadequate to the task of providing all the provisions required by the castle's now substantially expanded population) to the standards of the stables which now housed the Queen's horses (of which she complained she had too few, expecting further horses to be supplied for her use either by Queen Elizabeth or by Shrewsbury) to the quality of the rooms and furnishings set aside for the use of Mary and her attendants. It rapidly dawned on Shrewsbury (as it no doubt did on Bess) that housing Queen Mary in the style she demanded whilst at the same time following the strict instructions he had received regarding the necessity of keeping the Queen in close and above all effective captivity, yet still treating her respectfully as a queen would prove to be no easy task. With the cost of Mary's captivity largely falling on himself, within a few weeks of Mary's arrival, Shrewsbury was already beginning to express concerns about the rising expenses he was being forced to bear.

Bess in the meantime busied herself with attempting to keep the Scottish Queen amused. At this time, they seem on the whole to have enjoyed each other's company (they had a mutual interest in needlework and embroidery, which no doubt helped), and before long Mary and one or two of her ladies-in-waiting were often to be found in Bess's chambers sewing and gossiping about various domestic matters, matters which

Shrewsbury assured Sir William Cecil were "indifferent" and "trifling" and "without any secret dealing or practice".[1]

It was not long before the unhealthy conditions of Tutbury castle began to exact a toll on its inhabitants. Shrewsbury himself began to feel unwell, as did many of the castle's servants, probably due to the general dampness of the castle and its inadequate and unhealthy water supplies and sanitation arrangements, and within a few weeks, Mary too was complaining of stomach pains and other aches. Shrewsbury wrote to Queen Elizabeth and the Council advising them of the health problems

---

[1] At this point in her incarceration, in the early spring of 1569, Mary was prepared to be fairly passive so far as secret dealings on her part were concerned. A few months before, it had been suggested by some of her supporters that she should marry the Duke of Norfolk, who held the distinct advantages of being England's premier peer, from a family well known to have strong Roman Catholic leanings (though he himself had been raised as a Protestant) and extremely rich. Mary was for the time being content to allow her supporters to explore and advance that proposition on her behalf, not least because she somehow convinced herself that once she was married to Norfolk, she would be welcomed back to Scotland and able to regain her throne, hence the passivity. The fact that Mary was still married to Bothwell (by now incarcerated in a Danish prison cell) was not regarded as an impediment; it was anticipated that an annulment of the marriage would be easy to arrange. Norfolk himself was interested in the proposition; his leadership of the conference in York which had investigated the circumstances of Darnley's murder had apparently convinced him that in marrying Mary, he would not be marrying a murderess and he no doubt enjoyed the thought of being perceived as the King of Scotland. Unfortunately, the Scottish Parliament, unwilling to cooperate, declared Mary's marriage to Bothwell to be legitimate and made it clear that Mary's return to the throne was an impossibility. Even more unfortunately, especially from Norfolk's perspective, no one had bothered to inform Queen Elizabeth that the suggestion that he should marry Queen Mary was being explored seriously, which seems quite astonishing considering her reactions to not being informed of the marriages of Lady Katherine Grey and Lady Mary Grey only a few years before. When the Queen found out, as inevitably she did, in July 1569, there was a stormy scene at Court (it did not help that only a short while before, Norfolk had assured Elizabeth personally that he had no intention of marrying Mary). On 11th October 1569, Norfolk was ultimately despatched to the Tower for a time and Mary's hopes of returning to Scotland in triumph were dashed.

that were arising and suggesting that it would be advisable to move Mary to a healthier location, at least while improvements and further repairs were made to Tutbury. Permission was granted to move Mary to South Wingfield Manor, a manor and estate owned by Shrewsbury (but in which, under the marriage settlement between Bess and Shrewsbury, Bess possessed a life interest) about fifteen miles from Chatsworth and Bess was despatched there to make sure all was prepared for the forthcoming transfer.

Shrewsbury (with an armed guard), and at his own expense, supervised the transfer of Mary and her household[2] to South Wingfield Manor and they arrived there without incident around 20th April 1569. South Wingfield Manor, which had been originally built in 1441 was in many ways a far better place to hold Queen Mary in custody than Tutbury. True, as its name suggests, it was more a manor house than a castle, meaning it would be more difficult to resist a determined attack. On the other hand, having originally been built as a residence, its domestic facilities were more comfortable than those of Tutbury, and there was considerably more space to meet the needs of Queen Mary's household and that of Bess and Shrewsbury, though the water supplies and sanitary arrangements were still limited and primitive. Built on the basis of two courtyards, an inner one and an outer one, Mary and her attendants were housed in rooms overlooking the inner court whilst Bess, Shrewsbury, their servants and the guards were housed in rooms around the outer courtyard, and above the gatehouse which formed the principal entrance to Wingfield, so that a constant watch could be maintained on who was entering and leaving the house.

---

[2] Which after her arrival at Tutbury had expanded to over 60 people due to her being joined by various supporters, the cost of whose care fell on Shrewsbury. He was probably relieved and grateful when Sir William Cecil issued orders that her household was to be reduced to no more than 30, though Mary complained bitterly when she heard of it and essentially evaded the injunction, at least for a time.

Mary initially seems to have been pleased with the change, and the stomach pains she had complained about in Tutbury subsided, but shortly after her arrival she was permitted to meet in private with a messenger from Scotland. Exactly what news he had for her is unclear – probably confirmation that there was little sign that the Scottish people, and certainly not the Lords of the Congregation, wished for her return – and she reacted (as she would so frequently in the future when she received bad news) by bursting into tears, proclaiming herself once more ill, and retiring to her bed. Two doctors were summoned from London to attend to her, and under their ministrations, her health began to improve for a while. Then, towards the end of May, it worsened again, and it was decided that she should be moved temporarily to Chatsworth while South Wingfield Manor was subjected to a thorough cleaning. Mary was held at Chatsworth for a few days and her health seemed to recover but when the time came to return to Wingfield, Shrewsbury himself became ill, suffering some form of fever, and was forced to return to South Wingfield Manor on a horse-drawn litter. His illness continued for several weeks, with bouts of sickness, some of them sufficiently serious to cause Shrewsbury and Bess to fear that his life was in danger, interspersed with periods of apparent recovery. Upon hearing the news (for both Bess and Shrewsbury wrote to Sir William Cecil to advise him of the state of Shrewsbury's health), Queen Elizabeth wrote to Sir John Zouche (a neighbour of Bess and Shrewsbury, and a representative of a cadet branch of the la Zouche family) and Sir Ralph Sadler (a seasoned Tudor courtier well known to both Bess and Shrewsbury) instructing them to assist Bess in guarding Mary whilst Shrewsbury was ill. The Queen also wrote to the Earl of Huntingdon (conveniently located at Ashby-de-la-Zouche, some 30 miles or so from South Wingfield Manor) instructing him to stand by in readiness to take over Shrewsbury's custodial duties should that prove necessary.

Shrewsbury's bouts of sickness finally came to an end in late June 1569 and for a few weeks, Bess and Shrewsbury enjoyed a period of relative tranquillity at Wingfield, though Shrewsbury was now becoming ever more conscious of the costs he was incurring in housing Mary, and increasingly troubled by Queen Elizabeth's continuing refusal to provide him with actual funds, or even believable promises of further funds in compensation for the payments he was now regularly being forced to make. Nevertheless, Shrewsbury sought to carry out his duties as best he could, and it must therefore have been a rude shock in mid-July of 1569 when news of Queen Elizabeth's reaction to the discovery that the Duke of Norfolk had been contemplating marriage to Mary first reached his ears. The Queen effectively accused Shrewsbury of being untrustworthy and ordered that Mary should forthwith be returned to Tutbury, a decision against which Mary protested bitterly, but to no avail. To ensure the transfer happened without incident, Queen Elizabeth despatched the Earl of Huntingdon to South Wingfield Manor to effectively assume command there, which offended Shrewsbury deeply, but about which he could do nothing.

The Earl of Huntingdon was efficient and by September 1569, Queen Mary was once again ensconced in Tutbury, though under much stricter security than before. The number of guards assigned to her was doubled (naturally, at Shrewsbury's expense) and her household at last reduced to 30, which again caused Mary to collapse in tears and retire to her bed complaining of illness, though her histrionics seem to have failed to move Huntingdon to any discernible extent. Mary rapidly grew to hate and fear Huntingdon, and poured out her dislike for the man in a letter to the French ambassador dated 25th September 1569 which she contrived to have smuggled out of Tutbury, and in which she openly stated she considered herself "a poor prisoner in danger of her life ..."

As for Bess and Shrewsbury, Huntingdon (speaking with Queen Elizabeth's authority) made it clear that he considered that they had both been too lax in their treatment of Mary (apparently paying no heed to the strict instructions they had both received of the necessity of treating Queen Mary with the respect due to her rank). There was little Shrewsbury could say in his own defence save that he had been trying to carry out his duties as best he could and Bess no doubt felt much the same. Huntingdon appears to have regarded Shrewsbury with some contempt[3] and the working relationship between the two was not assisted by instructions they received from the Queen on 25th September declaring that they should jointly act as custodians of Mary.

In fact, they did not work together for very long; in November 1569, armed rebellion broke out in the north of England, in what became known as the Rising of the North. The rebels were largely English Catholics led by Charles Neville, the Sixth Earl of Westmorland and Thomas Percy, the Seventh Earl of Northumberland, supporters of the Duke of Norfolk who by now was imprisoned in the Tower. The intentions of the rebels were to seize Mary, depose Queen Elizabeth and place Mary on the English throne in Elizabeth's place. Together, the two earls raised a force of nearly 6000 men and advanced southwards towards Durham, which they captured on 14th December, intending to march from there to capture York and then to proceed to Tutbury. The Earl of Sussex, Elizabeth's Lord President of the North, hastened to assemble a force of soldiers loyal to Elizabeth and shortly had recruited 10,000 men, and when the rebels heard of this (and that another force of 12,000 men loyal to Elizabeth was being assembled in the south of England) they abandoned their plans to capture York and instead seized Barnard's Castle. By now though, the rebels' morale was beginning to collapse, and as Sussex began to march against them with his superior force, the rebels began to break up and retreat. On 20th December,

---

[3] The Earl of Huntingdon – a committed Puritan - was one of the few Tudor peers whose ancestry could match that of the Talbots, since he had Plantagenet blood, being descended from Edward III, and thus potentially could be considered an heir presumptive to the throne. He was loyal to Queen Elizabeth all his life, yet wary as she was of anyone who might conceivably supplant her as the reigning monarch, no matter how remote the likelihood, she was generally reluctant to trust him with assignments outside the Midlands. He had married a sister of Robert Dudley, Earl of Leicester, and once told Leicester the Queen would occasionally give his wife "a privy nippe especially concerning myself …" as a warning to Huntingdon not to allow his Plantagenet blood to cause him to develop ambitions for the throne. There is no evidence he held such ambitions, or if he did, he had the sense to keep them to himself and presumably he lived longer because of it (he died in 1595, aged around 60).

Westmorland and Northumberland fled across the border into Scotland and the rebellion was over.[4]

As for Queen Mary, when news of the rebellion reached Queen Elizabeth, she issued orders on 23rd November that Mary was to be removed to Coventry, her move there being supervised by Huntingdon and Shrewsbury (again at Shrewsbury's expense). The swift victory over the rebels meant that Mary was only held in Coventry for a few weeks; by 3rd January 1570, Queen Elizabeth and her Council decided it was safe to return her to Tutbury and so return she did. A few weeks later, the Earl of Huntingdon was released from his custodial duties, and responsibility for Mary's confinement fell solely on Shrewsbury and Bess once more. Henceforth however, their duties would be more onerous. Not only was Mary to be kept under closer guard than before, but Mary herself was now determined to engineer her escape from captivity by any means possible, no longer content to sit passively by as her supporters dreamed and plotted her release. Her intrigues now became more incessant, and Sir William Cecil ensured that a careful watch was kept upon all of Mary's activities, including the monitoring of her supposedly secret correspondence with supporters (and people she fancied to be her supporters). Inevitably Shrewsbury, and to an extent, Bess, were steadily drawn into this dangerous world of espionage and plot and counter-plot and the never-ending strain of this, coupled with the ongoing expenses he was being forced to bear, began to weigh heavily upon the Earl. By now, he must have been wishing he had never been selected for the "honour" of housing Queen Mary, and Bess may well have been thinking the same.

---

[4] But not the reprisals. Northumberland was eventually captured by the Scottish Earl of Morton (shortly to become Scottish Regent) in 1572, handed over to the English in exchange for £2000 and promptly executed in York. Westmorland, his titles attainted and his lands confiscated, contrived to escape to Flanders where he lived in poverty supported by a small pension paid to him by King Philip II of Spain until his death in 1601. As for the rank and file of the rebels, they too were not spared, with over 600 being executed.

Chapter 10
Death of Norfolk

The 4th of February 1570 marked the first anniversary of Shrewsbury's and Bess's assumption of responsibility for the confinement of Queen Mary and during that first year, the Scottish Queen and her household had been transferred from one set of lodgings to another six times (Tutbury to Wingfield to Chatsworth to Wingfield to Tutbury to Coventry and back to Tutbury once more). This practice of peregrination back and forth across the Midlands under Shrewsbury's eyes (and largely at his expense) would continue throughout the next fourteen and a half years, until August 1584 when Queen Elizabeth finally released Shrewsbury from his confinement duties, and appointed Sir Ralph Sadler to replace him; during the fifteen and a half years that Shrewsbury acted as Mary's custodian, she was moved in total 46 times. Transferring the Queen and her household from one location to another meant of course that Shrewsbury (often but not always accompanied by Bess) and their household (and Mary's guards) had to move as well. As Shrewsbury was under orders to remain in close proximity to Queen Mary, and not to leave his post without specific permission, he soon found that he was almost as much of a prisoner as Mary herself, at least so far as his physical location was concerned. This, in addition to the rapidly spiralling expenditure he was being forced to make, began to weigh on his mind,[1] not least because he feared that

---

[1] Queen Elizabeth initially agreed to pay £52 a week to Shrewsbury to meet the cost of housing and feeding Queen Mary and her entourage, but not only was this woefully inadequate, but Queen Elizabeth in fact paid less than this, with the result that by February 1570, Shrewsbury was already £308 out of pocket. Shrewsbury was also paying a significant fraction of the costs of the soldiers guarding Queen Mary. Moreover, the costs of keeping the Scottish Queen in captivity were not the only expenses Shrewsbury was obliged to incur during these years. He had been required to provide extensive funds in 1562 when his eldest son Francis (who would predecease his father) had married Anne

being obliged to spend long periods away from Queen Elizabeth and her Court might diminish his political influence as indeed it almost certainly did. Enforced attendance at the side of Queen Mary also fettered Shrewsbury's ability to attend to his various financial interests with the same degree of diligence as he had been accustomed to show in the past, and this too was a matter of growing concern for him.

To an extent, Bess, who naturally felt it her duty to support her husband, and who was expected to act as a companion for Queen Mary, at least some of the time, may also have suffered from the sensation of quasi-imprisonment at this time. Bess had more latitude than Shrewsbury, however, to attend to her own affairs and to family matters, which was just as well as the task of confining Mary was not the only challenge facing the Earl and Countess of Shrewsbury during those years. That being said, neither Bess nor Shrewsbury could have had any illusions that maintaining custody of Queen Mary was not their paramount task and that the achievement of this to the satisfaction of the exacting standards of Queen Elizabeth and her Council would require the utmost diligence on their parts.

This was exemplified by events which occurred a few months after the first anniversary of their custodianship. Once again, Tutbury had proved inadequate to the challenge of providing safe but secure accommodation for the combined households of Queen Mary and the Shrewsburys, and by the spring of 1570, there had developed a desperate need to implement a severe regimen of vital repairs and thorough cleaning of the entire castle. In May 1570, it was therefore decided that Queen Mary should be moved back to Chatsworth whilst this happened, and by 24th May, the move had been implemented, something that delighted Queen Mary, and presumably Bess and Shrewsbury. Mary was yet more delighted when it was decided that at

---

Herbert, a daughter of the First Earl of Pembroke, had provided money in 1568 as part of the marriage settlement for his son Gilbert and Mary Cavendish and yet more money when his daughter Grace had married Henry Cavendish. Shrewsbury's financial position was to worsen significantly during the 1570s.

Chatsworth the strict conditions of her incarceration which had been in force over the previous few months could be relaxed, at least to an extent. She was allowed to ride horses again, albeit in the company of Shrewsbury, and she had to keep within a few miles of Chatsworth, though she was allowed to ride on some of the local moors and she could receive visitors once again.[2]

It may or may not have been a coincidence, but it was around this time of lessened security that a handful of Mary's supporters concocted, or possibly resurrected, a plan which involved capturing Mary whilst she was out riding on the moors and spiriting her off to the Isle of Man, from whence she could presumably seek to escape back to Scotland or (perhaps more likely) head for France or Spain, either of which might well be prepared to offer her sanctuary. The plotters were led somewhat half-heartedly by Sir Thomas Gerard, a knight from Lancashire whose wife had inherited property at Etwall in Derbyshire, about 30 miles from Chatsworth. Other plotters included two brothers, Francis and George Rolleston and John Hall, a former servant of Shrewsbury's who had (according to later testimony) left the Earl's service as he had disapproved of the Earl's marriage to Bess.

Perhaps assisted by the relaxation of the security surrounding Mary, the plotters had somehow made contact with Mary's steward, a man called John Beaton, to whom they confided their plan. Beaton promptly dismissed the prospect of Mary being kidnapped from the moors, but offered the counter-suggestion that Mary might somehow escape from Chatsworth at night by means of a rope being lowered from a window. Whether the plan would have worked is doubtful; it would have been

---

[2] In one sense, this relaxation of the conditions of Queen Mary's incarceration is somewhat surprising, since only a few months earlier, on 25th February 1570, Pope Pius V issued the papal bull known as Regnans in Excelsis, in which he declared Queen Elizabeth to be a heretic, excommunicated her (and anyone who obeyed her orders) and essentially urged Catholics to rise up and depose her. As a result, anti-Catholic sentiment in England rose dramatically and the bull heightened the suspicions of those who saw Queen Mary as the focal point for rebellion against Queen Elizabeth.

astonishing if Shrewsbury had not set guards to watch the windows of Mary's apartment in Chatsworth both day and night, but in any event the plotters never had the chance to find out. Beaton made the mistake of approaching another of the Earl's servants, Hersey Lassells, with a view to recruiting him to Mary's cause, but Lassells, perhaps wishing to collect a reward or otherwise curry favour with his employers or the authorities, promptly informed Bess of the plot. Bess in turn told Shrewsbury who took steps to make sure no nocturnal departures by way of any of Mary's windows would be possible. Sir William Cecil was notified and the Rolleston brothers were imprisoned, as eventually were Sir Thomas Gerard and John Hall, whilst Beaton managed to avoid interrogation by dying, apparently from natural causes. Mary declared that she had never been a party to the plot, indeed had refused to approve when Beaton had approached her about it, which may well have been true, and she continued to enjoy the more relaxed regime at Chatsworth for several more months.

Although the plot had failed, the presence of John Hall as one of the conspirators led to some awkward questions being asked by Sir William Cecil[3] of both Bess and Shrewsbury, though they seem to have been able to convince him of their innocence of any wrong-doing. To be on the safe side though, Bess dismissed Lassells, who it transpired had been involved in passing secret letters back and forth between Mary and the Duke of Norfolk. Norfolk himself had been released from the Tower in August 1570, but kept under close surveillance and house arrest.

Queen Mary was moved to Sheffield Castle in December 1570, and then to Tutbury Castle, where she remained for several months before returning once again to Chatsworth in August 1571. During much of this time, Bess remained at Chatsworth, and saw little of her husband or Queen Mary. There seems to be no suggestion of a rift between Bess and her husband at this time (that came later), but it was the beginning

---

[3] Soon to become Lord Burghley – he was created a baron by Queen Elizabeth on 25th February 1571.

of a tendency for Bess and Shrewsbury to spend increasing periods of time apart.

Bess however, had much to keep her occupied during the spring and summer of 1571. Not only was she kept busy supervising the household of Chatsworth, but she was also increasingly concerned about her brother James. James had finally recovered his father's house and lands at Hardwick out of wardship in around 1547 and had married but had no legitimate children. He suffered from ill-heath, probably some form of bronchitis or other chest infection, and repeatedly ran into financial difficulties, requiring him periodically to turn to Bess for assistance, as he did in January 1565, just before the death of Sir William St Loe. Bess had generally provided him with funds when requested, typically in the form of loans, but she had understandable concerns about what would happen to the ancestral lands at Hardwick if James should die without an heir. Now, in the summer of 1571, James was facing financial difficulties once more, and had written to Bess asking for another loan and warning that if Bess could not help him, Hardwick Hall might have to be sold. Bess duly provided James with the desired funds but insisted not only on placing a mortgage on the Hall itself but (having seen the example of Shrewsbury's exploitation of mineral rights on Talbot lands) also on leasing coal and other mining rights under the lands at Hardwick. This represents an early foray by Bess into the business of mining, though as a general rule she preferred to own her mines and lease them to others to operate.

In the meantime, Queen Mary and the Duke of Norfolk had continued to exchange secret messages in the form of cyphered letters. Norfolk had also agreed to help Mary pass money to some of her supporters in Scotland, and, even more seriously, allowed himself to become enmeshed in what became known as the Ridolfi Plot, yet another attempt to depose and execute Queen Elizabeth and to place Queen Mary on the throne in her stead. The Plot was uncovered swiftly enough by Walsingham's spies in April 1571, but whilst the English authorities must have suspected the possible involvement of the Duke in the conspiracy, he was for the moment allowed to continue to live under house arrest.

Then, on 29th August 1571, two of Norfolk's servants, William Barker and Robert Higford, passed a bag of gold coins to a Shrewsbury draper named Thomas Browne, supposedly so that Browne could deliver it to another of Norfolk's servants, Laurence Bannister, who was based in the north of England. The money (which had been provided by De la Mothe Fénelon, the French ambassador to London) was intended to be passed on to several Scottish noblemen who claimed to be secret supporters of Mary. Browne became suspicious, opened the bag and found 600 gold coins and several cyphered letters. Browne reported his findings to Lord Burghley, and Barker, Higford and Bannister were promptly arrested, interrogated and tortured, and the cyphered letters at least partially deciphered. One of them appeared to reveal Norfolk's participation in the Plot[4] and Norfolk's servants eventually provided evidence to their interrogators implicating Norfolk. He was arrested on 7th September 1571 and conveyed to the Tower. A search was instigated of Norfolk's house where a hidden cyphered letter from Queen Mary to Norfolk and the cypher code were discovered. Norfolk was charged with treason and his trial scheduled for 16th January 1572.

Queen Mary, by now back in Sheffield Castle was ordered into close confinement when her correspondence with Norfolk was discovered, and Bess hastened to Sheffield to support Shrewsbury, who by now was becoming very wary of everything Queen Mary said or did. Then, as Norfolk's trial date approached, Shrewsbury was summoned to London in his capacity as Lord High Steward to preside over the trial. Bess elected to remain at Sheffield Castle, and Sir Ralph Sadler was appointed Queen Mary's temporary custodian in Shrewsbury's absence.

---

[4] It has been suggested that this may in fact have been a forgery planted on the orders of Burghley and Walsingham in order to incriminate the Duke.

Norfolk's trial date duly arrived, and Shrewsbury presided over a court packed with rivals and enemies of the Duke. The trial lasted one day; Norfolk was not allowed to cross-examine any of the witnesses who had testified against him (in fact the witnesses were not present in person, and the evidence against him consisted solely of written confessions and allegations), but he did confess that he had tried to marry Queen Mary without Queen Elizabeth's permission and that he had sent letters and money to Scotland on Mary's behalf "in doing whereof I did too much forget myself". He denied any involvement in the Ridolfi Plot or any other conspiracy aimed at removing Queen Elizabeth from the throne, and denied involvement in any form of rebellion. His denials did him no good, at the end of the day he was found guilty of treason and condemned to death by Shrewsbury himself, the Earl being seen to weep as he pronounced the death sentence on a man who he had considered a friend and whom he professed to have admired.

When news of Norfolk's death sentence reached Sheffield Castle, Sir Ralph Sadler thought it best that Bess break the news to Queen Mary. She duly went to her, but found the Queen "all be-wept and mourning", Mary already having heard the news from a servant. Bess tried, somewhat clumsily, to be supportive of Mary in a matter-of-fact manner, but in her emotional state, Mary interpreted Bess's mood and heard her words as demonstrating a deep lack of sympathy for the distress Mary was undoubtedly feeling. When Bess asked the Queen what ailed her, Queen Mary replied:

> "that she knew her ladyship could not be ignorant of the cause, and how deeply she must be grieved for the trouble of her friends, who fared worse for her sake ..."

She did confide in Bess that she was concerned that recent letters she had sent to Queen Elizabeth may have damaged Norfolk's case, but Bess replied that she might be sure that:

> "whatsoever she had written to the Queen's majesty could do the Duke neither good nor harm touching his condemnation; so if all his offences and reasons had not been great, and plainly proved

against him, those noblemen which passed [i.e. sat] on his trial would not, for all the good on earth, have condemned him".

Perhaps unsurprisingly, Queen Mary failed to derive any comfort from Bess's reply. Sadler later claimed in a letter addressed to Lord Burghley dated 21st January 1572 that Mary:

"thereupon, with mourning, became silent, and had no will to talk more on the matter, and so like a true lover she remaineth still mourning for her lover."

At that time, Norfolk remained locked in the Tower, awaiting Queen Elizabeth's signature on his death warrant.[5]

Mary, now viewed with deep suspicion, even hatred, by much of the English population, was ordered back into close confinement once again, and the somewhat more relaxed regime she had enjoyed in the summer of 1570 soon became a distant memory. When Shrewsbury returned to Sheffield Castle following the conclusion of Norfolk's trial, he found her ill and depressed (though this did not prevent her from seeking to stay in contact with her supporters – a cache of cyphered letters written by Mary was found outside Sheffield Castle a few days after Shrewsbury's return, and Shrewsbury was in no doubt of the continuing importance of keeping Mary confined). Shrewsbury's return was at least good news to Sir Ralph Sadler, who a little while before had written "I was never so weary of any service as I am of this …", that is, of guarding the Scottish Queen, and had added that Bess herself could

---

[5] Queen Elizabeth signed Norfolk's death warrant on 6th February 1572, by which time he was simply Thomas Howard, his dukedom having become attainted and all other honours stripped from him following his trial. Elizabeth seems to have been initially somewhat reluctant to order Thomas Howard's actual execution (he was, after all, her second cousin), and she for several months found various excuses justifying its postponement. Howard was eventually beheaded on Tower Hill on 2nd June 1572. One of the official witnesses of the execution was Shrewsbury, who (with Bess) had travelled to London for this purpose. Shrewsbury himself ultimately benefitted from Thomas Howard's attainder and execution, for in due course he was appointed Earl Marshal of England, an office Howard had held before his fall.

be no more eager for Shrewsbury's return than he himself was. Shortly after Shrewsbury's return, Sadler left with relief, but would again become embroiled with Queen Mary in due course.

Notwithstanding the stress suffered by both Shrewsbury and Bess as a result of having to keep Queen Mary in captivity, and the increasing periods when they were apart for one reason or another, the personal relationship between the two of them was at this time, close and intimate. This is demonstrated by a deed of gift that Shrewsbury entered into on 22nd April 1572, one which he would come to regret bitterly in years to come, but which he seems to have entered into willingly at the time. Under the deed, he passed ownership of lands Bess had brought into the marriage to her sons William and Charles Cavendish, subject to Bess's own life interest in the properties. This was not altogether an act of altruism on the part of the Earl. In return for signing the deed (which was unwitnessed), Shrewsbury was released from the obligation to pay:[6]

> "... some great somes of money which he the said Earle standeth chargeable to pay as well to the yonger children of the said Countesse as also for the debts of the said Countyesse and for dyvers other weighty consyderations ..."

The net result of the deed of gift was that Bess waived the right to be compensated by Shrewsbury for certain debts and received back lands which were valued at approximately £1050 a year (and which were settled on William and Charles, with Bess retaining her life interest). Shrewsbury himself was released from the obligation of making the

---

[6] It is now not entirely clear which debts are being referred to here; they may have been debts Bess incurred on the Earl's behalf with regard to the captivity of Queen Mary and for which Shrewsbury would have compensated Bess but for the making of the deed of gift. As regards the reference to Bess's "younger children", this presumably is a reference to a promise Shrewsbury made to Bess under their marriage settlement that he would settle money (about £20,000) on William and Charles when they respectively reached the age of 21, as William was due to do at the end of 1572. What the other "dyvers other weighty consyderations" were is unknown.

payments to William and Charles when they attained their majorities as he had promised under the marriage settlement, and may well in addition have received a cash payment under the deed of gift which might temporarily have eased his cash flow difficulties somewhat. Nevertheless, Shrewsbury was now finding the costs, both financial and emotional, of having to guard the Scottish Queen increasingly burdensome, and it was noted by some that he was beginning to manifest changes in his personality, such as becoming easily irritated and argumentative, especially when Bess was absent. Moreover, his troubles were intensified by the knowledge that rumours were beginning to circulate at Court to the effect that he and Bess were increasingly sympathetic to the plight of Queen Mary, and that as a result the security measures ordered by Shrewsbury were inadequate (though in fact they weren't).

News of the massacre of Huguenots in France in what has become known as the St. Bartholomew Day's Massacre, which started on the evening of 23rd August 1572 led to yet further tightening of the security measures in place for Queen Mary. To her intense annoyance, the number of her permitted attendants was reduced to sixteen and severe restrictions were placed on her ability to receive visitors. Then in October 1572, it was reported that Queen Elizabeth had been taken gravely ill by smallpox.[7] When this news reached Sheffield Castle, Queen Mary did not hesitate to point out to Shrewsbury that if Queen Elizabeth died, she, Mary, would be next in line to the throne and in the event of her ascending to it, she would remember who had been kind to her and who had not. This simply added to Shrewsbury's worries though, if only out of a sense of self-preservation, he and Bess (when

---

[7] She had already survived an attack of smallpox in October 1562, which may have left her with a degree of facial scarring which she thereafter hid beneath a layer of make-up comprised largely of white lead paint. Since, as a general rule, a person who has survived smallpox cannot contract it again, it has been suggested that in October 1572, Queen Elizabeth may actually have been suffering from chickenpox, the symptoms of which in a severe case can seem superficially to resemble those of smallpox.

she was in attendance) did try to make Queen Mary as comfortable as possible so far as their instructions permitted. In the event, Queen Elizabeth survived her illness of October 1572 and on 22nd October, she herself wrote to Shrewsbury (who had written urgently to Lord Burghley enquiring after the Queen's health) to say:

> *"... By your letters, we perceive that you had heard of some late sickness wherewith we were visited, whereof as you had cause to be greatly grieved, so that you heard of our amendment and was thereby recomforted yet for a satisfaction of your mind you are desirous to have the state of our amendment certified by some few words in a letter from ourself ..."*

Elizabeth went on to describe that she had been "... distempered, as commonly happeneth in the beginning of a fever ..." and that certain red spots had appeared on her face "... likely to prove the smallpox ..." but she hurriedly added that the spots had disappeared after four or five days, and stressed that she had fully recovered and that "her faithful Shrewsbury" should allow no grief to touch his heart for fear of her disease.

So far as Queen Elizabeth was concerned then, it was a case of carrying on business as usual, and she appears not at this time to have given much credence to the rumours of potential slackness of duty or even disloyalty on the part of Shrewsbury and Bess. One thing she would not agree to however, was a request from Shrewsbury around this time that another custodian of Queen Mary be appointed in his place, notwithstanding Shrewsbury's complaint that his own health was now beginning to suffer. For the time being, Shrewsbury was obliged to remain at his post. Over the next few years, a consequence of this would be the slow drifting apart of Shrewsbury and Bess.

Chapter 11

Birth of Arbella

It was Queen Mary's turn to be ill (again) in the summer of 1573. In one sense, this was actually quite convenient for Mary, as for some time she had been asking Queen Elizabeth for permission to visit the baths of Buxton, or as Mary liked to call them "La Fontayne de Bogsby", near to Chatsworth, the waters of which were famed as far back as Roman times for possessing healing qualities. In particular, during the Middle Ages, St Ann's Well in Buxton had come to be revered as a holy shrine and a place worthy of pilgrimage, especially by those suffering from various maladies from which they hoped to be delivered by the warm spring water that flows into the Well, much in the same way as Lourdes in France is venerated today. This practice had however fallen into disfavour during the time of Thomas Cromwell, and access to the waters by pilgrims had been forbidden. Access had been restored in the early 1570s, and Buxton was fast becoming a popular Elizabethan spa town (though not as popular as it would become in Georgian and Victorian times).[1] Nevertheless, even then it was a place for the fashionable and wealthy to visit (the Earl of Leicester was a regular visitor) and Queen Mary had set her heart on being able to do the same.

Unfortunately for Queen Mary, Queen Elizabeth had initially been reluctant to grant permission, fearing that security measures in Buxton might be lax and that whilst visiting, Mary might somehow contrive a means of escaping her captivity. As it happened, Shrewsbury was in the process of building a hall in Buxton close to the baths, and by the summer of 1573, it had been completed. Queen Elizabeth was

---

[1] Healing qualities attributed to the spa waters at this time included the ability of "strengthening the enfeebled members" and "assisting the lively forces". More prosaically, they were supposed to be efficacious in treating gout – both Shrewsbury and Lord Burghley sought relief from the waters for this condition at various times.

persuaded that Queen Mary could be accommodated securely in Shrewsbury's hall, and while she was still reluctant about the whole matter, Lord Burghley wrote to the Earl on 10th August 1573 saying that Queen Elizabeth did not feel that she could "in honour" withhold permission for Mary's visit, on condition that Mary be kept away from strangers.

Queen Mary, accompanied by Shrewsbury (who himself had recently been ill and wished to see if he could gain any benefit from the waters), arrived at Buxton for what became a five week visit on 22nd August 1573. Bess, who had been spending some time at Chatsworth, joined them a few days later, and the entire visit seems to have gone well. Thereafter visits to Buxton would become very important to Queen Mary, and she eventually made visits most years between 1573 and 1584, before Queen Elizabeth withdrew her permission.

Whilst Shrewsbury was kept busy with his guardianship duties, and struggled as best he could with the steadily increasing burdens that those duties imposed upon him, Bess was busy with matters of her own. High up the list of her concerns were the marital prospects of her daughter Elizabeth, eighteen years old and still unmarried at the beginning of 1574. Bess was determined to secure a good husband for Elizabeth, and had already begun to indulge in discreet (and sometimes not so discreet) matchmaking on behalf of her daughter; Shrewsbury had inevitably been dragged into some of these activities, and would in due course write to Lord Burghley saying "… there are few noblemens' sons in England that she hath not prayed me to deal for at one time or another …" By the beginning of 1574, these machinations by Bess on behalf of her daughter had yet to show any realistic sign of success, though in fairness, a year or so before, a distinctly promising possible match had temporarily come to the attention of Bess, namely the possibility that Elizabeth might become espoused to Peregrine Bertie.

He was the son of Bess's old friend Catherine, Duchess of Suffolk, widow of Charles Brandon, the Duke of Suffolk,[2] and Richard Bertie, who had married Catherine around 1553 despite the differences in their social ranks. Of relatively humble ancestry, Richard Bertie had been Catherine's Master of the Horse; Catherine for her part had clung to her title of Duchess, notwithstanding her marriage to Bertie – this retention of a title upon remarriage was a common practice in Tudor times when a titled woman subsequently married a man of lesser rank. There had been some discussions between the Duchess and Bess concerning a possible match between Peregrine and Elizabeth over the preceding twelve months, and the two families generally had been in approval, but in the event, the discussions had come to nothing, as Peregrine had already decided for himself that he loved someone else, and he later married Mary de Vere, daughter of the Sixteenth Earl of Oxford.

Then, in the summer of 1574, Margaret Lennox, the Dowager Countess of Lennox, mother of the murdered Lord Darnley, sought permission from Queen Elizabeth to visit her Yorkshire estate at Temple Newsam. Permission was granted on condition that the Dowager Countess refrained from visiting Queen Mary either at Sheffield or at Chatsworth; the Dowager Countess replied that she could not forget Darnley's murder, had no intention of visiting the Scottish Queen and preparations began to be made for her departure. At the same time, rumours began to spread as to the possible real reason for the trip, with the French ambassador, La Mothe Fénelon, reporting back to Paris that the Dowager Countess's true motive was to visit her grandson James in Scotland, and indeed possibly kidnap him (an accusation the Dowager Countess angrily denied when she came to hear of it). The Dowager Countess set off north in October 1574, accompanied by her sole surviving son, Charles Stuart. Before long, they had reached Huntingdon, where they visited Catherine, the Duchess of Suffolk and

---

[2] Peregrine Bertie would in due course inherit the Barony of Willoughby de Eresby as the Thirteenth Baron upon his mother's death, his barony being one of the rare examples of those that can pass down the female line.

Richard Bertie. When the Lennox party set off once more, the Duchess of Suffolk accompanied them as far as Grantham before returning home.

At Newark, the Dowager Countess received a message from Bess who, together with her daughter Elizabeth, had with what might seem suspiciously fortuitous timing decided to visit Rufford Abbey in Nottinghamshire, a property acquired by the Fourth Earl of Shrewsbury at the time of the dissolution of the monasteries. By that message, the Dowager Countess and Charles were invited to pay a visit to Rufford Abbey, which was some fifteen miles distance from Newark and they seemed to have accepted that invitation with alacrity.

Charles, then aged seventeen, was commonly known as the Fifth Earl of Lennox, though in fact the original earldom had passed to Charles' nephew James VI of Scotland (as had the Scottish lands associated with the title) upon the death of Charles' father on 4th September 1571. Shortly after the death of the Fourth Earl, the then Scottish Regent, the Earl of Mar, bestowed the earldom and the Scottish lands on Charles. Strictly speaking, this was a newly created earldom, meaning that Charles more properly should have been referred to as the first earl of the new earldom, but he continued to be referred to as the Fifth Earl, and this usage continued even after the Earl of Mar's successor as Regent, Regent Morton, declared the creation of the new earldom to be invalid. More to the point though, Regent Morton also ruled that the Scottish lands associated with the Lennox earldom remained in the possession of the Scottish Crown, thus denying Charles (and his mother) the benefit of the profits of those lands, significantly reducing their incomes. As a result, both the Dowager Countess and her son (who was still unmarried) had a powerful motive to find a wealthy wife for Charles.

With her invitation accepted, Bess herself rode out to meet the Lennoxes and escort them back to the Abbey. Once there, not only did Charles and Elizabeth make each other's acquaintance (probably for the first time) but the Dowager Countess suddenly claimed she had been taken ill, and took to her bed for five days. Bess no doubt was officially supposed to be acting as a chaperone to the young couple, but citing the necessity of nursing the Dowager Countess, appears to have left Charles and Elizabeth alone for much of the five days during which Margaret Lennox was supposedly bedridden. By the time the five days were up, Charles and Elizabeth had fallen in love, announced their betrothal to one another and their intention to marry as soon as possible, which they promptly did, in early November 1574, in the Chapel of the Abbey.

Both Bess and the Dowager Countess expressed their happy surprise at the match, whilst denying any element of matchmaking on their parts, but many people then and since have found this very hard to believe. Bess certainly had been searching for a suitable match for Elizabeth, and her daughter marrying Charles not only provided Bess and her family with kinship links to both the English and Scottish monarchs (something that socially would have been very important to Bess, who after all, for all that she was now a Countess, had still been born into an undistinguished Derbyshire family barely able to claim gentry status) but also, given that Queen Elizabeth was childless, and seemed increasingly likely to remain so, gave rise to the possibility that any child of the union could potentially ascend to the English throne itself. As for the Dowager Countess, whilst the Cavendish family certainly did not at that time possess the royal links that she and her son could boast, Cavendish wealth (especially when coupled to that of the Earl of Shrewsbury) more than compensated for this deficiency, as demonstrated by the fact that Bess around this time loaned Margaret Lennox a significant sum of money (at least £2000, which she subsequently repaid to Bess at the annual rate of £500 a year for the next four years) and Elizabeth herself would bring a dowry of £3000 into the marriage.[3] Given the obvious advantages of the match to both families, it seems likely that there had indeed been a degree of marriage plotting by Bess and Margaret Lennox (possibly involving the Duchess of

---

[3] This was supposed to be funded by Shrewsbury but he prevaricated about providing a dowry for Elizabeth, arguing that he had not agreed to the marriage, and the promised amount was only paid (to Elizabeth's daughter Arbella) several years after Elizabeth herself had died.

Suffolk as well), at least to the extent of manoeuvring Elizabeth and Charles into each other's company and gently encouraging their affection for one another. As for Shrewsbury, though he later claimed he had not condoned the marriage or been aware that it had taken place until after the fact (which may have been true), he later admitted (in a letter to Lord Burghley) that

> *"... As for the notion of marriage between [the Dowager Countess'] son and my wife's daughter, it was not ... hid from the world. It hath been in talk betwixt them more than a year past, and not thought of as a matter worth Her Majesty's hearing ..."*

Whether or not Shrewsbury had in fact been aware of discussions between the two countesses regarding a proposed marriage, once again it appears that no one appears to have considered that this would certainly have been a matter worth bringing to Queen Elizabeth's attention, especially having regard to her reactions to previous breaches of the Royal Marriage Act. Nor does anyone seem to have made allowance for the fact that Queen Elizabeth had never particularly liked or trusted the Dowager Countess, notwithstanding that she was the Queen's cousin, and that the Queen had long held suspicions that Margaret Lennox might have ambitions for the throne, either on her own behalf, or for the benefit of her children. It is especially surprising that Bess, who highly valued her relatively close relationship with the Queen, seems not to have been concerned about the Queen's likely reaction when she heard the news, which of course she did, a few days later. Bess may simply have calculated that the Queen's anger, at least against her, would possibly be mitigated by the closeness of their relationship and the fact that Shrewsbury was providing invaluable service as Queen Mary's gaoler. In any event, Shrewsbury learned of the Queen's extreme displeasure about the whole matter from a letter he received from Lord Burghley, and he seems suddenly to have fully realised the potential dangers of the match not only to the two countesses but potentially to himself as well. On 5th November 1574, Shrewsbury wrote a letter to Burghley in reply, trying to explain the marriage away as a simple matter that the Queen need not have concerns about whilst at the same time trying to avoid any suggestion of active involvement in the marriage himself. He depicted a scenario where, as a result of the Dowager Countess having been taken sick and forced to break her journey at Rufford Abbey, Charles and Elizabeth had met and:

> "... the young man, her son, fell into liking with my wife's daughter, before intended, and such liking was between them as my wife tells me, she makes no doubt of a match, and hath so tied themselves upon their own liking as cannot part. My wife hath sent him to my lady, and the young man is so far in love that belike he is sick without her. This taking effect, I shall be well at quiet ... and now this comes unlooked for without thanks to me."

The letter did nothing to reduce the Queen's anger, and in mid-November, the Dowager Countess, together with Elizabeth and Charles, were ordered to return to London immediately to explain themselves. Bess, for the moment, was not so summoned. The Lennoxes' journey took several weeks, partly because of bad weather and partly because the Dowager Countess was hoping (vainly as it transpired) that the Queen's anger might abate over the space of a few weeks.

In the meantime, Shrewsbury was hearing reports from Court that far from the Queen's anger abating, she was now actively suspicious that the marriage might be part of a clandestine plot to remove her from the throne. He fired off further letters to Lord Burghley protesting his innocence and loyalty, and wrote to the Earl of Leicester and to the Queen herself; to her he declared:

> "... I understand of late your Majesty's displeasure is sought against my wife for the marriage of her daughter to my Lady Lennox's son ... the truth is it was dealt with suddenly and without my knowledge ..."

He also tried to reassure the Queen that:

"… for my wife, she finding her daughter disappointed of young Bertie … and … that the other young gentleman was inclined to love with a few days acquaintance, did her best to further her daughter to this match, without having any other intent or respect relevant to your Majesty …"

Margaret Lennox finally presented herself at Court on 12th December, where she found the Queen still furious about the entire matter. The Dowager Countess tried to justify herself by pointing out that as instructed, she had avoided visiting both Chatsworth and Sheffield, that the marriage had resulted from a "sudden affection" of her son for Elizabeth Cavendish and that there had been no other "dealings or longer practices" concerning the matter; unfortunately, this contradicted Shrewsbury's assertion that there had been "talk betwixt" the two countesses concerning a possible marriage for more than a year and Queen Elizabeth, not unreasonably, concluded that the Dowager Countess was lying. The Earl of Huntingdon and Francis Walsingham (he only became Sir Francis Walsingham on 1st December 1577) were ordered to instigate a full enquiry into the whole affair and on 27th December 1574, the Dowager Countess was ordered to the Tower.[4] Charles and Elizabeth were placed under house arrest in Hackney (where the Lennox family maintained a house) and Bess was summoned to London.

In fact, there is no evidence that Bess actually travelled to London in January 1575, let alone that she was sent to the Tower as has been suggested by some biographers. The order summoning her may have been rescinded on the grounds that her daughter Mary (who had married Gilbert Talbot) was shortly due to give birth at Sheffield Castle, and indeed produced a son (who was named George) the following

---

[4] This led to her protesting that "Thrice I have been cast into prison, not for matters of treason, but for love matters. First when Thomas Howard, son of the Duke of Norfolk, was in love with me; then for the love of Henry Darnley, my son, to Queen Mary of Scotland, and lastly for the love of Charles, my younger son, to Elizabeth Cavendish."

month. Unfortunately, this event also annoyed Queen Elizabeth, who complained that the birth of the child must have led to strangers being present in close vicinity to Queen Mary (who was then at Sheffield) and that this had been expressly forbidden. In response to this criticism, Shrewsbury roused himself to write a letter to Lord Burghley dated 3rd March 1575 to protest that:

> *"... the midwife excepted, none such have, or do at any time, come within her [Queen Mary's] sight. And at the first, to avoid such resort, I myself with two of my children, christened the child ..."*

In the meantime, the enquiry being conducted by Huntingdon and Walsingham led to various servants in the Shrewsbury and Lennox households being investigated, with particular emphasis on whether there was some connection between the marriage and Mary, Queen of Scots. It was discovered that at least one of Shrewsbury's servants had been helping Queen Mary by assisting in passing messages from her to her supporters. This prompted yet further severe criticism of Shrewsbury from both Queen Elizabeth and the Privy Council and further orders that Shrewsbury be diligent in his duties. By now Shrewsbury was actively hoping that the task of guarding the Scottish Queen would be given to someone else, but for the moment, he was obliged to remain at his post, beset by worries and fears, which now were exacerbated by his concern that the marriage of his stepdaughter to Charles Stuart might cause him to fall into even more apparent disfavour with the Queen.

In fact, onerous though his duties were, and by now they were beginning to significantly affect his health (he increasingly was complaining of suffering gout, arthritis and other forms of "distemper"), there was at this time no real possibility that he would be relieved from his post as Queen Mary's gaoler; Queen Elizabeth and her Privy Council, for all that they criticised him, did not seriously doubt his loyalty to his monarch, and Queen Elizabeth in particular had no problem with the costs of Queen Mary's incarceration being subsidised by the Talbot fortune.

As for Bess, if she had calculated that her relationship with the Queen would help to shield her from repercussions over her daughter's marriage, she had calculated correctly. True, she had teetered on the edge of royal disfavour,[5] but the Queen's displeasure (at least so far as Bess was concerned) slowly ebbed over the following few months and Bess never suffered any sanctions over the marriage. This state of affairs was assisted by the fact that Huntingdon's and Walsingham's enquiries had failed to demonstrate any real link between the marriage and any plot involving Queen Mary; the whole affair no doubt served to highlight that Bess was an ambitious woman so far as her family's status was concerned, but this was hardly a secret and Queen Elizabeth might well have seen this as an asset, so long as she could rely on Bess's loyalty, which ultimately, she knew she always could.

The Dowager Countess was released from the Tower in March 1575, but Queen Elizabeth's distrust of her was unabating, and Margaret Lennox was ordered to remain under house arrest at Hackney with her son and daughter-in-law (who by now was almost certainly in the earliest stages of pregnancy). Margaret Lennox was still there in November 1575 when Elizabeth gave birth to a daughter, who was christened Arbella.[6] There

---

[5] Bess was very careful over the next few months to avoid any indication that she was anything but scrupulously loyal herself to Queen Elizabeth. To be on the safe side, Bess took special care in choosing her gift to the Queen for the 1576 New Year celebrations; she eventually selected at considerable cost a cloak made of watchet (blue) or peach satin, and a safeguard (an outer skirt) "... embroidered with some pretty flowers and lined with sundry colours ...", gifts which apparently were well received by Her Majesty, and did much to confirm to the watching world (or at least the world of the Court) that Bess's place in the affections of her sovereign was confirmed once more.

[6] Bess and Margaret Lennox might well have been hoping that Elizabeth would bear a son, but the fact that Arbella bore royal Stuart blood no doubt gave both a sense of satisfaction. As for Queen Elizabeth, (Arbella was her first cousin, twice removed) she was not exactly enthusiastic about the arrival of another

is some doubt as to Arbella's exact date of birth, and indeed where she was born. It seems likely that it was at the Lennox house in Hackney, but it has been suggested that Arbella might have been born at one of the Talbot properties in Nottinghamshire. As for the date, it must have been before 10th November 1575, for on that date the Dowager Countess wrote to Queen Mary, acknowledging and thanking the Scottish Queen for her "... good remembrance and bounty to our little daughter here ..." The letter (which includes a postscript from Elizabeth Lennox adding her own thanks to Queen Mary) concludes with the Dowager Countess referring to herself as Queen Mary's "... most humble and loving mother and aunt ..." The exchange between Queen Mary and the Dowager Countess at this time was in fact surprisingly warm, given that a year or so before, Margaret Lennox had been assuring Queen Elizabeth, Lord Burghley and anyone else who would listen that she could never forget the murder of her son Darnley and strongly implying she held Queen Mary responsible for his death. Moreover, given the likelihood of the letter being intercepted and read by agents working for Walsingham and Lord Burghley, and bearing in mind Margaret Lennox's recent sojourn in the Tower on suspicion (amongst other things) of possible complicity in plotting with Queen Mary, such a warm exchange might even be viewed as rash. In fact, it seems that the letter generated no repercussions for the Dowager Countess (and it may well be that by now, Margaret Lennox had somehow convinced herself that Queen Mary had not been responsible for Darnley's death). Moreover, the Dowager Countess was as much aware as anyone else that Arbella not only had a potentially powerful claim to the English throne, but also might be a conduit through which her family might reclaim some or all of the Scottish Lennox lands of which they had been deprived by Regent Morton and that the influence of the Scottish Queen in respect of that quest might be valuable. Viewed in that light, the

---

possible claimant to her throne, but she could at least content herself that as a female, Arbella was less likely to give rise to a possible conspiracy to oust her from her throne than if Arbella had been born a boy.

Dowager Countess might well have concluded that a degree of rapprochement with Queen Mary might be desirable.

Chapter 12

Lewd Fellows of the Peak

Once the controversy over her daughter's marriage to Charles Stuart had (largely) subsided, Bess spent much of 1575 at Chatsworth, where she once again concentrated on supervising the running and improvement of the estate, as well as overseeing further alterations to the house itself. Unfortunately, this meant that she was still spending time apart from Shrewsbury, who was finding separation from Bess increasingly difficult to deal with. They still wrote civilly, even affectionately, to one another when they were apart, at least during the first half of the year. Shrewsbury addressed Bess as "my dear None" in his letters, his affectionate nickname for her, as he had since the earliest days of their courtship. Bess did in fact leave Chatsworth to visit Sheffield Castle fairly frequently during this time, usually to oversee the "cleansing" of the castle, but this generally occurred when Shrewsbury had moved Queen Mary elsewhere. As 1575 progressed however, a peevish tone began to penetrate the Earl's letters to Bess, and gently at first, and then with slowly increasing aggression, he began to chastise and find fault with her, not only about her absences but also about the money she was spending on improvements at Chatsworth as well as her use of Talbot workers there which meant that they were unavailable for work on projects of his own. Then, over the summer of 1575, potential trouble arose over some of the Earl's tenants in the Peak Forest,[1] who were objecting to the enclosure of pastures and the removal of rights of way through the forest, changes that may well have been ordered by the Earl (or at least of which he was aware), but for which the tenants blamed Bess. The tenants threatened to take their complaints directly to Queen Elizabeth herself, and some travelled to London to present a petition at Court, causing the Earl yet further worry as to how he was

---

[1] "Lewd fellows of the Peak" according to Shrewsbury's son Gilbert; he also commented on their "doltish persuasions".

137

being viewed in London. Bess herself might have had concerns about how the enclosures might be perceived, as Queen Elizabeth and her Council were anxious to avoid rural unrest if this could be avoided. In the event, some sort of compromise seems to have been reached, though this would not be the last time Bess had trouble with the "lewd fellows" in relation to enclosures; as late as 1604, some of the tenants of the Peak Forest were petitioning about the improper enclosure of common pastures. Bess responded to these later claims by stating that they were simply untrue.

Making matters even worse (from Shrewsbury's perspective), in September 1575, Shrewsbury received the unwelcome news that Queen Elizabeth had decided (once again) that Queen Mary's household should be reduced and therefore proposed that the money provided to the Earl to (supposedly) meet the costs of Queen Mary's captivity be reduced from £52 per week to £30 per week. He wrote in protest to the Queen, pointing out that he had agreed to act as Queen Mary's custodian when every other man "shrank from it", and that £52 per week was less than half the amount Queen Elizabeth had been paying for Mary's keep before he had taken up the post, but to no avail; Queen Elizabeth appears to have completely ignored his protest (and nor did she take any steps to compensate him for back payments he was due but had not been paid or to compensate him for the expenses he himself had incurred).

Shrewsbury also was feeling financial and emotional pressures originating from his own family; his son Gilbert, who was married to Bess's daughter Mary, was close to Bess's son Charles and at that time got on well with his mother-in-law. Gilbert and Mary, especially with the arrival of their son, George, were now feeling the need for a house of their own, and Gilbert had been pestering Shrewsbury to provide one. In June 1575, Shrewsbury had reluctantly agreed to do so, but had done nothing about it, although he had sought Bess's advice on the matter. By October 1575, no house had yet been provided (or at least not in a form that was habitable) and Gilbert (who together with his wife and son seems to have been lodging in difficult conditions in Sheffield) was writing to Bess complaining that he had never "... longed for anything so much as to be from hence [i.e. his lodgings in Sheffield] ..." adding that "... truly madam I rather wish myself a ploughman than here to continue ..." In that same letter though, he added that his father:

> "... is continually pestered with his wonted business, and is very often in exceeding choler of slight occasion, a great grief to them that loves him to see him hurt himself so much ..."

Shrewsbury eventually offered his son the use of Goodrich Castle in Hereford[2] but by the time Gilbert and his family moved there, it was in a pretty poor state structurally and sparsely furnished to the point of being almost uninhabitable. Shrewsbury, who was now beginning to resent Gilbert and Mary, partly as a result of having to provide them with a home of their own and partly because he objected to Gilbert's continuing close relationship with the Cavendish family generally, and especially Bess and Charles, refused to assist by providing more than a few inadequate items of furniture and other furnishings from Sheffield Castle, despite Bess's urgings that he be more generous. Bess eventually lent her son-in-law and daughter furniture and tapestries from Chatsworth, and Gilbert wrote to Bess on 13th October 1575 to thank her, promising that:

> "... where it hath pleased your Ladyship to bestow of us a great deal of furniture towards [our] house, we can but by our prayers for your Ladyship shew ourselves dutiful as well for this as all other your Ladyship's continual benefits towards us ..."

He added that the items that Bess had provided from Chatsworth were of more worth than all the items which had been in Goodrich Castle when he had acquired it and those which had been sent by his father

---

[2] Originally of Norman origin (and possibly even earlier), the castle had first come into the possession of the Talbot family in 1326 when Richard Talbot, Second Baron Talbot had married Elizabeth de Comyn and seized the castle from the Despencers (who in turn had illegally appropriated the castle from Elizabeth the year before).

from Sheffield. He also mentioned that his father had refused to provide more than the cheapest cotton fabric to make sheets and clothing, with Shrewsbury claiming that other cloth which had been available to buy had been too expensive. Shrewsbury had also refused to provide Gilbert and Mary with plate from Sheffield that Bess had specifically set aside for them. Shrewsbury's financial concerns were starting to turn into penny-pinching miserliness, and his family was beginning to notice it.

Six months or so later, two new tragedies descended upon the family. In early April 1576, Arbella's father, Charles Stuart, died of tuberculosis, leaving Elizabeth a widow after only eighteen months of marriage. Then, only a few weeks later, Shrewsbury's daughter Catherine, who on 17th February 1562 (or possibly 1563) had married Henry Herbert, eldest son of the First Earl of Pembroke, also died after an illness of nearly two years. Catherine's death naturally caused Shrewsbury great distress, adding still more to his burdens; Bess too was upset, as she and Catherine had enjoyed a close relationship, but the death of Charles Stuart probably had a bigger immediate impact on her, for she was concerned to ensure, so far as she could, that her daughter Elizabeth's rights as the Countess of Lennox were recognised both in England and in Scotland. This was a concern also shared by Margaret Lennox, Charles' mother, who wrote a letter to Queen Elizabeth concerning the matter and pleading for her help.

In June 1576, Bess visited the Court for the first time since the scandal of the Lennox marriage and found herself warmly received by Queen Elizabeth. With the support of the Earl of Leicester, Bess too urged Queen Elizabeth to use her influence with the Scottish government and press for recognition of Elizabeth's (and Arbella's) rights in respect of the Lennox earldom. Queen Elizabeth was sympathetic enough to write to the Regent Morton to say that she found it very strange:

"… that any disposition should be intended of the earldom to the prejudice of the only daughter of the late Earl of Lennox …"

but it is doubtful that she (or indeed Bess) expected any positive results from this intervention and indeed there were none. As far as Regent

Morton was concerned, the earldom was vested in young King James VI, and would remain so unless and until the Scottish King determined otherwise.

Concern about the earldom was also shared by Mary, Queen of Scots. She had already drawn up a will purporting to set out the rules of succession to the Scottish throne (notwithstanding that she had abdicated the throne), and had included Charles as a possible successor. In February 1577, Queen Mary added a codicil stating:

> "I give to my niece Arbella the earldom of Lennox, held by her late father and enjoin my son, as my heir and successor, to obey my will in this particular ..."

Unfortunately, she omitted to execute the will or the codicil, meaning that they had no legal effect and anyway the Scottish government refused to accept that Queen Mary had the right to specify the succession to the Scottish throne or the disposition of the Lennox earldom in the first place.[3] Elizabeth's and Arbella's rights in relation to the earldom were therefore ignored north of the Scottish border as, needless to say, were any claims they might have in relation to Lennox lands in Scotland.

In the summer of 1577, the Earl of Leicester, who by now was approaching the age of 45 (he had been born on 24th June 1532), visited Buxton. Having been considered fit and handsome in his youth, middle age was now beginning to creep up on him. His weight was increasing, he had begun to suffer from various maladies, including gout, and was

---

[3] Just before the making of the codicil, when Arbella would have been around two years old, Margaret Lennox commissioned a painting of her, which now hangs in Hardwick Hall. At the Dowager Countess' insistence, the portrait defiantly bears the inscription "Arbella Comitessa Leviniae"; that is "Arbella, the Countess of Lennox". Notwithstanding this, on 16th June 1578, Regent Morton (himself shortly destined to be deposed as regent and thereafter executed) acting in the name of King James conferred the earldom on Robert Stewart, uncle of the young king.

hopeful (as were his doctors) that a visit to the spa town might be beneficial to him. In fact, it had originally been proposed that he might make the journey there in the company of Queen Elizabeth and her entourage as part of that year's Royal Progress, and Bess had been eager to have the opportunity of entertaining the Queen and Leicester at Chatsworth, which, though it would have been expensive, would have raised her status in the eyes of many even higher. Unfortunately for Bess, the plans for the Queen's Progress were altered and the Queen would never visit Buxton or Chatsworth. The Queen accepted though that Leicester might benefit from a visit to Buxton and he received permission to travel there without her. On hearing the news, Bess immediately proffered an invitation to Leicester to visit Chatsworth for a few days following the conclusion of his trip to Buxton, and Leicester was pleased to accept.

The offer by Bess was not entirely altruistic, though she certainly liked Leicester; she was canny enough to realise that being on good terms with the Earl might, politically and socially, be nearly as useful as remaining on good terms with the Queen herself. Moreover, she was determined that Leicester should see Chatsworth at its best, and in the months preceding his visit, she ordered a flurry of improvements be made to the house and estate. These were more in the nature of adding final polishes and refinements to the existing fixtures and finishings rather than major rebuilding works, though to Bess, necessary final polishes included adding new and expensive panelling and doors to rooms that were to form Leicester's suite, new timber floors, new screens for the great hall, new garden walls and improvements to the gardens generally. At one point during the summer just before Leicester's visit, she was employing over 80 labourers (at considerable expense) to make the last-minute improvements, which once more annoyed Shrewsbury, who was obliged to remain at Sheffield in charge of Queen Mary. In his absence, and with Bess supervising the work at Chatsworth, the role of acting as host to Leicester during his Buxton visit fell to Gilbert Talbot who seems to have done a good job; though Leicester boasted in a letter to Lord Burghley that he and his brother (who had accompanied him) were living moderately and contenting themselves with meals consisting of only "one or two dishes", the list of produce sent by Bess to Gilbert in Buxton for the benefit of Leicester suggests otherwise. Included in the items shipped for consumption by the Earl and his party were a hogshead[4] of clear wine, two hogsheads of beer and two hogsheads of ale. Fresh food was also provided daily, including (and this was just for the first day of Leicester's visit): "1 buck, 24 rabbits, 4 fat capons and 12 quails ...", together with bread, clotted cream, butter, venison pastries, peascods and other items. It should be added that Gilbert did more than merely ensure that Leicester was (more than) adequately plied with food and drink; no doubt acting on Bess's instructions, he also raised the issue of the Lennox earldom once again, and Leicester promised that when he met Bess at Chatsworth, he would advise Bess as regards how best to write to the Queen about the matter (though in fact nothing seems to have come of this).

After leaving Buxton, Leicester stayed three days at Chatsworth before departing to return to London. Although he apparently enjoyed his visits to Buxton and Chatsworth immensely, declaring that he wished he could have stayed three weeks longer, it is doubtful whether his sojourn in the Midlands did him much good so far as his health was concerned; he developed a boil on the calf of his leg and when the time for his departure came, he had to be borne away on a horse-litter. This did not however prevent him from writing enthusiastically to Queen Elizabeth praising the Shrewsburys for their hospitality, which in turn led the Queen to write a letter of thanks from Greenwich on 25th June 1577 to Shrewsbury (intending that Bess should also see it):

"Our very good cousin,

Being given to understand from our cousin of Leicester how honourably he was not only lately received by you our cousin [and] the Countess at Chatsworth and his diet by you both discharged at Buxton, but also presented with a very rare

---

[4] Essentially a cask containing (in England) about 66 gallons of liquid.

present, we should do him great wrong (holding him in that place of favour we do) in case we should not let you understand in how thankful sort we accept the same at both your hands not as done unto him, but to our own self, reputing him as another ourself; and therefore you may assure yourself that we, taking upon us the debt not as his but our own, will take care accordingly to discharge the same, in such honourable sort, as so well-deserving creditors as you are, shall never have cause to think you have met with an ungrateful debtor.

In this acknowledgement of new debts we may not forget our old debt, the same being so great as a sovereign can owe to a subject; when through your loyal and most careful looking to the charge committed to you, both we and our realm enjoy a peaceable government, the best good happe [i.e. good fortune] that to any prince on earth can befall. This good happe then growing from you, you might think yourself most unhappy if you served under such a prince as should not be ready graciously to consider of it as thankfully to acknowledge the same, whereof you may make full account, to your comfort, when time shall serve. Given under our signet at our manor of Greenwich the 25th Day of June 1577 and in the nineteenth year of our reign ..."

It would be interesting to know how Shrewsbury reacted to the Queen's references to new and old debts; he was still no closer to obtaining recompense for the expenses he had been forced to incur whilst guarding Queen Mary. Regardless of this however, he seems to have prized the letter, adding a handwritten note to it himself stating that it was to be kept as "the most precious jewel". It no doubt served to provide him with some reassurance that the Queen did, after all, appreciate his service as Queen Mary's gaoler even if she was not willing to pay fully for that service.[5]

A few weeks later, around the end of July 1577, a disagreement, perhaps their first significant one and which was referred to in some detail in letters from Gilbert Talbot to Bess dated sometime in late July and 1st August of 1577, erupted between Bess and her husband. Bess by now had joined Shrewsbury at Sheffield and had arranged for a group of "embroiderers" to carry out some work at Sheffield Manor Lodge, another Talbot property sometimes used to house Queen Mary. For reasons not entirely clear, one of Shrewsbury's servants, John Dickenson, the Keeper of the Earl's Wardrobe, had refused to allow the embroiderers to stay overnight in the lodge, and they had complained to Bess's groom, a man called Owen, who had sought to challenge Dickenson, but to no avail. News of the altercation reached both the Earl and Bess, Shrewsbury flew into a rage and there was a vigorous argument between the two, following which Shrewsbury departed to visit one of his properties at Bolsover. Bess in the meantime departed Sheffield to return to Chatsworth without informing Shrewsbury of her plans. The following day (as Gilbert later recounted to Bess in his letter of late July 1577), Gilbert rode over to Bolsover with a view to riding back to Sheffield with his father, who took the opportunity of venting his feelings about Bess, complaining that the words he had used to her during the argument were not as cruel and bitter as some of those Bess had delivered to him in the past. Bess, he alleged, was surrounded by "varlets" who were always seeking to foment trouble by telling false

---

[5] There exists the draft of another far less formal letter written by the Queen to Shrewsbury and Bess a few weeks before, on 4th June 1577, in which she teased them by effectively stating that she hoped that the Shrewsburys were not overfeeding Leicester and his brother, for if they were, her debt to Shrewsbury might grow so large that the Queen herself might become bankrupt. Queen Elizabeth seems however to have had second thoughts about Shrewsbury's likely reaction to some of her comments, and the letter was never sent.

tales, specifically referring not only to the embroiderers but also to Owen (whom the Earl disliked; he had been urging Bess to dismiss him, but she had refused). Shrewsbury added that he was expecting to see Bess on his return to Sheffield, forcing Gilbert to tell him that Bess had already departed back to Chatsworth, news that caused Shrewsbury "… to marvel greatly …" and say that her malice was such that she would not "… tarry one night for my coming …" He refused to accept Bess might have legitimate reasons for returning to Chatsworth (as Gilbert had tried to argue), though he thawed a little when Gilbert explained that he had seen that Bess was very upset about the quarrel, and now believed that Shrewsbury was only happy when he was apart from her, and most unhappy when they were together.

Shrewsbury responded that Gilbert knew to the contrary and added what was presumably becoming an old refrain, namely that he had often cursed the building at Chatsworth which drew Bess away from his side and that he would not have done that to her. After this, Shrewsbury had fallen largely silent for the remainder of their journey back to Sheffield, but Gilbert in his letter to Bess assured her that Shrewsbury desired "… reconciliation if he knew which way to bring it to pass …"

Gilbert's letter is the first real detailed evidence we have of the rift that was opening up between Bess and Shrewsbury, but it suggests that the argument of the lodging of the embroiderers was merely the latest of a series of disagreements between them; clearly Shrewsbury begrudged the expense and troubles caused by Bess's building activities at Chatsworth, and resented that that she spent so much time there away from him. No doubt he felt a need for her support as he grappled with his duties as Queen Mary's keeper. Bess for her part seems keen to present herself as the injured party while remaining reasonable and measured in the face of Shrewsbury's accusations.[6] We do know however that on receipt of Gilbert's letter of late July, she did not immediately return to Sheffield (as Shrewsbury wished), but rather remained at Chatsworth, dealing with her own affairs, for in his letter of 1st August 1577 (which was also signed by Bess's daughter Mary), Gilbert recounts that he (having just returned from a visit to Chatsworth himself) had spoken again with his father about Bess's absence. On this occasion the Earl had not been so inquisitive about Bess's activities but had asked at various times when Gilbert had thought Bess might return to his side. Gilbert said that he had explained that at times, Bess suffered badly from rheumatism (a complaint that she would plague her from time to time in the years that would follow) and that when this happened, she simply did not know when she might be able to travel again. (One might think Shrewsbury should have known this.) He added that he had also told Shrewsbury that he thought that at other times, when Bess was well, Bess would prefer "some respite" for several months at Chatsworth, since she was under the impression that Shrewsbury was better pleased with Bess's absence rather than her presence, a charge which Shrewsbury earnestly denied. Gilbert also informed Bess that he had told his father that she meant to dismiss Owen as her groom, as he had clearly offended the Earl, but that he had also said that Bess did not know what offence Owen had committed, that he was a "simple, true man" and that Bess would be glad to understand exactly what Owen had done wrong so as to justify his dismissal. Shrewsbury had simply replied that Owen's dismissal was his will for diverse reasons, which he refused to specify, but that he doubted that Bess would be willing to accept any man he might suggest as her new groom.

---

[6] Some biographers have speculated that Bess might have become suspicious that her husband was becoming too close to Queen Mary (after all, they inevitably spent a lot of time together) and was growing jealous as a result. There is no real evidence to support the suggestion that Shrewsbury was developing any form of romantic attachment for the Scottish Queen at all.

The letter of 1ˢᵗ August 1577 ends with a brief postscript concerning Gilbert and Mary's son George, then about two and a half years old, who apparently was well and drank every day to his "lady grandmother". Ten days later, little George died, apparently from a convulsion of some sort.

There is no doubt that both Shrewsbury and Bess deeply grieved the loss of their grandson, though perhaps Shrewsbury was more intent on concealing his emotions, at least publicly, than Bess. On 12ᵗʰ August 1577, the Earl wrote to Lord Burghley (who only a few days before had been visiting Chatsworth and entertained by Bess for a couple of days) to give him the sad news but adding "I doubt not my wife will show more folly than need requires" and asking that Burghley write to her. In a separate letter to Walsingham, he wrote that:

> "… my wife (although she acknowledges no less) is not so able to rule her passions and has driven herself into such a case by her continual weeping as is likely to breed in her further inconvenience …"

adding that he was seeking permission to join Bess at Chatsworth, taking Queen Mary with him. Permission was granted and Bess and Shrewsbury, for the moment, came together once again. They stayed together at Chatsworth for several weeks, and then Shrewsbury, together with Queen Mary, departed once more for Sheffield. It looked like Bess and Shrewsbury were more or less reconciled, even though they were largely living apart once more, but this was something of an illusion, as there were tensions (spoken and unspoken) between them, not least to do with family affairs. Whether they liked it or not, their respective children were slowly being drawn into the simmering dispute between the two, and both Bess and Shrewsbury found it difficult when one or more of their own children appeared to be inclined to support the other. Couple that with the stress that Shrewsbury was under and his continuing and growing resentment at Bess's determination to focus on her own affairs (especially the continuing improvements at Chatsworth and her now increasingly apparent dynastic ambitions for her children and Arbella), and her eagerness to be her own mistress,[7] at least so far as Chatsworth and the Cavendish family were concerned, and a dispassionate observer might well have concluded that the writing was on the wall so far as Bess's and Shrewsbury's marriage was concerned. But for the moment at least, they both contrived to maintain the illusion that as far as was possible, all was well between them.

To complicate matters, the issue of the Lennox earldom (never far from Bess's mind) took centre-stage once more with the death in London, on 7th March 1578, of Margaret, the Dowager Countess of Lennox. Not only was this a shock to Bess, for the two of them had been friends for many years, but Margaret had been at least as eager as Bess in the efforts to procure that Elizabeth's and Arbella's rights in relation to the earldom were recognised. With Margaret's death, Bess had lost an important ally in the battle for the earldom. Interestingly, on 4th March 1578, and thus before Margaret Lennox's death, Shrewsbury (perhaps at Bess's urging) had written to Lord Burghley, who was now the Master of Wards, "requesting" his interest in the wardship of Arbella, which gives rise to the suggestion that Margaret Lennox's imminent death had been anticipated. Indeed, on 26th February, after she had been taken ill, she had rewritten her will and though in the process she had emphasised she was in "perfect mind" and "in good health of body", the latter declaration must at least be open to debate. In any event, Queen Elizabeth (aware of Arbella's proximity to the throne), elected to award the wardship of Arbella to herself but assigned actual custody of the child to her mother Elizabeth, which came as a great relief to Elizabeth, for she had feared Arbella might be taken from her. On 17th March 1578, Bess wrote to Queen Elizabeth to thank her for this act of seeming kindness (which of course had cost the Queen nothing) and took the opportunity (again) of asking that the Queen give her gracious

---

[7] She seems to have been far more willing to defer, or at least of giving the impression of deferring, to Shrewsbury's wishes when they were together at one or another of the Talbot properties than when she was at Chatsworth.

consideration to her daughter Elizabeth's "case". As before when the issue had been raised, there was in practice little the Queen could do, even if she had wanted to, and in any event, within a few months Regent Morton would bestow the earldom on Robert Stewart.

Queen Elizabeth may not have liked Margaret Lennox very much, but she no doubt saw an opportunity of enhancing her own prestige by ordering that the Dowager Countess be buried with pomp and splendour appropriate for the funeral of someone closely connected to her throne. The Dowager Countess' funeral took place at Westminster Abbey on 3rd April 1578, something Margaret Lennox had anticipated would happen in her will. It was effectively a state funeral and Bess travelled to London to attend as one of the principal mourners. It seems likely that she consoled herself that whilst the Lennox earldom and Lennox Scottish estates were, at least for the moment, out of reach for her daughter and granddaughter, they would at least be able to claim the Lennox lands sited in England. If she did think this, she was to be disappointed; Queen Elizabeth had her own reasons for agreeing to stage a state funeral for Margaret Lennox but she had absolutely no intention of paying for it out of her own pocket, or at least more than she had to. Nearly all of the Lennox English estates were seized by the Crown, to help to meet the funeral costs and to pay off the Dowager Countess' debts, leaving Elizabeth and Arbella with little more than a small estate at Smallwood in the county of Cheshire. This seemingly generated an income of around £300 a year, which even Queen Elizabeth (when pressed) finally conceded was insufficient income to support the dignities of persons so close to the throne. Queen Elizabeth eventually agreed to provide a couple of pensions (£400 a year for Elizabeth Lennox and £200 a year for Arbella), which when added to the Smallwood income was still inadequate but better than nothing. As a result of these dealings, both Elizabeth and Arbella remained very short of money.[8]

There was also the issue of the Dowager Countess' will, particularly with regard to personal items of the Dowager Countess. After some specific bequests to various individuals (including, incidentally the gift of a bed and bedstead to her grandson King James) and some charitable donations, and specifying that the body of her son Charles, then entombed in the church at Hackney, should be exhumed and laid with hers in Westminster Abbey (which was done), the will essentially provided that the residue of her personal estate, principally consisting of around 20 sets of jewels (many of them including diamonds) should be given to Arbella when she turned fourteen. In the meantime, the jewels were placed in a casket and Margaret Lennox entrusted it to Thomas Fowler, her steward and ultimately sole executor of the will, for safekeeping. The following year, on 19th September 1579, Queen Mary sent a warrant to Fowler ordering him to:

> *"… deliver to the hands and custody of our right well-beloved cousin, Elizabeth, Countess of Shrewsbury, all and every such jewels …",*

confirming that they should be given to Arbella upon attaining the age of fourteen, as had been specified in the will, but adding that if Arbella died before her fourteenth birthday, the jewels should be given to King James (which the will had not specified).

The warrant may have been issued at the urging of Bess; it seems that Elizabeth Lennox (and hence Bess herself) may have grown suspicious of the probity of Thomas Fowler and concluded that Arbella's jewels would be safer in Bess's hands. If this is so, their suspicions were well-

---

[8] Around this time, the Scottish government began to agitate for the income from the Lennox English estates to be paid to them. They received from Queen Elizabeth shrift that was as short as the replies they themselves had made when asked to yield income from the Lennox Scottish estates.

placed, for Fowler had travelled (without permission) to Scotland, taking the jewels with him. When he received the warrant, he replied that on his journey north, he had been waylaid and the jewels stolen. Strangely, many of them subsequently made their way into the possession of King James, who despite promising to return the jewels to Arbella (when his possession of them became known), signally failed to do so. Thus, Arbella was denied yet another significant portion of her inheritance.

As for Thomas Fowler, he seems to have suffered no repercussions for his actions; in 1581, he became the Earl of Leicester's steward before retiring to Scotland a few years later following Leicester's death in 1588. Fowler died in 1590.

1. Bess of Hardwick

2. Bess of Hardwick

3. Lady Arbella Stuart

GEORGIVS TALBOTVS
COMES SALOPIÆ
AN·ÆTATIS 58
S·H
1580

4. George Talbot, 6th Earl of Shrewsbury

5. Sir William Cavendish

6. Mary, Queen of Scots

7. Mary I of England and Philip II of Spain

8. Robert Dudley, Earl of Leicester

9. Elizabeth I

10. William Cecil presiding over the
Court of Wards

11. Hardwick Hall, "More glass than wall"

12. Tapestries inside Hardwick Hall

Chapter 13

A Growing Estrangement

Bess paid another trip to Court in October 1578. The Court at this time was at Richmond Palace, having moved there to escape an outbreak of the plague in London, and Bess had been pleased with the accommodation found for her there by the Earl of Leicester. Indeed, on 24th October, Bess wrote to Lord Burghley praising the rooms she had been allocated (a "very good chamber" attached to another little room according to Bess) in Leicester's own lodgings. "I would rather have albeit it never so little a corner within the Court than greater easement further off" she added.

Bess had set off for Richmond on 9th October 1578. She went via Dunstable, about 30 miles north of London, which she reached on 11th October. Elizabeth Lennox and Arbella were then living there with friends, and Bess spent four or five days visiting them before setting off for the remainder of her journey to Richmond. At Court, Bess seems to have attempted (with Leicester's support) to persuade the Queen to increase the pensions allotted to Elizabeth and Arbella, but to no avail.[1]

Notwithstanding this, in other respects, Bess's visit to the Court was a success; the Queen spoke kindly to her and been pleased to see her (perhaps wishing to hear details of how Queen Mary was faring) and

---

[1] It has been suggested by some biographers that Arbella may have accompanied Bess to Richmond, presumably in the hope that the sight of Arbella might soften the Queen's intransigence on the issue of the pensions but there is no evidence for this; it would have been a long and difficult journey for a three year old, and Bess (and Elizabeth Lennox) would have been reluctant to expose Arbella to possible danger in the event that the London plague outbreak reached Richmond during her stay. In any event, if Arbella did accompany Bess to London (and there is no evidence that Elizabeth Lennox accompanied Bess on her trip to Court either, also suggesting that Arbella remained with her mother in Dunstable during this time), the ruse clearly failed.

Bess seems to have been popular generally throughout the Court; Leicester wrote to Shrewsbury commenting on this around this time.

Bess remained at Court for the rest of October and much of November, before departing on 20th November 1578 back to the Midlands, as she had promised Shrewsbury she would join him (and Queen Mary) for Christmas at Sheffield Castle. She travelled back via Dunstable once more, picking up Arbella (assuming Arbella did indeed remain in Dunstable whilst her grandmother was in Richmond), and possibly Elizabeth Lennox as well, although this is unclear, and they made their way to Derbyshire. The original plan may have been for all three of them to spend Christmas with Shrewsbury at Sheffield, but the Queen's strict prohibition on "strangers" being in close proximity to Queen Mary still held sway, and Bess was forced to detour to Chatsworth where Arbella and presumably Elizabeth would spend Christmas. Bess left them at Chatsworth and hastened back to Sheffield, arriving back on 24th December. On 29th December 1578, she wrote to Sir Francis Walsingham, commenting on the health of Queen Mary, saying that Mary had been taken ill once again, and had been staying in her bed, except on Christmas Day itself. Bess explained that Queen Mary had "grown lean and sickly" and was complaining that "want of exercise" was responsible for bringing her to that "weak state". Bess said that she hoped there would be advised consideration of the state of the Scottish Queen's health. In a footnote to the letter, Bess added some details of her "little Arbell": "I came hither on Christmas Eve" she said, "and left my little Arbell at Chattysworth." She declared too that she thanked God that Arbella had coped very well with travel.

For Bess and Shrewsbury, little really changed as the months of 1579 passed by. Bess continued to add what she considered to be finishing touches to Chatsworth, while also continuing to press the Queen for additional financial support for Elizabeth Lennox and Arbella, though none was forthcoming, and it was around this time that Elizabeth Lennox settled permanently, at least for the foreseeable future, at Chatsworth, no doubt with Bess's blessings, Bess also continued to monitor the affairs of Court from afar. Gilbert and Mary Talbot were frequent visitors to the Court and kept her (and Shrewsbury) informed as regards important developments.

Relations between Bess and Shrewsbury continued to worsen, although they were still writing to each other in relatively civil tones, principally about family and other domestic matters. Particularly as Shrewsbury's health began to deteriorate again, and as his financial concerns grew, he also increasingly resented Queen Elizabeth's parsimony when it came to the expenses of guarding Queen Mary. He sought permission on several occasions to travel to the Court to discuss his financial woes with Queen Elizabeth in person, but his requests were refused. His resentment over Bess's continual absences at Chatsworth also grew, as did his sense of fury at what he regarded were examples of her extravagance, and that of her children. Bess of course was in the relatively unusual position of having independent income of her own, which she was using to increase the resources of the Cavendish family, as and when opportunities arose, though she also asked Shrewsbury for money from time to time (as was her right under their marriage settlement). From Bess's perspective, this was understandable and prudent; all that Shrewsbury could seemingly see was that Bess and her family were spending money which he believed could and should have been used to alleviate at least some of his financial concerns. At this time, he was in fact still considerably richer than Bess, at least in terms of actual capital, but her financial assets were slowly and steadily increasing, whist he was now being obliged to pay several thousand pounds a year out of his own pocket for the keeping of the Scottish Queen, and the knowledge of that financial drain was almost always in the forefront of his mind. Couple that with the deterioration of his marriage to Bess, and his ever-present concerns as to how he was perceived by the Queen and her Council, and it seems possible that Shrewsbury might well have been on the way to a nervous breakdown by the end of 1579.

Some of his financial concerns were self-inflicted. In the 1570s, he allowed himself to become embroiled in several building projects of his own, which cannot have helped his financial circumstances. One example of this were the improvements he ordered to be made to Shrewsbury House in Chelsea, upon which Gilbert Talbot commented with approval in a letter to his father and Bess dated 28th February 1579. Shrewsbury House had been built or acquired by the Fourth Earl of Shrewsbury sometime around 1519 (there are reports of the Fourth Earl living there in that year). Made of brick, it was built in the form of three sides of a quadrangle and stood by the River Thames at Cheyne Walk. At some time during the 1570s, Shrewsbury decided that improvements were needed, especially new and improved glass windows and new decorated plasterwork in several rooms, including the great chamber. This work was carried out at considerable expense and would be finally completed sometime in early 1580, but now the master craftsmen carrying out the improvements wanted payment for their services to date and were pressing the Earl hard for their money.

Serious as this was, it paled into insignificance compared to the expenses arising from Shrewsbury's decision, possibly inspired by Bess's work at Chatsworth, to build a new great prodigy house of his own at Worksop Manor in Nottinghamshire. Worksop Manor had been owned by the Talbots since the fourteenth century and Shrewsbury's father had begun building a new manor house on the estate before his death on 25th September 1560 brought the project to a premature end, leaving the house incomplete. In 1577 (although some preliminary work may have commenced before then), Shrewsbury had ordered that construction begin once more, but on a much larger scale than his father had envisioned, and (probably on Bess's advice) had secured the services of the master mason Robert Smythson to design the new house and oversee the building works.

Worksop would eventually become one of the great Elizabethan prodigy houses, arguably greater than Chatsworth as it stood in Bess's day.[2] Although the original plans for the house as designed by

---

[2] It would become the principal seat of the Eighth and Ninth Dukes of Norfolk (the dukedom having been restored to the Howards in 1660) before it burnt down in a fire in 1761

Smythson have not survived, we know that when it was finally completed in 1585, it was highly admired by Shrewsbury's contemporaries; it was tall and imposing (having at least four floors above ground) and in 1590, when visiting Worksop, Sir Robert Cecil described its gallery (224 feet long) as being the fairest in England. Completion of the new house undoubtedly enhanced Shrewsbury's reputation socially, but given the costs inherent in its construction and maintenance, the question has been asked by many as to why Shrewsbury commenced the work at all, particularly at a time when he was complaining incessantly about his financial circumstances. After all, it was not as if he needed another house; he already had seven principal residences, namely Buxton Hall, Rufford Abbey, Sheffield Castle, Sheffield Manor Lodge, Tutbury, Welbeck Abbey and South Wingfield Manor, as well as two houses in London, Shrewsbury House in Chelsea and numerous other smaller manor houses, principally situated in the Midlands. It seems that there may have been several reasons for his ordering the commencement of his building works of the 1570s, and especially at Worksop.

First of all, not all his houses were in good repair; as already noted, Tutbury required considerable work to bring it up to a standard to allow it to be considered to provide satisfactory lodgings for Queen Mary, even as a captive, and Shrewsbury may well have considered that some of the houses he owned or otherwise controlled (some were leased from the Crown or other noblemen) were insufficient to sustain his own dignity as an earl, at least as a primary residence. This concern may have been exacerbated by the thought that it was by no means impossible that Queen Elizabeth might one day decide to descend upon him during one of her Royal Progresses and if that happened, he would need somewhere sufficiently grand to entertain his sovereign.

Then too, the fact that he was living in an age when it was increasingly fashionable for the wealthy and well-connected to embark on large building projects may also have been a factor; it was a way many important families of the time sought to demonstrate their social significance and power and there is no reason to think that Shrewsbury was immune from this desire.

Thirdly of course, he may well have had the desire (sub-conscious or otherwise) to compete with Bess in the building and re-building of great houses. Whilst he continued to complain bitterly that Chatsworth consumed so much of Bess's attentions, money and he may well have thought, affections, not to mention the services of his own workmen, he would not have been ignorant of the fact that Bess took great pride in Chatsworth, and may have wished to enjoy that feeling for himself. If his creations outshone those of Bess, well by this stage he may not have objected to that either.

Whatever his motivations, by early 1580, he must have been regretting the expenditure on his building projects (indeed work on Worksop was temporarily halted in the early 1580s for financial reasons). Adding to his concerns, new disputes had arisen with some of his tenants in the Peak District in the summer of 1579. Perhaps as a consequence of his financial concerns, and notwithstanding the reactions of the lewd fellows of the Peak back in 1575 when attempts had been made to enclose common pastures and to close forest rights of way, his bailiff had been instructed to raise the rents of some tenants (primarily those living in Glossopdale and neighbouring Ashford), and to revoke other leases, presumably so they could be reissued at a later date to new tenants on terms more favourable to Shrewsbury. The tenants objected vociferously. Their anger was primarily focussed on Shrewsbury's bailiff, Nicholas Booth, though Shrewsbury and indeed Bess, who strictly speaking was the primary landlord in Ashford, came in for considerable criticism as well. Indeed, in a letter dated 22nd June 1579 and written from Chatsworth, Shrewsbury complained to Lord Burghley about allegations that some of the Ashford tenants had been making against Bess, and asking for them to be punished for their presumption. Bess added a postscript to the letter essentially saying that the Ashford tenants at least had nothing to complain about and her only concern was that Queen Elizabeth and Lord Burghley might be troubled over the matter.

As a matter of fact, they were, as the letter had been prompted by some of the tenants making their way to the Court to petition for redress and their complaints were heard by the Privy Council. The Privy Council (whose members reportedly were astonished at the new rent levels Shrewsbury was seeking to impose) found in favour of the tenants; as before in 1575, neither the Council nor the Queen were eager for rural unrest, particularly in an area so close to where Queen Mary was being imprisoned and they also seem to have felt that the tenants (by and large) had justice on their side. For Shrewsbury, it seemed like yet another example of a lack of support and understanding on the part of Queen Elizabeth and her Council.

By the spring of 1580, people were beginning to notice that all was not well with the marriage of the Shrewsburys. Shrewsbury had begun to be far more critical of Bess in front of others, friends and servants alike, focussing much on her extravagance, the demands for money she and her children continued to make of him and alleging that she was seeking to alienate him not only from her children, to whom he was step-father (and father-in-law in the case of two of them) but his own children as well. News of the growing rift had now percolated through to the Queen and the Privy Council, raising concerns that disagreement between Bess and Shrewsbury might somehow jeopardise the security arrangements in place for the Scottish Queen. In the summer of 1580, (following receipt of correspondence from Shrewsbury to Queen Elizabeth in which he listed some of his grievances against Bess) the Queen despatched Leicester (following a visit to Buxton) to visit Bess at Chatsworth, to try to ascertain the exact state of relations between the Shrewsburys, and if possible, to effect some sort of reconciliation. Leicester subsequently reported (to Shrewsbury) that he had found Bess in a distressed state, though when he had gently asked her if reports by Shrewsbury that she had threatened to reveal defamatory information about him, presumably about his dealings with Queen Mary, were true, she had calmy denied it, and had declared that she had no intention of making any public utterances against Shrewsbury. She had however observed that she herself had been subject to treatment that would alienate the heart and duty of any wife. She also had stated that she was not the cause of the estrangement, but had hinted darkly that she suspected other people had been seeking to turn her husband against her.

Bess went on (Leicester later recounted) to point out other actions of the Earl which had caused her, and other members of the family, distress. One incident related to Arbella, who had been living at Sheffield Manor Lodge with Gilbert and Mary Talbot. Apparently out of spite, Shrewsbury had ordered that Arbella be removed from the Lodge and returned to Chatsworth at once. This arbitrary decision had so upset Mary (who was pregnant) that she moved back to Chatsworth immediately to be with her mother. When Gilbert announced that he wished to accompany his wife to Chatsworth, Shrewsbury had forbidden him to go, threatening to cut off Gilbert's funding (he received an annual allowance of £200 from the Earl) if his order was disobeyed. Gilbert in fact had disobeyed his father and secretly visited Chatsworth to see his pregnant wife; he was there at the time of Leicester's visit and they briefly met; when Shrewsbury learnt of this, Gilbert's disobedience seemed to him further evidence that Bess was seeking to alienate him from his family and that Gilbert and Mary in particular were in league with Bess against him.

By the reference she made to "other people" during her conversation with Leicester, Bess almost certainly meant the Queen of Scots. Bess had seen relatively little of her over the previous few years, and they were certainly not as close as they once had been, partly because of Bess's lingering suspicions of an affair between her husband and Queen Mary, something that Shrewsbury continued firmly to deny. By this time though, Queen Mary for her part seems to have developed a distaste for Bess and may well have sought to sow seeds of dissension between Bess and her husband, partly out of a desire to cause trouble for Bess, and also in the hope that disagreement between the Shrewsburys might create opportunities that she could herself exploit.

Leicester departed Chatsworth without bringing about any sort of reconciliation between Bess and Shrewsbury, and shortly thereafter

Mary Talbot gave birth to a daughter, also named Mary.[3] Over the next year or so, relations between Bess and Shrewsbury continued to worsen; they had a significant argument in October 1581 over money, with Shrewsbury complaining that Bess never ceased demanding money from him and that she only enjoyed the lands she held (that is, Chatsworth and other properties) as a result of his generosity. Bess in turn complained that Shrewsbury was failing to honour the terms of their marriage contract. Rumours about the possible imminent collapse of the Shrewsbury marriage continued to spread and grow, and to make matters worse, there were concerns about the health of Queen Mary, who had been thrown from her horse as she set off for one of her periodic visits to Buxton and hurt her back. Queen Elizabeth and her Council grew so concerned about the situation in Sheffield that in November 1581, they sent Robert Beale, Clerk of the Privy Council (and Walsingham's brother-in-law) to Sheffield to investigate the situation there for himself (he was also to question Queen Mary about correspondence she had initiated with the King of France about the possibility of her regaining the Scottish throne and ruling jointly with King James as co-monarch). Bess was ordered to be present (it must have been an uncomfortable visit for both her and Shrewsbury), but together they presented something of a united front when Beale arrived at Sheffield at the start of what would be a three-week visit, warning him of the Scottish Queen's deviousness and manipulative cunning.

Upon his arrival at Sheffield, Beale found that Queen Mary was confined to her bed once more, complaining of an illness in her side, and he found her difficult to interview. Perhaps the strangest interview took place on 23rd November, for as he was led into the Queen's chamber, all the candles suddenly blew out, leaving the room in darkness. All that Beale could hear was the sound of the Queen's women sobbing, and the voice of Queen Mary emanating from the bed declaring weakly that she was dying. Beale, perhaps genuinely concerned that the Scottish Queen

---

[3] She went on to become Mary Herbert, Countess of Pembroke and died in 1649. Mary, Queen of Scots was her godmother.

really was seriously sick, left the bedroom, sought out Bess, and asked her to go and check on the Queen herself. When Bess entered the bedchamber (the candles had presumably been relit by now), she found Queen Mary seemingly lying asleep, or feigning it. Bess returned a little later to check on Mary once again; Mary was now awake, complaining, but in the opinion of Bess, as she later said to Beale, she had known the Queen "... far worse than she presently was ..." Beale eventually did manage to see Queen Mary in daylight, and later reported to the Council that she did seem pale, was overweight and suffering from rheumatism.

Beale's visit accomplished little; he got a token promise from Queen Mary that she would be more circumspect in her dealings with foreign governments but little more than that, and he was unable to report back to London that the Shrewsbury marriage rift showed any signs of ending. Moreover, he had been obliged to listen to Shrewsbury complaining about his financial woes; he dutifully recounted Shrewsbury's litany of complaints to Queen Elizabeth and her Council, but they were ignored once again. Perhaps the person who most benefited from his visit was Queen Mary herself; Queen Elizabeth on this occasion at least accepted the fact of Queen Mary's illnesses and agreed to a relaxation of the regime under which she was being held. In particular, she was allowed the use of a carriage and six horses for rides in Sheffield Park and received permission to attend the occasional play or masque in Sheffield Castle to relieve the monotony of her captivity.

Bess had other troubles in 1581 apart from her marriage. Sometime around April 1581, she received the unwelcome news that her brother James, then aged 55, had died in Fleet Prison where he had been imprisoned for debt. James had been married twice but died without a legitimate heir (he left an illegitimate son who was not entitled to inherit the family lands). As a consequence, the Hardwick lands had been seized by receivers tasked with paying off James' creditors as best they were able (including of course, Bess, who had the benefit of holding mortgages on the Hardwick estate). Bess was eager to acquire the land herself (or rather, to acquire it in her son William's name, retaining a life interest for herself); to pay for this, she asked Shrewsbury for money due to her under the marriage settlement, which he refused to pay, leading to Bess writing in complaint to Lord Burghley. Eventually, Bess contrived to purchase the Hardwick estate out of bankruptcy for £9,500 in June 1583.

Chapter 14

"I had the certain promise of the Countess"

Trouble and tragedy continued to beset Bess in 1582. Scarcely had the year begun when her daughter Elizabeth Lennox, who had been attending a Twelfth Night party at Sheffield Manor Lodge, was taken ill. Her condition swiftly worsened, so much so that on 16th January 1582, she updated her will, and she died five days later, at three o'clock in the morning of 21st January. She was 26 years old, and on the evening of her death, Shrewsbury wrote to Walsingham to report that Bess was taking Elizabeth's death "... so grievously and so mourneth and lamenteth that she cannot think of aught but tears ..."

Elizabeth's death meant that Arbella was now almost totally dependent upon Bess, both in the parental sense and financially. Her death also meant that the £400 annual pension that Elizabeth had been receiving would cease. Knowledge of this had been preying on Elizabeth's mind over the last few days of her life, and in her will, she had pleaded that Queen Elizabeth take pity on Arbella, asking that Bess be appointed Arbella's legal guardian and requesting that the £400 pension should continue to be paid to Arbella. Perhaps in the hope of encouraging this, Elizabeth bequeathed "her best jewel set" with a great diamond to Queen Elizabeth, who promptly took it, and granted Bess guardianship of Arbella but remained silent as regards the pension.[1]

There seems no doubt that Bess was indeed grief-stricken at Elizabeth's death, but this did not prevent her from rousing herself to fight for what she regarded were Arbella's rights. A week after Elizabeth's death, on 28th January, Bess was writing to both Lord Burghley and Walsingham,

---

[1] Elizabeth also left her white sable coats to Bess, and touchingly, after thanking Shrewsbury for being a good father to both herself and Arbella, left him a gold salt cellar.

reiterating the request that the £400 annual pension be continued and essentially claiming that the money would be vital in helping to ensure that Arbella received the quality of education that her future position in life would require. At around the same time, Bess's son William wrote in a similar vein to the Queen, but to no avail. Bess, having by now returned to Chatsworth, wrote once again to Sir Francis Walsingham on 6th May 1582 to press Arbella's claim. That same day she also wrote to Lord Burghley, stressing more firmly the point that Arbella had royal blood in her veins, but the Queen remained unmoved and the pension remained stopped. As far as Queen Elizabeth was concerned, Arbella's own yearly pension of £200 was sufficient, and if further funds were required for the child's upbringing and education, it was not unreasonable that Bess (and Shrewsbury) should provide them.

Elizabeth's death was the cause of yet another clash between Bess and Shrewsbury; shortly after Elizabeth's death, Bess had asked Shrewsbury to take into his employment some of Elizabeth's servants, a request which had infuriated the Earl and which he firmly declined, stating that he already had "too many spies" in his house.[2] He might also have said to himself that he already also had too many expenses. The result was that Bess abruptly departed Sheffield to return to Chatsworth, even though her daughter Mary was at Sheffield Manor Lodge and about to give birth to another child, which she did, reportedly the day after her mother's departure. The child was a girl, and perhaps predictably in all

---

[2] Shrewsbury certainly feared that some of the Shrewsbury servants were more loyal to Bess than to himself and he particularly disliked a gentleman servant called William Marmyon who formed part of Bess's household and who he considered to be little more than a spy for Bess. Marmyon may or may not have been reporting back to Bess on Shrewsbury's activities, but he certainly wrote to Sir Francis Willoughby in the early 1580s describing the poor state of the Shrewsbury marriage (he referred to it as being like a civil war) and saying that he wished to leave Bess's service and join Sir Francis' household at Wollaton Hall which he eventually did. In fact, he re-joined Willoughby's service as he had previously worked at Wollaton between 1572 and 1578.

the circumstances, was christened Elizabeth. (She went on to become Elizabeth Grey, the Countess of Kent.)

By now, all of Bess's surviving children had reached adulthood and she was closer to some than others. Her eldest daughter Frances had long been married to Henry Pierrepont and spent much of her time on the Pierrepont family estate at Holme Pierrepont in Nottinghamshire. By 1582, Frances had given birth to two daughters, Grace and Elizabeth (the latter would have serving in the household of Mary, Queen of Scots at this time); Frances would go on to give birth to a son, Robert, in 1584. Busy as both Bess and Frances were, they seem to have seen each other reasonably regularly and remained on good terms until Bess's death.

That was emphatically not true of Bess's relationship with her eldest son Henry. Henry, having married Grace Talbot, had grown up to be a disappointment, even a cause of shame, for Bess, perhaps made worse because he was heir to Chatsworth. Aged 31 in the summer of 1582, to someone who did not know him well, he may have seemed a relatively successful man. Unlike his brothers he did not go to university but in 1572, after having completed a tour of Europe in the company of Gilbert Talbot, he had contrived to get himself elected as MP for Derbyshire (and would be re-elected in the next four successive elections, probably thanks to the influence of Shrewsbury). Not content with this, in 1574, he volunteered to fight in the Low Countries against the Spanish, initially as a Captain and later as a Colonel, taking with him 500 men recruited from the various Cavendish and Talbot estates. In December 1582, he was appointed High Sheriff of Derbyshire. Shrewsbury thought highly of him, or at least more highly than he did of Bess's other sons, and not only praised him to Queen Elizabeth but also allowed him and his wife to reside at Tutbury for several years.

There was however another side to Henry. He and his wife Grace endured a most unhappy marriage; they had no children together, but Henry became notorious for his womanising and sired so many illegitimate children that he became known as the "common bull of

Derbyshire and Staffordshire".[3] To Bess, this would have been bad enough, but making matters worse was the fact that Henry was financially profligate (by 1584, his debts would exceed £3000), notwithstanding that on attaining his majority, he became entitled to claim income from lands that his father had settled on him, income that hitherto had been claimed by Bess. He gambled extensively, and his financial position was made worse by the debts he had incurred while fighting in the Netherlands. By the early 1580s, Bess had virtually written Henry off as a waste of both her time and money (he was her "bad son" she later proclaimed), though judging from their correspondence, she and Grace appear to have maintained a good relationship. In some ways he probably reminded her of her dead brother James. Henry in his turn grew increasingly resentful of his mother, and in the quarrels between Bess and Shrewsbury he generally could be relied on to side with the Earl.[4]

Bess's growing disillusionment with Henry caused her to focus more of her attentions on her second son William and to an extent her third son Charles so far as her financial and dynastic ambitions were concerned. In 1580, William had both married and been knighted, and now was residing with his first wife Anne, first at Chatsworth and later at Hardwick Hall, and essentially kept himself busy for much of the time assisting his mother with her various financial interests. He seems at this time to have been a dutiful though dull man, and while he developed a

---

[3] He had at least eight illegitimate children, one of them being the ancestor of a line that would eventually become the Barons Waterpark in the Peerage of Ireland.

[4] Even though Henry was a disappointment to Bess, she seems sometimes to have found him useful. In 1589, he spent several months travelling on the continent, ending up at Constantinople, and it has been speculated that he may have gone partly at Bess's behest in order to investigate possible trade opportunities. He may also have been instructed to purchase Persian and Turkish carpets; Hardwick certainly had some by 1601 (and still possesses two from that period) and these may have been brought back by Henry. As for foreign trade opportunities, if any were identified by Henry, there is no evidence that Bess decided to pursue them.

reputation for meanness as the years went by, it seems clear that Bess knew that she could rely on him to carry out her instructions. As his mother's second son, he must have watched with increasing interest the growing estrangement between Bess and Henry and realised that careful attention to his mother's demands could prove to be financially beneficial to him and his family, as ultimately proved to be the case.

Charles, the third son, was also obedient to Bess's wishes when called upon to be but had a livelier personality than his older brother William. He grew up to be very close to his stepbrother Gilbert, frequently taking his side when Gilbert became embroiled in feuds or other quarrels (which happened fairly often as Gilbert had a disputatious side to his personality). Especially when Charles was young, he was capable too of getting into trouble on his own account. In 1575, for example, after Charles had gone out poaching with several servants, Shrewsbury had written to Bess complaining that Charles was "easily led to folly" and told her that she should "advise him from those doings". That said, there was a lighter side to Charles. He seems to have been more popular than his brother William (unlike William, Charles could be generous with both time and money when he wished to be, though he never incurred debts on the scale that Henry contrived to do) and he had a reputation for being a skilled horseman and swordsman. He took a keen interest in music too, and in later years became a patron of the madrigalist John Wilbye, who in due course would dedicate his first book of madrigals (published in 1598) to Charles. He also shared Bess's interest in building. Bess had provided him with a house, Stoke Manor (later Stoke Hall) situated on the edge of the village of Grindleford, in Derbyshire, but in due course he would begin building projects of his own. Charles, like his eldest brother Henry, also served for a spell (in 1578) fighting the Spanish in the Netherlands and was knighted in 1582.

In 1581, he had become engaged to Margaret Kitson. She was the daughter of Sir Thomas Kitson, of Hengrave Hall in Suffolk, a wealthy landowner, and Bess had played an active role in encouraging the marriage, and indeed in the negotiation of the marriage settlement. There had been some dispute as to the terms of the settlement, but eventually an agreement was reached and the marriage proceeded that same year.

As for Bess's youngest surviving daughter Mary, she and Bess enjoyed a close and loving relationship throughout much of their joint lives (though that relationship grew strained in the years following Shrewsbury's death in 1590 which would lead to a dispute between Bess and Gilbert Talbot with regard to Bess's rights as Shrewsbury's widow). For the most part, her marriage to Gilbert seems to have been happy as well, though tensions between the two understandably grew during the years of Bess's dispute with Gilbert. By the end of 1582, she and Gilbert had produced two surviving children, Mary and Elizabeth, and another daughter, Alethea (later the Countess of Arundel) would be born in 1585. Of all Bess's daughters, Mary seems to have been most like Bess as regards strength of character and determination, though she was possibly less wise in some of her judgments than Bess, even though she was better educated. She was also far more arrogant than Bess, which caused many people to dislike her. It was a trait which in later years would lead her into serious trouble.[5]

Though relations between Bess and Shrewsbury were now approaching breaking point, May of 1582 saw a brief interlude of relative mutual civility, possibly even affection, between the couple, one of the last there was to be. Exactly why this happened is not exactly clear, but sometime around early May, Bess mentioned to Shrewsbury that she was in need of a horse-litter and Shrewsbury wrote on 15th May 1582 to Thomas Baldwin, his London agent, instructing him to procure a "very handsome one" for Bess, specifying the form it was to take in considerable detail. It seems that Shrewsbury was genuinely desirous of pleasing Bess, at least in this matter and went to some trouble to do so. Baldwin duly obliged; he was well used to overseeing Shrewsbury's business interests in London and with Shrewsbury forced to remain

---

[5] She would later convert to Catholicism and (after Bess's death) be imprisoned in the Tower of London for a number of years.

much of the time guarding Queen Mary, Baldwin played an essential role in assisting with the Earl's affairs. Bess in due course took possession of a fine new litter, but it was not long before relations between Bess and Shrewsbury began to worsen once again.[6]

Death returned to haunt the family in 1582. In early July of that year, Bess's daughter-in-law Margaret, who had married Charles only a year or so before, died after giving birth to a son, who was christened William (and subsequently died in infancy). Margaret's death once again galvanised Bess into writing letters intended to protect the financial interests of family members; before long she was writing to Sir Thomas Cornwallis, Sir Thomas Kitson's father-in-law, seeking re-assurance that Kitson, who now had only one surviving daughter, Mary, but no sons of his own, would treat Charles as his son, notwithstanding Margaret's death (and, more to the point, honour the outstanding terms of the marriage settlement, which principally related to certain pieces of land which were supposed to have been transferred to Charles and Margaret). Whether or not Kitson took any steps to comply with the outstanding terms is unknown, but when he died (in 1603), without further issue of his own, his fortune was shared between Mary and Charles.

Then, around the end of August 1582, Shrewsbury received the news that his eldest son and heir to his earldom, Francis, had died of the plague whilst visiting family members in Belvoir Castle. Francis, who had been born about 1550, had been married but had no children. Shrewsbury therefore had to accept that not only had his eldest son died but also that it was now likely the Talbot lands and titles, including the earldom, would be inherited by Gilbert, with whom he was now on

---

[6] Baldwin's surname was sometimes spelt "Baldwyn". He would be arrested and sent to the Tower in December 1584 for (perhaps innocently) having become involved in the passing of secret coded messages from Queen Mary to her supporters. He was incarcerated there for three years. When he was released, he retired to his estate at Diddlebury which he had inherited from his father while in the Tower. He died in 1614.

increasingly poor terms. Not only that, but Mary Talbot, whom he regarded as being in league (like Gilbert) with Bess to his own disadvantage, would now most likely one day become Countess of Shrewsbury in her own right. Shrewsbury appears to have seen his eldest son's death as some sort of victory for Bess and a weakening of his own position, and in correspondence with friends, subsequently hinted that he dated his final estrangement from Bess from the date of Francis Talbot's death. The fact that Francis died leaving many debts Shrewsbury was expected to cover simply added to the increased sense of persecution that the Earl was now feeling. Making matters even worse, there were now rumours that Mary Queen of Scots had conceived Shrewsbury's child. On hearing of these rumours, Queen Mary and Shrewsbury discussed the matter, and concluded that Bess, William and Charles were responsible for the rumours (Queen Mary, now determined on making mischief between Bess and Shrewsbury for reasons of her own, may have planted the notion in the Earl's mind).

Notwithstanding all this, Bess and Shrewsbury were still capable of acting in concert should a real emergency arise, and a potential one did in early 1583. In September 1581, Bess's nephew John Wingfield, had married Susan Bertie, the daughter of Catherine Brandon, Duchess of Suffolk and her second husband Richard Bertie. On hearing the news, Queen Elizabeth took the view that she should have been asked for her consent and news of her displeasure reached the ears of both Shrewsbury and Bess (indeed, Bess, still an inveterate matchmaker, may have encouraged the marriage in the first place). Sixteen months later, the Queen's anger about the marriage had shown no sign of abating and on 6th February 1583, Shrewsbury wrote to Walsingham from Sheffield asking him to help in reconciling Queen Elizabeth to the fact of the marriage. The following day, Bess (who was also at Sheffield) also wrote to Walsingham from Sheffield making a similar appeal. Whether Walsingham succeeded in tempering the Queen's displeasure at that time is unknown, but the Queen did eventually come to accept the fact of the marriage, perhaps assisted by the fact that John Wingfield volunteered to fight in the Netherlands, where he fought with some distinction and where he was knighted in 1586.

After that, Bess may or may not have remained at Sheffield for the next few months, but she was certainly there in July 1583 when Mary Talbot gave birth to a boy (John, who died shortly thereafter). At the time of John's birth, Bess and Shrewsbury seem to have been civil to each other, and according to later statements made by Bess, when they subsequently parted, they did so on amicable terms, with Shrewsbury promising to send for her again in a few days' time.

He never did, and shortly after her departure, he halted all payments due to Bess under their marriage settlement (though he continued to collect rents from the lands Bess had brought into the marriage and which were now under his control). He also forbade her access to Sheffield Castle or any other Talbot property. He sought to justify his actions by claiming Bess had breached the terms of the deed of gift of 22nd April 1572 by disposing of some land without his permission which (he argued) invalidated the gift. In essence, Shrewsbury had decided that he had suffered enough from what he saw were hostile actions by Bess (and her sons William and Charles) and was determined to fight back and reclaim what he regarded was his.

We can get an image of Shrewsbury's state of mind around this time from a letter written by Gilbert Talbot to Bess dated 19th September 1583, in which he reported the outcome of a meeting between himself and his father, who was ill at the time. Gilbert reported (amongst other things) that Shrewsbury, in the course of a long, rambling and at times incoherent conversation had told him that matters were "hard" between Bess and himself, and that he forbade Gilbert to take Mary to London as he feared that Bess would join them there and all three would "exclaim against" him. He claimed too that Sir Walter Mildmay (Chancellor of the Exchequer and founder of Emmanuel College, Cambridge) and the Master of the Rolls (at that time, Sir Gilbert Gerard) were wholly on Bess's side in the matter of the estrangement and would have had an "order" made against him save for the fact that the Lord Chief Justice would not consent (the exact nature of the order is unclear). He also complained that William Cavendish had tried (improperly in Shrewsbury's opinion) to claim £1800 for "lot and cope" (essentially fees paid by lead miners to the owners of lands on which lead mines were situated); according to Gilbert, the Earl made such a matter of this as "was never heard" and spoke "so out of purpose" that it would be in vain to write of it. Henry Cavendish, on the other hand, was praised by Shrewsbury for maintaining his honour (one would love to know what Bess thought of that statement). Somewhat bizarrely, given the poor relationship between Gilbert and his father, Gilbert too came in for some praise from Shrewsbury, with Shrewsbury assuring him that he loved him best of all his children, and that Gilbert had never given any offence save for staying too long at Chatsworth.

Perhaps significantly, Gilbert told Bess that whenever he had tried to reply to the points raised by Shrewsbury, he had been interrupted and he had been unable to express his point of view or raise counter-arguments. The Earl was essentially ranting against Bess and unwilling (or unable) to consider any viewpoint other than his own.

Shrewsbury was now trying to assemble allies for his forthcoming battles with Bess. Henry Cavendish clearly was on his side, and his comments to Gilbert about him being the favourite of all his children may have been a clumsy attempt to recruit him as well, though if it was it did not succeed. In July 1583, the Earl had given orders to Baldwin to summon his two younger sons, Henry and Edward Talbot, back to England from France where they had been enjoying themselves on a break from Oxford, instructing him to inform them that when they returned, they were to be "stout" with Bess, William and Charles. Shrewsbury also wrote to others seeking support, such as Leicester and Walsingham, seeking to set out his case against Bess; probably wisely, most, if not all, of those he contacted sent sympathetic but non-committal replies and kept their heads down. No one wanted to get caught in the middle of a fight between Shrewsbury and Bess.

Bess for her part reacted in a calm yet apparently sorrowful manner to Shrewsbury's allegations and actions, and would write from London on 26th August 1584 to Shrewsbury to protest that she had tended to his happiness in every way that she could, that no allegation made against her justified separation and asking for liberty to come to see him, a request that Shrewsbury firmly denied. Bess also made other pleas for reconciliation, or at least a chance to meet and talk through the differences between herself and Shrewsbury, none of which elicited a favourable response from the Earl. It is difficult though to tell whether Bess was genuinely seeking some sort of rapprochement with Shrewsbury, or whether she was quietly happy to separate from him, and making her pleas simply to create an image of herself as the wronged wife and to elicit as much support from her friends (many of whom were also Shrewsbury's friends) and especially the Queen, as she could. One aspect of the separation which certainly irked her however was Shrewsbury's halting the payments due to her under the marriage settlement and his seizing rents from lands which she regarded as being payable to her. She and Shrewsbury began a long series of claims and counter-claims as to how much the other owed them.

Shrewsbury may have been surprised and saddened not to have received more support (moral or otherwise) in his fight with Bess from the Earl of Leicester, who he had hitherto regarded as not only a close political ally but also a friend. He had known of course that Leicester was also a close friend of Bess; what he probably did not know in late 1583 and early 1584 was that his separation from Bess had not dampened her dynastic ambitions. Indeed, it may have encouraged them to the extent that they might enhance her power base. This time, she was focussing her attentions on Arbella, then eight years old, and her plans for her granddaughter also involved Leicester, and especially Leicester's son.

In June 1581, Leicester's wife Lettice had given birth to a boy, Robert, Lord Denbigh (a "noble imp" according to Leicester) and over the winter months of late 1583 and early 1584, Bess and Leicester had been in secret discussions concerning a possible marriage between Arbella and Robert. Such a marriage would have brought advantages to both families. From Leicester's perspective, given Arbella's place in the royal succession, the marriage might well have placed his son on the throne of England (or at least adjacent to it), as well as linking his family to the ever richer Cavendishes. From Bess's perspective, the marriage would provide her family with even better access to powerful parties at Court, including of course, Leicester himself (still the Queen's favourite, but perhaps not as much as he had been before his marriage to Lettice Knollys), connections which would not only be useful in her battles with Shrewsbury but also generally in the future. The marriage might also induce the Queen to look more favourably at the possibility of naming Arbella as her heir.

The problem though was that the proposed marriage might also anger the Queen given her known sensitivity about the succession and so, initially at least, Bess and Leicester kept the proposed marriage a secret from her. Queen Mary was also not informed of the proposal, which clearly had potential implications for herself and her son. Realistically as well, even in Tudor times, an actual marriage service involving an infant of two and a half (or thereabouts) would almost certainly be declared to be legally invalid (and of course the requirements of the Royal Marriage Act had to be considered, given Arbella's proximity to the throne) and so there was in practice no way that the proposed marriage could take place in the foreseeable future even if Bess and Leicester had wanted this to happen. They may therefore have decided to proceed slowly, perhaps with a view of introducing the idea to the Queen at what they considered to be an opportune moment, one at which royal ire at the suggestion was least likely to be roused. They seem however to have thought it a good idea that the two children should at least be seen to be formally betrothed to one another and so at the end of February 1584, they decided to proceed with a betrothal "ceremony" for Arbella and Robert, something that wasn't uncommon in Tudor times, at least for the wealthier members of society. Unsurprisingly, rumours of the ceremony quickly began to spread and by 4th March, Lord Paget was writing to the Earl of Northumberland stating that:

> "The Queen should be informed of the practices between Leicester and the Countess for Arbella, for it comes on very lustily, insomuch as the said earl hath sent down a picture of his baby son."

Queen Mary was furious when she heard the news, and on 21st March 1584 she wrote to Michel de Castelnau, the Sieur de la Mauvissière and the French ambassador to Queen Elizabeth that:

> "... nothing has ever alienated the Countess of Shrewsbury from me more than this imaginary hope, which she has conceived, of setting this crown on Arbella her granddaughter, by means of marrying her to the son of the Earl of Leicester ..."

Up until now, though the friendship between Bess and Queen Mary (if indeed there had really been one) had effectively evaporated, Queen Mary had largely been content simply to seek to cause division between Bess and Shrewsbury, but there is no real evidence of any other significant actual direct personal hostility from Queen Mary towards Bess. Having said that, on 5th January 1584, Queen Mary had written to Mauvissière saying:

> "... you will have somewhat understood by my aforesaid letters, my intention of involving indirectly the Countess of Shrewsbury ..."

which could have been a reference to seeking to cause strife between Bess and Shrewsbury, possibly by encouraging the notion that Bess was one of those responsible for spreading the suggestion that Queen Mary had borne Shrewsbury's child. In that same letter though, Queen Mary made reference to having in writing details of:

> "... such acts and practices of her and hers to reveal, in which the Earl of Leicester and others of his faction are deeply involved ...",

suggesting that Queen Mary may have assembled a collection of allegations (imaginary or not) against Bess for use should the need arise.[7] (It might also suggest that Queen Mary had somehow become aware of the discussions between Bess and Leicester about the marriage proposals for Arbella and Robert earlier than March 1584). In any event, from now on, now that news of the betrothal was public knowledge, Queen Mary would openly become an implacable enemy of Bess, and (as far as she could) be determined to do her harm. Indeed, in the letter of 21st March to Mauvissière she urged the ambassador to tell Queen Elizabeth about the betrothal. She also made statements about Bess which if believed, could easily be regarded as proof of treachery on the part of Bess, no doubt intending that they be passed on to Queen Elizabeth:

> *"… I had the certain promise of the Countess, that if at any time my life was in danger or if I were removed from here, she would provide the means of my escape and she herself would easily avoid danger and punishment in so doing. She made her son Charles Cavendish swear before me that he would live in London, particularly to be of service in passing on all that happened at Court and that he would keep two strong geldings ready especially to carry speedy news of the death of the Queen who was ill at the time …"*

Despite Queen Mary's entreaties, Mauvissière (probably wisely) chose not to pass on to Queen Elizabeth all the details of the allegations made by Queen Mary about Bess, or to mention the betrothal. There was no need; Queen Elizabeth was quite capable of learning of the betrothal herself and when she did (sometime in mid-March), she was indeed annoyed (especially with Leicester) but she restrained her anger. She doesn't seem to have imposed any form of punishment on Bess and she certainly didn't expel Leicester from the Court (as she might well have

---

[7] Some biographers have speculated that the reference to details of acts and practices may be a reference to the contents of the so-called scandal letter. See Appendix 2.

done if any other courtier but he been involved), for a few months after the betrothal, Leicester was accompanying the Queen on one of her Progresses around the Thames Valley.

It was while he was on this Progress that Leicester received news that his son Robert had died on 19ᵗʰ July 1584, dashing any hope of a marriage alliance between the Dudleys and the Cavendishes. Bess would have to look elsewhere for an advantageous match for Arbella. Robert's death also meant that Leicester would die without a legitimate successor and his son's death was a blow from which Leicester never really recovered.[8] Shrewsbury wrote him a letter of condolence (which has not survived); Leicester's reply to it has however and in it he urged Shrewsbury not to pursue a quarrel with Gilbert. Shrewsbury responded to this with another letter expressing his hatred of Bess and Mary Talbot and declaring he saw Bess as his "professed enemy".

Shrewsbury's actions that summer show that he meant exactly what he had said. In July 1584, he instructed one of his bailiffs to ensure that the tenants on the lands Bess had acquired from St Loe should henceforth pay their rents to him and not to Bess "at their uttermost peril". At Ashford (later known as Ashford-in-the-Water), about 5 miles from Chatsworth his bailiff Nicholas Booth (who seems to have nursed a hatred of Bess and the Cavendishes generally nearly as deep as that of Shrewsbury) led a party of men to seize supplies of lead and attacked Charles Cavendish, who for his own safety was obliged to seek refuge in the steeple of the local church where he remained for 24 hours. The Earl's men also demolished the walls around his pastures at Stoke Manor, injuring some of Charles' servants in the process. Demands for rent from the tenants were also made at Stoke, notwithstanding that

---

[8] Leicester had a surviving illegitimate son by Lady Douglas Sheffield with whom he had an affair in the 1570s. That son, who became Sir Robert Dudley, would later try to argue that Leicester had secretly married his mother and that he was entitled to claim the Dukedom of Northumberland and the Earldoms of Warwick and Leicester; his claims were not recognised in England, and he died in Italy in 1649.

many of the tenants had already paid their due rents to Bess's agents; those who refused to pay again had their animals seized by the Earl's men and in some cases were expelled from their tenant properties. Law and order in the area was clearly beginning to break down.

Bad as this was, worse would happen at Chatsworth. In July 1584, Shrewsbury was preparing to lead a party of armed men to seize control of what he later described to Lord Burghley was *his* house at Chatsworth. He later argued that in seeking to gain control of Chatsworth, he was simply acting in the interests of Bess's "… eldest and best deserving son …", namely Henry, who after all was still the heir to the Chatsworth estate. On hearing the news, Bess hurriedly moved to the old family house at Hardwick. William Cavendish supervised the transfer of valuable plate and furnishings from Chatsworth to Hardwick and then returned to defend Chatsworth as best he could.

Shortly thereafter, Shrewsbury arrived at Chatsworth at the head of a party of 40 armed men and tried to gain entry to the house. William, armed with a pistol and halberd, together with several retainers, refused him entry (using "lewd language" in the process according to Shrewsbury), whereupon Shrewsbury's men broke in. This, to Shrewsbury, was armed resistance to a lawful authority, that is himself, (he also regarded the removal of the valuable plate and furnishings from Chatsworth to Hardwick as theft on the part of Bess and William) and the result was that William found himself under arrest for "insolent behaviour", ordered to appear before a judge to explain himself, and in the meantime was transported to the Fleet Prison (which is why Bess was in London when she wrote her letter to Shrewsbury on 26th August asking for liberty to see him). William was shortly to be released after a judge had heard his defence for his actions. The events in Derbyshire, in the meantime, were the subject of immense gossip at Court.

Ironically, while all this was going on, Shrewsbury was about to find one of his deepest desires realised. On 2nd August 1584, Bess wrote to Lord Burghley, warning him what was happening, stressing that

Shrewsbury intended to seize Chatsworth by force and asking him to intervene, essentially claiming that a letter from him to the Earl would be more likely to have effect than one from any other living subject. This letter simply served to confirm to the Council, if confirmation was by now required, that it was no longer feasible, practical or wise for Shrewsbury to continue to act as the Queen of Scots' custodian. Indeed, even before Bess wrote her letter, it had been decided that Shrewsbury should cease to be the gaoler of Queen Mary, and on returning to Sheffield from a visit to Buxton at the end of July 1584 (where he had accompanied Queen Mary on what was to be her last visit to the spa town), Shrewsbury found to his pleasure that he was to be replaced, at least as a temporary measure, once again by Sir Ralph Sadler. Queen Mary was to be moved to South Wingfield Manor. Sadler and Shrewsbury were to escort her there in early September, following which Shrewsbury was permitted, finally, to come to Court.

Chapter 15
Execution of a Queen

As soon as he had taken his leave of Mary, Queen of Scots, at South Wingfield Manor, Shrewsbury headed for Oatlands Palace (near Weybridge in Surrey), where the Court was assembled, for a meeting of the Privy Council. Shrewsbury of course was a member of the Council (though he had not attended an actual meeting for many years), but before he took his seat, he demanded to know if any member of the Council "… would charge him with any lack of duty to Her Majesty …" None of them would and he duly took his seat.

The Queen, when she met him, no doubt recognising that Shrewsbury was now an ill man, both physically and mentally (he may have been suffering from early onset dementia), was notably gentle with him when they met; she called him "her good old man" and ordered that a footstool be provided for him while they talked. During their conversation, the state of Shrewsbury's marriage naturally arose, though the Queen apparently refused to take sides, at least explicitly. Shrewsbury, according to a report attributed to the Spanish ambassador, thanked her for delivering him from "… two devils, the Scottish Queen and his wife …". As a matter of fact, he was free from neither, though admittedly he no longer had custodial responsibility for Queen Mary. She did however continue for a while to be held at several of his residences. Rumours that Queen Mary had borne Shrewsbury's illegitimate child (who, it was now being claimed had died shortly after birth and been buried secretly) were also continuing to spread both within and without the Court, and Queen Mary was loudly demanding that steps be taken to investigate whether Bess and her sons William and Charles were responsible for this, as she asserted. It was therefore decided that the Council should investigate the matter once and for all. Queen Mary is said to have rejoiced when she heard Bess was to be investigated. That hearing was scheduled for November 1584.

At around the same time, the Queen and her Council decided that the estrangement between Bess and Shrewsbury not only had serious implications for the couple themselves, but also for the security of the realm, and that a commission of enquiry (composed of the Lord Chancellor, Sir Thomas Bromley, and two chief justices) should be established to investigate the rights and wrongs of the matter. The commission was scheduled to convene in December 1584. Thus, as the winter of 1584 approached, Bess, William and Charles faced two separate enquiries. Shrewsbury apparently was delighted; he believed that he would be vindicated in both of them.

He wasn't. When Bess and her sons appeared before the Council that November, they denied on their knees and on oath that they had been responsible for inventing or spreading the rumour of Queen Mary's supposed pregnancy, declared that they considered it to be a "false and malicious invention" and they stated in writing that "… the Queen of Scotland had never, to their knowledge, borne any child or children since she had been in England …" The Council believed them and considered the matter closed. Bess and her sons considered themselves vindicated. Shrewsbury no doubt considered it a miscarriage of justice (though one good result from his perspective was that after the Council's investigation, rumours of his improper relationship with Queen Mary began to fade away). In any event he could do nothing about it. As for Queen Mary, she had no choice but to accept both the findings of the Council and that on this occasion at least, she had failed to harm Bess. As it happens, her own troubles were about to engulf her, and she would soon have greater concerns than trying to damage the reputation of the Countess of Shrewsbury. From this time on, she essentially vanished out of Bess's life.

The commission of enquiry into the Shrewsbury marriage first convened on 23rd December 1584, and was a far more substantive set of proceedings than the Council hearings the month before. It was, to all intents and purposes, a civil trial, and Bess and Shrewsbury were each represented by counsel. At the heart of the enquiry were the allegations of financial impropriety that both sides had made against each other, and at the centre of those was the 1572 deed of gift. Shrewsbury initially tried to argue (through his lawyers, as he was away from London when the enquiry commenced), that it had been forged; that argument failed, as it was clearly genuine. He then tried to argue that the deed of gift had been for Bess's benefit alone and not for William and Charles, and yet they had benefited from it (he failed to remember that by agreeing to it, he had been released from the obligation of making substantial cash payments to William and Charles when they attained the age of 21). According to the Earl's figures, on Bess's orders William and Charles between them had spent more than £25,000 on property purchases in the Midlands over the preceding 12 years, using his money to which they were not entitled; moreover, Bess had been receiving from him an annual income of £5000, five times the amount to which she was entitled under the marriage settlement. Furthermore, he alleged she had become adept at extracting other sums from him when he was sick and unable to fully comprehend what he was agreeing to, and he argued he should be recompensed for those supposed improper payments.

Bess countered that the property purchases made by William and Charles had been made using their own money (and that they were now in debt as a result) and that the other claims made by the Earl (such as those relating to her annual income) were wildly exaggerated. She argued too that it was Shrewsbury who was in breach of the marriage settlement and that he had acted illegally in extorting rents from her tenants which were not due to him. It must be admitted that Bess was not above indulging in a little exaggeration herself from time to time (though not as much as Shrewsbury). The commission was aware of this but its task was to discover which set of arguments was the more persuasive and where between the two opposing sets of arguments the truth was most likely to lie.

The commission considered the matter over the early months of 1585. Bess spent much of this time in Derbyshire, mostly at Hardwick and took care to continue to appear patient and long suffering; Shrewsbury too remained away from the Court for the first two months of 1585, but then moved to his house in Chelsea in March from where he spent much of his time lobbying anyone he could think of who might assist his case.

The commission made its decision in mid-April, and Sir Francis Walsingham was delegated the task of announcing it to Shrewsbury on 24th April. Shrewsbury was summoned to the Court at Oatlands to hear the findings (Bess seems to have remained in Derbyshire) and he was dismayed to learn that, to a significant extent, the commission had found in favour of Bess. Based on the findings of the commission (Shrewsbury was told) the Queen was ordering that Shrewsbury was to make his peace with Bess and to take her back into his house, the properties William and Charles had purchased over the preceding twelve years were to remain theirs (subject to Bess's life interest where she possessed one) and Shrewsbury was to return £2000 in compensation for the rents he had improperly seized. Furthermore, Bess was to retain control over all the lands which had been passed to her under the 1572 deed of gift and Shrewsbury was to drop all outstanding claims against the Cavendishes and their servants. The only minor victory that Shrewsbury could claim was that henceforth Bess was required to pay the Earl £500 each year as rent for properties she occupied under the marriage settlement but which belonged to him. To put it bluntly, in the eyes of the Queen and the Court, Bess had won and Shrewsbury had lost.

Shrewsbury, unsurprisingly, was bitter about the verdict, and wrote to Leicester in protest but in essence confirmed he would abide by the Queen's rulings even though he considered they effectively made him his "wife's pensioner". He declared that no "… curse or plague on earth could be more grievous …" to him. Strangely, no one seems to have thought to tell Bess of the result of the enquiry; Leicester only remembered to write to Bess to give her the news in July.

It did not take Shrewsbury long to reach the conclusion that the reason for the unjust verdict (as he saw it) was that Leicester, Walsingham and others had conspired with Bess against him. The fact that Bess made her way to Court after hearing the news from Leicester and stayed there for the rest of the summer and autumn of 1585 was simply further proof to him that this must be so, and consequently he made no attempt at all to comply with the Queen's orders. He refused to take Bess back into his house despite several requests from Bess that he do so (Shrewsbury responded to these requests by sending her vituperative letters in return), refused to pay the money due to her, continued to harass her tenants and continued to pursue legal claims against her sons and servants (and he was not above bribing witnesses in pursuit of those claims). He ordered his own servants to be rude to Bess when they encountered her, to the extent that she was eventually obliged to complain to Walsingham about this. He also wrote incessantly to the Queen, Leicester, Burghley, Walsingham and anyone else who would listen complaining about Bess's behaviour and demanding that she be dismissed from the Court. The summer and autumn of 1585 was clearly a trying time for any person of consequence who was an acquaintance of Shrewsbury.

Bess continued her approach of seeming to be patient and reasonable, even when she asked Walsingham, Burghley and others to do all they could to persuade Shrewsbury to cease his harassment and to comply with the Queen's orders. But all appeals to Shrewsbury for him to see sense (and even Queen Elizabeth appealed to him) fell on deaf ears. Eventually, the Queen's patience snapped; acting on Lord Burghley's advice, in November 1585, she ordered that a second commission of enquiry into the state of the Shrewsbury marriage be held.[1] This time, the commission would be headed by Sir Francis Willoughby of Wollaton Hall (who was an old friend of Bess) and John Manners (Shrewsbury's brother-in-law). It assembled at Ashford in Derbyshire on 12th January 1586 and covered much the same ground as the first commission; William and Charles appeared as witnesses on their

---

[1] Although it is doubtful Shrewsbury appreciated it, perhaps mindful of his long years of service guarding Queen Mary, Queen Elizabeth was in fact being merciful to him in ordering that a second enquiry be held. Just about anyone else who so flagrantly disobeyed her orders on the scale demonstrated by Shrewsbury would have been sent to the Tower.

mother's behalf, and Shrewsbury appeared to put forward his side of the argument. The commission's deliberations were essentially over by mid-March; once again, Shrewsbury was confident that the commission would find in his favour, once again he was disappointed. On 8th May 1586, the Queen at Greenwich issued an order commanding Shrewsbury to obey the orders given to him following the first commission (save that Shrewsbury was given permission to sue William Cavendish for the furnishings and plate that had been removed from Chatsworth when Bess had fled to Hardwick in 1584). This time, the order was counter-signed by Walsingham and Lord Burghley.

The order was delivered to Shrewsbury accompanied by a letter from the Queen herself stressing that she considered that as queen, she could not allow two persons with the standing of Shrewsbury and Bess to live in such a degree of discord. In the circumstances, the letter was kindly worded but coupled with the order, it would be clear to any reasonable person that Queen Elizabeth was serious.

Still Shrewsbury refused to fully comply with the Queen's rulings (he did repay £850 of the £2000 he owed William and Charles for the rents he had improperly seized but the harassments and legal suits continued), and he went to London to protest in person and to accuse Lord Burghley, Walsingham and Sir Thomas Bromley of accepting bribes from Bess and again to demand that Bess be expelled from Court (where she was now residing; she still had duties as a Lady of the Privy Chamber). Lord Burghley's and Bromley's responses to this charge of bribery (if indeed they responded at all) are unknown; Walsingham denied the accusation vehemently. In any event, Shrewsbury's continuing lack of compliance led to the Queen issuing a decree in early July 1586 confirming (again) that Shrewsbury had to obey the orders given to him.

This time, Shrewsbury reluctantly signalled that he would comply, but the issue of the plate and furnishings would be a further issue of contention between Bess and the Earl. At the beginning of August, Shrewsbury provided Bess with a list of items he claimed should be returned to Chatsworth at once. The problem was that some of the items claimed by the Earl simply could not be returned. He claimed for instance for bed sheets which had been made seventeen years earlier and become worn out and discarded years before, as well as items which had been passed to William and Charles at the time of the 1572 deed of gift. Other items had been gifts that Bess had given to Shrewsbury in the past but which he had returned to her as he disliked them. Still others had been given by Bess to other people in earlier, happier years with Shrewsbury's express approval and some were items Bess had acquired before her marriage to Shrewsbury and which rightly belonged to her. Bess went through the list provided by Shrewsbury and carefully annotated it, pointing out which items she thought Shrewsbury could legitimately claim and those which he could not and then added as a postscript: "these parcels above demanded by the Earl are things of small value and mere trifles for so great and rich a nobleman to bestow on his wife in 19 years". Shrewsbury did not agree with the points raised by Bess and he and Bess were summoned before Burghley, Bromley and Walsingham to thrash out an agreement, which eventually they did. The Queen approved, but this time Shrewsbury was warned that further non-compliance would lead to him being fined £40,000.

Under the agreement, Bess was to go to the Earl's house at Chelsea and then proceed to South Wingfield Manor the day after. Shrewsbury was to join her there for a few days and then Bess was free to return to Chatsworth if she so wished. Shrewsbury was to meet the costs of staying at Wingfield and forgive William and Charles (but only after they had apologised to him). Bess duly departed the Court in accordance with the agreed terms and then Shrewsbury showed he was still not as compliant as had been thought. He was soon writing to Burghley to protest that while he had agreed that Bess might visit his houses in Chelsea and Wingfield, he had not agreed to "bed and board" with her and helpfully he drew up for Burghley a list of reasons why he should not do so. Around the same time, he wrote a letter to Bess declaring that although she might have been "... cleared in Her

Majesty's sight for all offences …", she had not been cleared by him and he would not trust her until she confessed that she had offended him and had returned to him all properties he considered to be rightfully his.

Lord Burghley's response to this latest diatribe can be imagined; Bess for her part seems to have headed for the safety of Hardwick Hall. Shrewsbury was clearly in breach of his agreement with Bess; by right, he should have been fined £40,000 (about £14 million today) but this seems not to have happened and indeed as autumn of 1586 progressed, notwithstanding all that had passed before, a strange lull seemed to settle over the ongoing dispute between Bess and Shrewsbury. It was not that their disagreements faded away (and they certainly were not forgotten), but rather that the government (and Shrewsbury) suddenly had more important matters to consider. The cause of this distraction was Shrewsbury's other old bête noire, Mary, Queen of Scots.

After Sir Ralph Sadler replaced Shrewsbury as Queen Mary's custodian in September 1584, she was held at South Wingfield Manor for three months. Sadler no doubt took his responsibilities seriously (he was an experienced diplomat and courtier), but he seems to have been a relatively kindly man (though he did once describe Queen Mary as "this most wicked and filthy woman") and despite orders from the Council to continue to keep Queen Mary under close confinement, he allowed her various small privileges, such as riding in the park and going hawking. News of this soon reached Queen Elizabeth and her Council, who over recent years had been growing increasingly concerned about the possibility of open warfare breaking out between England and Spain, which they feared might lead to an invasion of England.[2]

---

[2] By now Queen Elizabeth had for several years secretly (and sometimes not so secretly) been providing aid in the form of "volunteer" soldiers and supplies to the Dutch Protestants who were trying to free their country of the Spanish (not to mention tacitly encouraging attacks by English "pirates" on Spanish shipping) but open warfare had not yet broken out. War would break out in August 1585.

Consequently, the international situation coupled with the news of Sadler's lax regime, as it was now perceived to be by the Queen and her Council, exacerbated pre-existing fears that Queen Mary might somehow escape captivity and pose a genuine threat to Queen Elizabeth's throne and the cause of Protestantism in England and Wales. There were some members of the Council who openly believed that the safest course of action (so far as Queen Elizabeth was concerned) would be for Queen Mary to be killed on one pretext or another. Lord Burghley certainly thought this, as did Walsingham, but Queen Elizabeth was not (yet) ready to countenance such an action, certainly in the absence of clear and compelling evidence that Queen Mary deserved such a fate. It was therefore decided in January 1585 that Queen Mary should be moved back to Tutbury Castle, and Sadler be replaced by Sir Amias Paulet, who was a very different man to Sadler.

Paulet was a seasoned diplomat and administrator, having acted both as Governor of Jersey and as Queen Elizabeth's ambassador to France. He was also a zealous Protestant (to the point of puritanism) and fiercely anti-Catholic. He loathed Queen Mary and she soon came to loathe him because Paulet followed his instructions that she be kept in close confinement to the letter. One effect of this was that Queen Mary found herself unable to communicate with her supporters by secret correspondence; hitherto she had generally contrived to do this by one means or another, though sometimes such correspondence had been intercepted by Walsingham's spies. This in turn made her even more desperate and eager to escape her captivity; after all, by May 1585, she had been held captive in England for seventeen years. It also made her determined to find some way of re-establishing contact with her supporters.

An apparent opportunity to do this arose in early December 1585. Queen Mary's health had been declining again as a result of the move to Tutbury; not only that but Tutbury was once again in desperate need of cleaning (the middens were reported as stinking to high heaven). Furthermore, the French had been applying diplomatic pressure for Mary to be moved somewhere more salubrious and it was decided that she (whilst remaining in Paulet's custody) should be moved to Chartley Manor in Staffordshire, a moated manor house which belonged to the Earl of Essex. Essex objected strongly to his house being used to hold the Scottish Queen, but to no avail, and Queen Mary had been transferred there by the end of December 1585.

Queen Mary was not overly eager about the move (though admittedly Chartley from her perspective was better than Tutbury). She grew more enthusiastic however when some of her attendants found a possible way of smuggling letters in and out of the manor by hiding them in beer barrels. What neither they nor she knew was that this was a ruse set up at Walsingham's instigation; the smuggled letters were intercepted by his agents, deciphered and copied before the originals were sent on to their intended recipients. Once the system was established, all that Walsingham, Lord Burghley and others who wished to see Queen Mary's final downfall had to do was wait for Queen Mary to incriminate herself, as they were sure she would.

At more or less the same time, Walsingham's agents became aware of yet another plot to assassinate Queen Elizabeth. This has become known as the Babington plot. Born in 1561, Anthony Babington was the son of a wealthy gentry family in Derbyshire with Catholic sympathies. They were neighbours and friends of both the Talbots and the Cavendishes and Babington himself had served both as a pageboy to Bess at Chatsworth and as a pageboy to Shrewsbury at Sheffield, and whilst doing so, had met Queen Mary. He had married and then departed on a tour of France. Whilst there, he had been contacted by Thomas Morgan, a staunch Catholic who not only essentially acted as Queen Mary's agent in Paris but also had previously worked as Shrewsbury's secretary. Before long, Morgan had introduced Babington to other supporters of Queen Mary; unfortunately for them both (especially Babington), Walsingham's spies had been keeping a close eye on Morgan and Babington now came to Walsingham's attention.

Back home in England, Babington became involved in the smuggling of letters in and out of Chartley. He also became involved with a group of

Catholics who were plotting to assassinate Queen Elizabeth and replace her with Queen Mary, and before long, Babington had agreed to help. Indeed, he volunteered to be one of those tasked with assassinating the Queen. In July 1586, Babington wrote to Queen Mary (using the beer barrels as the mode of delivery) informing her of details of the plot; Queen Mary wrote back and though she worded her reply carefully, it was clear (when her letter was intercepted and deciphered) that she fully supported the plot and would cooperate with the conspirators. It was the evidence that Walsingham and Burghley were waiting for. Babington and his fellow conspirators were promptly arrested;[3] for the moment, no action was taken against Queen Mary. Then, in August she was allowed to go riding in Tixall Park, a few miles from Chartley; while she was away from Chartley, her rooms were searched and her correspondence confiscated. She was then informed that the conspiracy had been discovered and arrested for her part in it. On 21st September she and a few servants were sent to Fotheringhay Castle in Northamptonshire, where she was to be put on trial for her life.

Her trial was scheduled to begin on 11th October 1586, at a tribunal presided over by 36 commissioners, including the Lord Chancellor. As Earl Marshal of England, Shrewsbury had to be there. Sir Ralph Sadler was also there, sitting in judgment of his former prisoner. Queen Mary initially refused to appear before the tribunal at all, arguing that as she was a queen and not one of Queen Elizabeth's subjects, the tribunal had no jurisdiction over her, but she finally agreed to appear on 15th October. She was charged with breach of the Bond of Association of 1584, as modified by the Act for the Preservation of the Queen's Safety which had been passed by Parliament as recently as 1585. The former essentially specified that anyone who threatened the life of the Queen (or indeed successfully assassinated her) was to be put to death, the

---

[3] They were ultimately executed, in two groups. The first group (including Babington) were hung, drawn and quartered; the second group (after it had been decided that hanging, drawing and quartering was too savage a punishment even for the attempted assassination of the Queen) were simply sent to the gallows in the usual way.

latter specified the nature of any tribunal established to ascertain whether any breach of the Bond of Association had taken place. Queen Mary was denied the right to counsel or the right to call witnesses in her own defence, and the result of the trial, which lasted two days, was a foregone confusion. On 25th October, the commissioners, with the exception of Shrewsbury, who remained at Orton Longueville near Peterborough (in a house owned by his son Henry, where he had been staying for the duration of the trial), assembled in the Star Chamber in London to consider their verdicts. Shrewsbury's excuse for not travelling to London was that he was too ill; Lord Burghley wrote to him sharply warning him that any failure to attend might revive the rumours of improper association with Queen Mary, but it seems illness really did preclude the Earl from travelling to London. At the meeting of the Star Chamber, all but one of the commissioners voted to send Queen Mary to the executioner's block.[4] The exception was Lord Zouche, who professed himself unconvinced of Queen Mary's guilt.

The tribunal of commissioners may have found Queen Mary guilty and deserving of death, but her actual execution required the signature of Queen Elizabeth on a death warrant, and this (to the dismay of Lord Burghley and others) was not immediately forthcoming. Queen Elizabeth hesitated for several months, not wanting to be seen as having authorised the execution of a fellow monarch. Indeed, at one point, Walsingham (presumably acting on Queen Elizabeth's behalf) asked Sir Amias Paulet (who was still Queen Mary's custodian at Fotheringhay) whether it would be possible for him to arrange Queen Mary's assassination so as not to force the Queen to make a decision at all. Paulet gave a dignified refusal, stating that he could not:

---

[4] At Burghley's request, Shrewsbury wrote a letter confirming he believed Queen Mary to be guilty; Burghley ordered that it be recorded in the tribunal records.

"… make so great a shipwreck of my conscience, or leave so great a blot to my poor posterity, as shed blood without law or warrant …"

Queen Elizabeth eventually signed the death warrant on 1st February 1587, but even then, she hesitated to authorise its despatch to Fotheringhay, handing it to her secretary Davison for safe-keeping. Lord Burghley had anticipated this however, and procured a letter signed by several members of the Privy Council ordering Robert Beale, clerk of the Council to deliver the warrant to Fotheringhay. Shrewsbury and the Earl of Kent were also ordered to Fotheringhay; they were instructed to supervise the execution.

Nobody had told Queen Mary that her death was imminent, and this task fell to Shrewsbury on the evening of 7th February. Queen Mary had already retired to bed, and Shrewsbury delivered the news that her death warrant had been signed to her in her bedchamber. Queen Mary received the news calmly. She had been told that she had been found guilty in November and had been expecting to be executed. She probably however anticipated more notice of her execution than she was given. When she asked when the execution would take place, Shrewsbury replied that it was scheduled for eight o'clock the following morning.

In fact, it took place at about ten o'clock, in the Great Hall at Fotheringhay. Several hundred people were gathered to witness the execution; one of them was Gilbert Talbot. Shrewsbury, as Earl Marshal, was responsible for signalling the executioner to proceed once Queen Mary's neck was on the block. He did so by raising his staff of office; at the same time, he turned his head away so he did not have to see the axe fall. It took two strokes to all but sever the Queen's head from her shoulders (the executioner misjudged the first stroke and the edge of the axe buried itself in the back of her skull), but even after the second blow, some sinews still attached the head to the body and these had to be cut using the axe as a saw. When the deed was done, the Dean of Peterborough (one of the observers) cried out: "So perish all the Queen's enemies". The Earl of Kent came to stand over the body and declaimed: "Such be the end of all the Queen's and all the Gospel's enemies". Shrewsbury remained silent but was in tears.

There was one more tragic sight for Shrewsbury and the others to witness. Queen Mary had a little male Skye terrier which somehow had managed to accompany her into the Great Hall and had been hiding beneath her petticoat (she had been stripped of the long skirt she normally wore). The dog had been there when the axe had fallen; now discovered cowering and covered in blood, in shock, he refused to be enticed away from the body of his mistress until the body itself was ready to be removed. The poor creature died shortly thereafter.

Queen Mary's execution, and especially being obliged to supervise it, had a powerful effect on Shrewsbury. He had been anxious to be rid of his custodial duties, he may well have been ambivalent about his feelings about her, but watching and indeed directing the death of someone with whom he had lived in close proximity for sixteen years must have been almost more than he could bear. After it was over, he probably wanted nothing more than to escape back to the sanctuary of one of his houses, but instead in early March, he found himself summoned back to London. Queen Elizabeth was angry.

Chapter 16

"Look to her well …"

When Queen Elizabeth heard of the execution of Queen Mary, she reacted with an outbreak of fury that lasted for months. She accused her Council members, she accused just about everyone, of betraying her, particularly those who had signed the letter authorising the despatch of the death warrant to Fotheringhay. Lord Burghley and Leicester were banished from the Court (in Burghley's case, the banishment lasted four months – it was the worst quarrel he and Queen Elizabeth ever had) and other members of the Council found it advisable to be ill at home for a while. Eventually of course, the Queen calmed down and tacitly accepted that from her perspective, Queen Mary's execution had removed a dangerous rival,[1] but when Shrewsbury arrived back at Court in March 1587, all he knew was that the Queen was still raging and he must have feared he was about to be punished for obeying the Council's instructions that he should supervise the execution. To make matters worse, when he arrived at Court, his audience with the Queen was delayed for several days, which must have raised his level of anxiety even higher.

In fact, when he finally had an audience with the Queen, in early April 1587, he discovered she wanted to talk about the state of his marriage to Bess, rather than the execution. Bess was then in London herself, and had been complaining about Shrewsbury's continuing non-compliance with the Queen's orders. When Shrewsbury arrived for his audience

---

[1] In time, the Council members were forgiven, and official blame for the execution fell on poor Davison who was imprisoned in the Tower for nineteen months and fined 10,000 marks. Interestingly, we have no record of Bess's reaction to Queen Mary's execution when she came to hear of it, though given Mary's attempts to damage her, it is unlikely she wasted too much time grieving. On the other hand, Bess wasn't a vindictive woman so it is unlikely too that she celebrated wildly (unlike most of the rest of the country; Queen Mary's execution was by and large popular with many ordinary Protestants).

with the Queen, he found Gilbert and Mary Talbot also waiting, and (as Gilbert subsequently reported to John Manners) the Queen pointedly asked Mary what her mother wanted. Mary began to reply that Bess simply wished to resume her married life with Shrewsbury. Shrewsbury interrupted her and made it clear he had no intention of living with Bess ever again, blaming Bess's attitude towards himself as the reason for this.

Mary and Gilbert[2] then left, and the Queen once again set about encouraging reconciliation between Shrewsbury and Bess. Exactly what she said to Shrewsbury is not clear (and Queen Elizabeth by now must have been becoming very tired of Shrewsbury's continuing obduracy, notwithstanding that she recognised that he was still ill and had been stressed nearly to breaking point) but after a talk with the Queen reported to have lasted about an hour, Shrewsbury agreed (again) to allow Bess back into his Chelsea house, following which the two of them were to head for South Wingfield Manor where they were to "keep house together". He was also to allow her housekeeping provisions and pay her an annual allowance of £300. He agreed to drop all his outstanding lawsuits against the Cavendishes and their servants in exchange for the return of the furnishings and plate removed from Chatsworth.

This time, Shrewsbury did indeed keep his word, in a fashion and for a time. Bess went to the house at Chelsea and Gilbert commented in a letter that since the audience with the Queen,

> "... my Lord has been at Chelsea with my Lady and promises never to hear anything he dislikes about her without sending her word and receiving her answer ..."

A few days later, Shrewsbury must have left Chelsea, for in a letter which is undated but believed to have been written in the middle of

---

[2] Gilbert was having troubles of his own around this time. His debt problems were now becoming acute, and Shrewsbury was refusing to help him.

April, Bess herself wrote from Chelsea to Shrewsbury, thanking him for a letter he had sent her which she said she had found a great comfort and stating that apart from his presence, nothing could have been more welcome than to receive it. She also called him sweetheart. To an outside observer, it might have seemed that for the moment at least, the Shrewsbury marriage was in a better state than it had been for a number of years.

If that was the case, that happy state of affairs did not last for long. Around 22nd April 1587, Shrewsbury and Bess did go to Wingfield together, but by 26th April (or possibly earlier), Shrewsbury had taken himself off to Sheffield Manor Lodge. To be fair to Shrewsbury, he may have gone to tend to business of his own; moreover, following the Babington Plot, there had been a general crackdown on "recusant Catholics", and Shrewsbury was involved in this. Indeed, in mid-May, he was back at Wingfield where he interrogated a suspected Catholic priest. In a report to Walsingham summarising the results of his interrogation, Shrewsbury went out of his way to emphasise that he and Bess were present together at Wingfield.

Thereafter though, Shrewsbury began to avoid Bess more and more until, on 6th October, Bess was forced to write to Lord Burghley to complain that since "coming to the country", Shrewsbury had only visited her at Wingfield on three occasions, and never for more than a day at the time, which, if true, suggests that Shrewsbury had been being economical with the truth when he wrote and told Walsingham that he was staying with Bess at South Wingfield Manor in mid-May; Walsingham would have interpreted Shrewsbury's statement as meaning Shrewsbury and Bess had been staying together for several days at a time at least. Moreover, Bess complained that Shrewsbury had failed to provide her with household provisions as the Queen herself had ordered.

Now though, there was little that the Queen, or Burghley, or anyone else could do to repair the Shrewsbury marriage. Not only was the Queen and her Council now preoccupied with other, greater matters, such as the war with Spain, and preparations for a possible invasion of the country, but Shrewsbury's health was worsening again (he was particularly suffering from gout and arthritis once more which made it difficult for him to walk at all). He settled himself at Handsworth Lodge in Sheffield, from where, when not distracted by his housekeeper and mistress, Eleanor Britton, he tried to focus as best he could on his business affairs. He still received occasional instructions from the Queen and the Council, particularly in early 1588 when it became apparent Spain was preparing a great Armada tasked with the invasion of England; as Earl Marshal, Shrewsbury was expected to play an active role in the maintenance and expansion of the country's defences. In practice, his ill-health meant that much of the actual work in making such preparations was carried out by Leicester, whose own health was poor and getting worse. And he continued his pursuit of recusant Catholics.[3]

As for Bess, she seems to have accepted that her marriage to Shrewsbury was over (albeit they remained legally married) but took comfort from the fact that nobody would blame her for this state of affairs (apart from Shrewsbury, that is). This may have been her secret objective over the previous few years in the first place, though publicly, she continued to take some pains to let it be known that she was still in favour of reconciliation on reasonable terms if only Shrewsbury would agree to it. Nevertheless, now effectively free of Shrewsbury, and with her own wealth and income more secure, she was ready for a new project. And that project would take her back to the place where her story started – the original Hardwick lands.

Much as she loved Chatsworth, during the second half of the 1580s. Bess had been forced to accept that thanks to Shrewsbury's campaign of harassment against her, there was no real possibility of her residing there in the near future, and in the years before the final attempted

---

[3] He also made a point of setting spies to report on Bess's activities; she seems to have been aware of this, as she was of her husband's relationship with Eleanor Britton.

reconciliation with Shrewsbury in 1587, when in Derbyshire, she had largely based herself at what in time would become known as Hardwick Old Hall, the old manor house of the Hardwicks, the inhabitation of which she sometimes shared with her son William and his wife.[4]

The problem was that the Old Hall was too small to accommodate the combined households of both Bess and William comfortably, notwithstanding that Bess's brother James had commissioned some extensions and other improvements so it was now somewhat larger than the house Bess had lived in as a young child. By 1584, when Bess moved there from Chatsworth to escape Shrewsbury's attentions, it was essentially a dowdy four storey half-timbered manor house, with a detached kitchen, a small cluster of buildings to the east of it and a great hall built in the typical Medieval style. Bess decided that improvements were necessary, including replacing the great hall (which wasn't great enough for Bess) with a new larger transverse hall (that is, the hall ran the width of the house rather than lengthwise as had been more traditional in earlier times) and adding a new long gallery and a new three (later four) storey east wing, the work on which may have commenced when her brother James had been living there. By July 1587 (which is the date of earliest building records relating to the Old Hall which are known to exist), work was already underway repairing the roof and completing the east wing, which was to include a set of rooms for Bess (though during the earliest days of building, Bess had been obliged to proceed fairly slowly and economically thanks to Shrewsbury's seizure and withholding of monies due to her. It no doubt helped that to a very significant extent, Bess was able to utilise building materials originating from her own lands). Work on a new west wing (including new kitchens and a set of rooms for William and his family) commenced early the following year, and continued during the

---

[4] For a year or so after April 1587, when in Derbyshire, she based herself at South Wingfield Manor as she had promised to do, though she made the occasional visit to Hardwick. By the late summer of 1588, she was increasingly dividing her time in Derbyshire between Hardwick and South Wingfield Manor.

tumultuous summer months of 1588 when England and Wales were first threatened by, and then delivered from the Spanish Armada. Work on improving the Old Hall would continue for several years after that, with the house only being deemed truly fit for habitation in late 1592. Even after that, further improvements would continue to be made until 1599.

The result was a substantial imposing property, which some people found reminiscent externally of Worksop and spectacularly decorated inside, but Bess was dissatisfied with it. True, the extension and alteration work had principally been carried out with a view to solving a specific problem, that is, to provide Bess (and William and his family) with accommodation suiting their stations in life, but no architect had been consulted about the building work, and the work itself had been carried out in a haphazard manner as time, funds and opportunity permitted. In particular, the interior layout of the various rooms left much to be desired. The kitchens, for example, had been sited in the west wing, and smells and sounds from them could penetrate much of the rest of the house when the winds were blowing in the wrong direction, including into William's set of rooms which were immediately above them. Bess's own bedchamber in the new east wing was north facing and cold in winter and her personal withdrawing chamber was inconveniently situated on the floor above. The various grand public rooms (such as the long gallery and the great chambers (there were two of them)) were also haphazardly scattered about the house.

The renovated Hardwick Old Hall therefore would serve its purpose (for a while) but even while work was still being carried out on it, Bess concluded, possibly as early as 1588, that she would need to commission a new house, a new Hardwick Hall, and she would cause it to be built within sight of the Old Hall. And this time, she would consult one of the best architects (if not the best) in the country before starting work.

The architect she chose to advise her was Robert Smythson, who had previously worked for Bess at Chatsworth, designing a tower, and had advised Shrewsbury on the plan of Worksop Manor. By now, Smythson had developed a fine reputation as the designer of Elizabethan prodigy houses (he had assisted in the design of Longleat and had designed Wollaton Hall in Nottinghamshire, which had been completed as recently as 1588). It seems likely that Bess consulted him sometime in 1588 and she was determined that her new hall would address the deficiencies she had identified in the original Hardwick Hall. It was not until November 1590, however, that she ordered construction work to begin on Hardwick New Hall, and the foundations began to be excavated. Bess had other distractions around this time to keep her busy. One of these was her granddaughter Arbella.

Arbella was in her twelfth year in the summer of 1587. After the death of her mother in January 1582, she had tended to be moved about to be cared for by various relatives, Mary and Gilbert Talbot, in particular, and (when convenient) Bess herself (and when cared for by Bess, Arbella slept in Bess's bedroom). Arbella may have been staying with Bess when Bess had been obliged to flee from Chatsworth in 1584. Sometimes though, no relative was available to care for her and on these occasions, she was generally looked after by servants. Though she had several cousins, after the death of George Talbot in 1577, she had none that were broadly the same age as her other than her cousin Grace Pierrepont, but Arbella and Grace were raised in different households and seem to have seen relatively little of each other during their respective childhoods. Nor does Arbella appear to have had (or perhaps been allowed to have) other children of a similar age as playmates. Consequently, whichever household she was staying in, she tended very much to adopt the role of being an only child in the company of adults, which may have affected her personality as she developed. She grew up with the knowledge that she was closely linked to the throne (she once wrote that she was "… not ignorant of either [her] birth or [her] desert …") and this could on occasions (especially as she grew older) lead her into seeming haughty and arrogant.

Her education was certainly not neglected during her childhood (both Bess and Mary Talbot were insistent on this), with a particular emphasis (when Arbella grew old enough) on foreign languages such as French and Italian (and later Spanish) as well as the classics (which required her to become skilled at Latin and Ancient Greek) and history generally. She also learned some Hebrew. Her handwriting, once she mastered the skill was beautiful, she was adept at embroidery and had some musical skills, playing the viol, the virginals and the lute. She was a more than competent dancer. Her grandmother also insisted that she learn to keep her own accounts, though she was less keen on this than Bess.[5]

By the summer of 1587, there was increasing speculation as to the possibility of Arbella one day succeeding Queen Elizabeth, particularly after the execution of Queen Mary which had edged Arbella a little closer to the throne. Queen Elizabeth herself was quite aware of this, though given her customary unwillingness to discuss the succession or to commit herself to favouring any particular successor, she refused to confirm or deny what she thought of Arbella's prospects for the throne. Nevertheless, the Queen decided that it would be advisable to meet Arbella, no doubt so she could assess Arbella's qualities for herself. This in itself was quite unusual. Queen Elizabeth had not met Queen Mary before her execution; nor had she met (and she never would meet) James VI and it may be that at this time, she secretly thought more favourably of the possibility of Arbella being her successor than would subsequently be the case. She may also of course simply have been curious to meet Bess's granddaughter. In any event, as Arbella was now approaching the age of twelve, she might have concluded that it was simply time for Arbella to make an appearance at Court.

Arbella's age was also significant for another reason, for she was now old enough for her marriage prospects to become an important diplomatic consideration. This had already been a topic of discussion

---

[5] The general approach to her education seems to have been modelled on that which Queen Elizabeth had enjoyed as a young princess, which is understandable, considering the possibility that she might ascend to the throne herself. Arbella would develop a reputation of being a learned woman and retain an interest in books and learning throughout her life.

for the Queen and her Council, and several possible candidates for Arbella's hand in marriage had been and would continue to be mooted. These would include Ludovic Stuart, the Second Duke of Lennox, his brother Esmé Stuart (who would succeed to the dukedom following his brother's death in February 1624) and even King James VI, though for various reasons, none of these suggestions came to anything. Now though, in 1587, and with war with Spain raging, Queen Elizabeth and her counsellors saw the possibility of making use of the prospect of Arbella's marriage as a means of furthering their war arms, and possibly ending the war altogether. The suggested bridegroom this time was Rainutio Farnese, the son of the Duke of Parma who was then commanding the Spanish forces fighting in the Low Countries, and it was hoped that if the marriage could be arranged, this might lead Parma to cease his support of King Philip II and quite possibly lead to peace talks. This proposal (which in fact came to nothing but would be considered again several times in the years that followed) seriously alarmed King James VI when he heard of it in early 1587; he had become convinced that he was the only viable candidate for Elizabeth's throne, and now he feared that Arbella's marriage to Farnese (whose mother, the Infanta Maria of Portugal, was a descendant of John of Gaunt and hence herself had hereditary links to the English throne) might increase Arbella's chances of succession considerably. Following his mother's execution, King James had therefore demanded that Queen Elizabeth should publicly name him as her heir. He also demanded that he be given veto rights over any proposed marriage for Arbella. Queen Elizabeth dismissed James' demands out of hand, but another reason why she summoned Arbella to Court that summer may have been to send a message to King James that he should not try to meddle in the succession.

The summer of 1587 was the period of the supposed reconciliation between Shrewsbury and Bess, and Bess was residing at South Wingfield Manor. Arbella was staying with Mary Talbot in London when the order that she should come to Court was issued. The Court was then assembled at Lord Burghley's Theobalds in Hertfordshire, a house which had been completed only two years before. Arbella was taken to Theobalds by Gilbert and Mary Talbot; Charles Cavendish was already present and he dutifully sent a letter to Bess describing Arbella's reception. During her stay, she was addressed as "your highness" and served on bended knee. She was presented to the Queen twice, and dined with her, attracting much attention and many favourable comments from the other courtiers present, including Lord Burghley and Sir Walter Raleigh. As for the Queen, on this occasion, she seems to have approved of what she saw in Arbella, and is reported to have said to the wife of the French ambassador: "Look to her well, she will one day be even as I am and a lady mistress. But I will have gone before", which is probably as definitive a statement as Queen Elizabeth ever made about the prospects of Arbella succeeding her.[6] Whether Bess took this as truly being an indication of the Queen's intentions is doubtful, for she knew how the Queen enjoyed making potentially misleading pronouncements whilst committing herself to nothing, but Arbella at this time seems to have taken it seriously. She later declared that the Queen had "... by trial pronounced me an eaglet of her own kind ... worthy ... even yet to carry her thunderbolt ..."

Arbella's first appearance at Court thus was widely regarded as successful, and when her visit came to an end in mid-August 1587, it was generally accepted that she would be invited back the following year. In fact she was, returning to the Court at Greenwich with Mary and Gilbert Talbot in June of 1588, at a time when the Spanish Armada had already set sail but had not yet been sighted off the Lizard (that happened on 19th July). This time, though Arbella's visit seems to have begun well, she soon found herself in trouble when she objected to her position in a line of leading ladies of the Court making their way to Chapel; she claimed that she should be ranked as a Princess (that being,

---

[6] Apart from the Queen's declaration when she was on her deathbed having been asked who should be her successor: "I tell you my seat hath been the seat of kings" she said. "I will have no rascal to succeed me and who should succeed me but a king ..." which dashed any final hope of Arbella succeeding her once and for all.

she is alleged to have said, the very lowest position that could be given her) and argued publicly with the Master of Ceremonies. The Queen apparently took offence at this impertinence and Arbella was unceremoniously dismissed back to Wingfield in some disgrace, leaving London on 13th July. It would be more than three years before she was invited once more to Court. Bess was reportedly unamused by her granddaughter's arrogance and the incident was remembered by many in the years to come (the Venetian ambassador mentioned it in a despatch to the Doge and Venetian Senate as late as 1603).

That incident alone may not have been the only reason that prompted Arbella's dismissal from the Court. Though the Armada had not yet been sighted from England, it was known to be on its way and Queen Elizabeth and her Council were desperately seeking possible ways of reaching an acceptable peace agreement, if not with Philip II of Spain, then at the very least with the Duke of Parma and it is in this context that once again, the possibility of a marriage between Arbella and Parma's son was mooted. Whilst there seemed any prospect that this might be possible, there were perhaps some advantages to Queen Elizabeth in having Arbella close at hand. When it became apparent at the end of June that there was no possibility of the marriage, Arbella's usefulness at Court came to an end, and there was little point in her remaining, especially if she was proving to be troublesome. It may also have been concluded that if the Spanish did succeed in landing an invasion force on English shores, Arbella might well be safer in Derbyshire than at Greenwich.

There was quite possibly a third reason for the dismissal as well. Also present at Court that summer for the first time was Robert Devereux, the nineteen-year-old Second Earl of Essex. His mother was Lettice Knollys who after the death of her first husband, the First Earl of Essex, had married Leicester. Essex was many things, including young, handsome, brave, hungry for glory and status, irritating and arrogant, but he rapidly made a strong impression on Queen Elizabeth, and by the middle of the summer of 1588, he was well on the way to becoming one of her principal favourites, a process that would intensify following the death of Leicester himself on 4th September 1588. Unfortunately, Essex also seems to have stirred something in Arbella, who was perhaps not as discreet about her feelings as she might have been, for her infatuation with Essex that summer soon was noted by others. Essex may initially have inadvertently encouraged this infatuation; at the time of the Chapel incident, he seems to have playfully urged Arbella to claim what she considered to be her rightful position, but he was soon warned of the dangers of damaging his standing with the Queen by seeming to be too close to Arbella. Prudently, he began to keep his distance from her as best he could. Before long, Arbella was complaining to Mary Talbot that

> "... the Earl of Essex durst scarcely steal a salutation in the privy chamber where it pleased Her Majesty I should be disgraced in her presence ..."

The Queen, who could indeed be jealous of her favourites showing attention to other women (or vice versa), may therefore have concluded that sending Arbella away would be the simplest way of nipping her infatuation with Essex in the bud.

Chapter 17

Death of an Earl

Early November 1588 therefore saw Arbella ensconced permanently back at South Wingfield Manor under the care of Bess's servants. Bess was then visiting Hardwick, and she was there on 5th November when her steward at Wingfield, Nicholas Kinnersley, wrote to her to warn her that a man known to work for Shrewsbury and later, "a boy in a green coat", had been seen loitering about the Wingfield estate and asking questions about Bess's activities (presumably part of Shrewsbury's continuing attempts to spy on her). Kinnersley added that he did not know the reasons for the questions unless it was to:

> *"... bring my Lord [i.e. Shrewsbury] words of your absence here so that he might come upon you sudden and find you away ..."*

He also took the opportunity to report on Arbella. According to Kinnersley: "My Lady Arbella at eight o'clock this night was merry, and eats her meat well ..." but he also told Bess that she had been refusing to go to "school" (presumably he meant attend her tutors as she did not go to school in the traditional sense) for the previous six days (which suggests Bess must have been absent from Wingfield for at least six days). Kinnersley thought it advisable for Bess to come back to Wingfield at once if there was no other matter to prevent her from doing so. Arbella was continuing to show a haughty, rebellious and no doubt sometimes moody streak, and may not have been best pleased when her grandmother arrived at Wingfield and promptly whisked her back to the still incomplete but habitable Hardwick Old Hall. From some surviving correspondence, it seems as though Bess was becoming a little tired of Arbella's increasing recalcitrance; though she still continued to consider Arbella to be "her jewel", from this time on, Bess appears to have been less inclined to tolerate what she considered to be poor behaviour from Arbella than she had in the past.[1] This was noticed by other people, including Shrewsbury, who in 1590 is said to have told a servant that Arbella:

> "... *was wont to have the upper hand of my wife and her daughter Mary, but now it is otherwise (as it is told to me), for they have been advised by some of their friends at the Court that it was misliked ...*"

In Arbella's defence, she was by this time on the cusp of becoming a teenager, had grown used to being deferred to and even spoiled, and no doubt found the contrast between her glamorous experiences both at Court and in London generally and the more isolated life she was now forced to endure in Derbyshire (whether at Wingfield or at Hardwick) difficult to deal with. On the other hand, from Bess's perspective, she may well have privately considered that when *she* was Arbella's age (assuming of course Nathaniel Johnson's account of Bess's service is true), she would already have commenced her service in the la Zouche household, where one suspects poor behaviour from any household member, let alone a teenager[2] would not be tolerated for very long, if at all.

Shrewsbury in the meantime, was still capable of impinging on Bess's life. Over the years, since she had successfully established her right to claim her widow's dower from the Barlow estates following the death of her first husband, Bess had been receiving her dower payments from those estates, which by 1589 were worth about £100 a year. The estates had finally been retrieved by the Barlow family from the wardship of Sir Peter Frencheville, and for 20 years from 1568 to 1588, the estates had been owned by Peter Barlow (the son of George Barlow, who had

---

[1] Indeed, the following year, Bess would commission another painting of Arbella, again, with a Latin inscription referring to her as the Countess of Lennox; Bess was still eager to assert what she considered to be Arbella's rights by way of inheritance. It now hangs in Hardwick New Hall.

[2] Though in Tudor times, they did not really have the concept of the teenage years being a distinct and separate period of development as we do today.

inherited the estates underage when Robert Barlow, Bess's first husband, had died). Peter Barlow himself died on 11ᵗʰ April 1588 and was succeeded as the owner of the estates by his brother James. The estates though were encumbered with considerable debts (they probably had never recovered from the economic damage inflicted by Frencheville's wardship) and after a year or so of struggle to run the estates in the face of considerable pressures from creditors, James must have decided that the prudent course of action was to sell the family lands. Those lands adjoined land owned by Shrewsbury and were known to contain valuable lead deposits. In May 1589, Shrewsbury commenced negotiation to purchase the Barlow lands, and the transaction was completed in September 1589.

He paid £8000 for the Barlow lands and moreover took over responsibility for £7000 worth of Barlow debts. That was a high price for the land (Gilbert Talbot would later write "… queer what a dear purchase [Barlow] is …" when he learned the details of the acquisition), and the question arises as to why Shrewsbury bothered to buy the land at all, and especially at that price. True, the lead deposits were useful (the Barlow family had already begun to mine them), but in truth the Earl had little need of them. It has been speculated that Shrewsbury liked the thought of having some control over at least part of Bess's income stream, but he did not take any steps to halt the payment of her dower's third (she no doubt would have resisted him through the courts if he had tried) and in any event he must have known that even if he could have prevented those payments, by this time it would have made very little material difference in a financial sense to Bess. Alternatively, the decision to purchase the Barlow lands may just have been yet another example of Shrewsbury's mental state at the end of the 1580s; by this time, he was declining fast both mentally and physically. Bess for her part seems not to have made any public comment of which she thought of Shrewsbury's purchase.

Shrewsbury's health continued to worsen through the rest of 1589 and most of 1590. In December 1589, Queen Elizabeth found time to write to him, calling him her "very good old man" and enquiring after his health,

"… especially at this time of the fall of the leaf …" She also asked him to allow Bess to see him occasionally, claiming it was something "she hath now of a long time wanted". So far as Shrewsbury was concerned, there was no chance of that happening and it didn't; what was somewhat surprising was that a few months later, in April 1590, Shrewsbury who for many years now had been almost as antagonistic towards Mary Talbot as he felt towards Bess, suddenly penned Mary a kind letter (which is how Gilbert Talbot subsequently described it). Mary had been ill and Shrewsbury ascribed the cause of her illness to Mary's "… extraordinary pains taken in visiting and comforting others …" He called her a "good daughter" and asked that she let him hear from her more often.

Perhaps he had an intimation that his own days were numbered and he wished to heal the rift between himself and Mary, if not with Bess. On 12th October, he received a letter from the Bishop of Lichfield and Coventry urging him to be reconciled with Bess; the Bishop conceded that he had heard some say that Bess was a sharp and bitter shrew, but added that if:

> "… shrewdness or sharpness may be a just cause for separation between a man and his wife, I think that very few men in England would keep their wives long …"

Shrewsbury never replied to this letter, he was now confined to bed, and on 18th November 1590, he died. He was 62 years old, about the same age as Bess. His burial did not take place until 13th January 1591 at the Church of Saint Peter and Saint Paul in Sheffield; the delay was due to needing to arrange appropriate ceremony for the funeral of England's Earl Marshal, and it was indeed organised on an impressive scale, as if Shrewsbury truly had been a "Prince of the Peaks". Over 20,000 people attended (three of whom were killed by a falling tree), and the inscription on the ornate tomb in which he was laid to rest stressed his service to Queen Elizabeth, denied any improper association with Mary, Queen of Scots, and omitted any reference to Bess. The date of his death was left blank; it seems that his executors failed to procure that it be added.

As for Bess, there is no record of her reaction when she heard her husband had died, leaving her a widow for the fourth and final time (although she and Arbella did attend the Shrewsbury's funeral service). She had however been married to Shrewsbury for more than 22 years and it seems likely that she would have genuinely mourned at least a little, if not for Shrewsbury as he had been when he died, then for Shrewsbury as he had been when they had married. On the other hand, she no doubt told herself that she could enjoy Chatsworth freely once again, once more focus on her business ventures and seek to strengthen the financial future of her family. She could seek to pursue her dynastic ambitions for Arbella. She would have the benefit of income from Talbot lands which she could claim under her marriage settlement with Shrewsbury (it has been estimated that by the mid-1590s, her annual income entitlement from the various Talbot properties alone amounted to £3000). Those properties included South Wingfield Manor (where there were valuable iron works and glass works), Bolsover Castle (which had valuable coal deposits) and other properties scattered throughout Staffordshire, Derbyshire and Yorkshire. Once again, she also was free to enjoy the income from her Barlow, Cavendish and St Loe lands. All these things should be possible, she would have concluded, because she was now free of Shrewsbury and his harassment; indeed, on 19th December 1590, she wrote to Lord Burghley to say:

> "I hope my good Lord, that all disagreement (in this family) died with him [i.e. Shrewsbury], quiet is my principal desire and I shall rather suffer than enter into controversy."

What she probably did not anticipate was that although family strife caused by Shrewsbury had now ceased, it was about to erupt in a new form and from a new direction, namely serious disagreement with Gilbert Talbot (now of course the Seventh Earl of Shrewsbury) and, to an extent, with Mary (now the new Countess of Shrewsbury).

The underlying cause of these disagreements was the parlous state of the finances of the Talbot family. Notwithstanding his father's extensive litany of complaints of the costs of housing and guarding Mary, Queen of Scots, Gilbert Talbot appears to have been genuinely surprised to find that at the time of his death, his father had been in debt to a greater extent than he had anticipated (and of course Gilbert had significant debts of his own as well) and whilst the Talbots still had very significant landholdings, his father's estate was cash poor. This state of affairs was exacerbated by the behaviour of Eleanor Britton and her nephew who, upon Shrewsbury's death immediately began to appropriate what they could from Shrewsbury's properties in Sheffield. Items such as jewels, plate, furniture and bedding, not to mention such cash as they could find (including it was alleged, £8000 in silver coins and £10,000 in gold), were purloined. Gilbert managed to retrieve some of the stolen items from Eleanor and her nephew, but not all. He tried to bring felony charges against the Brittons but seems to have failed; it is not entirely clear what ultimately happened to the Brittons but it seems likely that they managed to escape Gilbert's attentions and lived to enjoy their stolen gains.

To make matters worse, at least from the perspective of Gilbert and Mary, there were also issues arising as a result of Shrewsbury's will which he had made on 24th May 1590. It made no mention of Bess, but then no one had thought that it would; everyone would have expected her to be satisfied with her income rights under the marriage settlement (as indeed she would have been). The will had named Gilbert's younger brothers Henry and Edward Talbot as executors (acting under the guidance of supervisors including men such as Lord Burghley, Lord Derby and others) but Henry and Edward declined to act; they almost certainly foresaw potential trouble with Gilbert, the primary beneficiary of the will and a man whose reputation as being someone quick to take offence and respond in anger was by now well established, and they were right to do so. When Henry and Edward refused to act as executors of their father's will, the supervisors suggested that Bess become sole executrix. She accepted but Gilbert objected strongly to this and Bess agreed to step aside in favour of Gilbert, who then became sole executor of the will himself. As he discovered the extent of the financial problems facing him, Gilbert began to quarrel with other members of his family over money issues, including Henry and Edward and especially with Bess when she made it clear she expected to receive everything to which she was entitled from the Talbots. Gilbert flatly refused to pay Bess the sums she was (legitimately) claiming, effectively arguing that the Talbot estates could not bear the expense. Furthermore, he declared, Bess was claiming Talbot lands to which she was not entitled under the marriage settlement.

Until now, Bess had generally been a supporter of Gilbert but she had no intention of being denied her due rights. She applied pressure on Gilbert, and on three occasions she thought she had reached an accord with him, and three times Gilbert failed to abide by the terms they had agreed. Bess wrote to Lord Burghley to complain of this on 11th April 1591, stressing the three occasions upon which she had tried to reach a reasonable settlement with Gilbert and adding that she would be loath to speak to him a fourth time. In truth there was little Lord Burghley could do to help Bess (and Bess probably knew this, she had been writing just to apprise Burghley of the situation and no doubt to let off some steam). If Bess wanted to enforce her rights, she knew she would have to pursue Gilbert through the courts, which in due course is what she would do. Gilbert for his part made it clear he was prepared to go to court himself to challenge Bess's claims under the marriage settlement (though it is difficult to see the grounds for such a challenge). Unsurprisingly, relations between herself and Gilbert (and to an extent, Mary too) worsened rapidly from this point on.

In the meantime, Bess's financial position had been strengthened considerably by the return of the Barlow, Cavendish and St Loe lands and other properties which she either owned outright or over which she had lifetime interests, and there was now no financial barrier to her proceeding with the construction of Hardwick New Hall. It is no coincidence that the work of laying the foundations for Bess's new house began two weeks before Shrewsbury's death (which presumably she anticipated). The construction of Hardwick New Hall would take more than seven years to complete.

By November 1591, four and a half years had passed since Bess had last attended Court, and with the rebuilding of Hardwick Old Hall approaching completion, and work on the New Hall now underway, Bess had decided (probably sometime in the autumn) that it was time for another visit. She had several good reasons for reaching this decision; first of all, now Shrewsbury was dead, there was no reason why she should remain indefinitely in Derbyshire. Then too, she may well have been conscious that she and Queen Elizabeth were both becoming elderly ladies, at least by Tudor standards, and it might be the last opportunity for the two of them to meet and for her to seek to advance the prospects of various members of her family, including of course Arbella. In particular, Bess wanted to procure Arbella's re-introduction into Court life after the faux-pas of her previous visit in 1588 and this time Arbella would attend the Court under the watchful eyes of her grandmother. Furthermore, although it would again ultimately come to nothing, the prospect of Arbella possibly marrying Rainutio Farnese had once more been raised and as before in 1588, Queen Elizabeth (and no doubt Bess) could see advantages in having Arbella present at Court whilst the matter was under consideration. Bess also wanted to consult lawyers about her legal claims against Gilbert. And finally, she wanted to indulge in a spot (well actually a lot) of shopping for items which would be needed (or desired) once her construction works at Hardwick were complete.

As the rich Dowager Countess of Shrewsbury, Bess's plans for her journey to London (she planned to stay at Shrewsbury House in Chelsea, in which she had a life interest) were elaborate and substantial. She travelled in considerable style with a retinue of about 40 people, some (including Bess) travelled in lumbering carriages, others seem to have travelled on horse-drawn litters or on horseback. The luggage train accompanying the retinue was comprised of twelve wagons; Bess intended that her visit should be a prolonged one, and in the event, it lasted eight months. Those who travelled with her included Arbella and her lady-in-waiting, Sir William Cavendish and his wife, Sir Charles Cavendish, Jane Kniveton and Mrs Elizabeth Digby[3] (both of whom acted as ladies-in-waiting to Bess), Bess's steward (Timothy Pusey) and her lawyer (Edward Whalley), and of course, servants of various types to attend upon them all, many of them clad in light blue Cavendish livery. The journey to Chelsea took about a week and to onlookers, it probably resembled something of a Royal Progress, with riders being sent on ahead to arrange for church bells to be rung in celebration as the retinue passed, and to make necessary arrangements for overnight accommodation and entertainments and the provision of food and other necessary supplies. Bess herself liberally dispensed charitable payments (typically 40 shillings) for the benefit of the poor of the various towns she passed through along the way and seems to have enjoyed the journey. The route of Bess and her party led them through Nottingham, Leicester, Market Harborough, St Albans, Dunstable and Barnet; they finally arrived at Shrewsbury House in Chelsea on 25th November 1591.

Shrewsbury House had been little used over the previous few years and required some attention before it could be considered suitable as the official residence of the Dowager Countess of Shrewsbury for the duration of the visit. Servants, including a carpenter, a blacksmith and a bricklayer, and provisions and other supplies, had been sent ahead, as had two fat oxen and 40 sheep. Work was carried out creating extra accommodation by boarding up the long gallery (making temporary extra bedrooms) and converting part of the stables into a dormitory. Firewood had been ordered and stored and the house was cleaned and scrubbed. By the time Bess and her party arrived in Chelsea, the house was ready.

Bess had the use of at least two other houses in London, but her choice of Shrewsbury House as her residence on this visit was shrewd. At this

---

[3] Incidentally she was about six months pregnant at the time; given the state of the roads and the fact that the carriages used for the journey were unsprung, it must have been a particularly uncomfortable journey for her.

time, Chelsea was little more than a village and not really considered part of London at all, but its riverside location offered the promise of (relatively) easy access by river to Whitehall, where the Court was assembled that Christmas. Greenwich, Westminster, Richmond and Hampton Court, should there be a need to visit any of them, were also easily accessible by the same means, which also permitted easier transportation not only of day-to-day supplies which might be needed at Shrewsbury House, but also made it much more convenient for important personages to visit Bess. The availability of fields of pasture close to the house was clearly also a factor, for this was where the 40 sheep and two oxen were set to graze until they were needed.

Almost immediately upon her arrival, Bess turned her attentions to two important priorities. The first was to ensure that she, Arbella and other ladies of her party who were to appear at Court were suitably, and fashionably clothed (an important consideration in Elizabethan times). To this end, Bess summoned tailors, haberdashers and jewellers to Shrewsbury House and before long, she had ordered yards of materials such as damask, satin, black taffeta, lace and other cloths which were soon transformed into elegant gowns. She also ordered items of gold and silver jewellery such as chains and bracelets. Not all the materials she ordered were destined to form Court clothes for Bess, Arbella and the other ladies; her accounts show that in December 1591, she paid the Queen's own tailor, William Jones, £59 and 14 shillings to make a gown (intended as a Christmas present for Queen Elizabeth), and she paid John Parr, the Queen's embroiderer, a further £50 for embroidering it.

The second important task she set herself was to make sure she was as up-to-date as possible with the state of affairs at Court; while away in Derbyshire over the previous four and a half years, Bess had primarily relied on reports from friends and family as to developments there (in particular reports from Gilbert and Mary Talbot, and when he was present, her son Charles) but now she must have felt more information would be helpful. One of the very first visitors she received once she arrived was Mary Scudamore, her cousin by marriage and a Gentlewoman of the Queen's Bedchamber, who not only discussed with

Bess the issue of a suitable Christmas gift to be given by Bess to the Queen (hence the commissioning of the gown prepared by Jones and Parr), but also provided Bess with the latest Court gossip.

The make-up of the Court had changed significantly since Bess had last visited it, and several influential courtiers whom Bess had known well in earlier years had recently died, or were destined to do so in the not too distant future. Leicester, for instance had died on 4th September 1588, even as victory over the Spanish Armada was being celebrated, Sir Francis Walsingham had died on 6th April 1590 (possibly of kidney cancer) and Sir Christopher Hatton, a particular favourite of the Queen, almost (but not quite) in the same league as Leicester in that regard, had died as recently as 20th November 1591, while Bess was enroute to Shrewsbury House. As for Lord Burghley, he was still alive (he would die on 4th August 1598), but he was now becoming an elderly gentleman, and more and more beset by illness, and finding the burdens of his service to his Queen harder to bear as the years passed, he was increasingly obliged (with the Queen's permission) to avoid the Court and work from home.[4]

New faces at Court had replaced those no longer seen. Lord Burghley had been training his second son Robert Cecil to be, he hoped, his successor and by November 1591 Robert had already become a member of Parliament, been knighted and appointed a member of the Privy Council, where he effectively acted as his father's deputy. He would continue to rise through the Tudor political ranks over the next few years, until Queen Elizabeth appointed him as her Chief Secretary (Walsingham's post before he died) in 1596. Unfortunately, Robert Cecil's rise provoked much jealousy amongst rival courtiers who were not eager to see the Cecils increase their influence at Court, and that jealousy was becoming more overt even as early as November 1591. Amongst those actively seeking to replace the Cecils were Sir Walter

---

[4] On one of these occasions, he commented to his son Robert Cecil: "I must keep my chamber, not as a potentate but as an impotent and aged man."

Raleigh and the Earl of Essex, the latter of whom by now was revelling in his position as the Queen's principal favourite, having been made Master of the Horse and a Knight of the Garter. Essex though was absent from the Court when Bess arrived, having been sent to France to fight the Spanish, at which he proved to be very bad. He returned to Court in January 1592. Yet another opponent of the Cecils was Francis Bacon (Robert's cousin) who had become Essex's confidential adviser. Bess's visit to Court thus coincided with the start of a period of intense rivalry between the Cecils and their opponents, a rivalry that would continue for several years.[5] Bess seems to have made a point of seeking to remain on good terms with all these rivals; she knew it would be helpful to have powerful allies at Court in her forthcoming struggle with Gilbert Talbot.

Bess and Arbella attended the Court at Westminster, travelling there by the river, for most of the traditional period of the Twelve Days of Christmas, commencing on Christmas Day itself, and no doubt enjoyed the seemingly never-ending round of feasts, masques, dancing, plays (possibly including one by William Shakespeare) and jesting (particularly perhaps the jesting, for Bess gave the court jester £1 as a gift at New Year). Arbella behaved herself, and in addition to presenting the Queen with her present of a gown, Bess made generous cash gifts to her family, servants and friends (Gilbert and Mary Talbot received £100 notwithstanding the simmering feud over Bess's marriage settlement;

---

[5] By November 1591, Raleigh had already effectively ruled himself out of the competition by seducing, making pregnant and in the autumn of 1591 secretly marrying Elizabeth Throckmorton, who also had the nickname Bess. More to the point, she was also one of Queen Elizabeth's Gentlewomen of the Privy Chamber. When the Queen finally learned of the secret marriage (as she did in May 1592) Raleigh and his wife were placed under arrest, sent to the Tower and ultimately banished to Sherborne Castle, Raleigh's estate in Dorset. Their banishment lasted for five years. As for Essex, Arbella might well have been tempted to resume her romantic pursuit of him save for the fact that in 1590, Essex had married Frances Walsingham, the daughter of Sir Francis Walsingham and the widow of Sir Philip Sidney, an act which caused Essex to fall into temporary disfavour with the Queen. Even so, there was some gossip about Arbella and Essex during the early months of 1592.

William Cavendish only received £26 but then Charles and Henry only received £20).

Mary Scudamore was not the only person to visit Bess at Chelsea. Other visitors included friends such as Anthony Wingfield (husband of Bess's half-sister Elizabeth), Lady Cobham (an old friend of Bess's who died the following year) and Roger Manners. Lady Bacon (mother of Francis Bacon) and Lady Cheke (a Lady of the Privy Chamber) also came to pay their respects (and each borrow £50). Lord Howard of Effingham (later created the Earl of Nottingham), the Lord High Admiral who had commanded the English Fleet at the time of the Armada, Fulke Greville (the statesman and poet) and Lord Buckhurst (who would succeed Lord Burghley as Lord High Treasurer in May 1599) also visited Bess. And there were many others.

One intriguing visitor, who dined with Bess on 4th January 1592, was Sir William Cordell, the Master of the Rolls. Cordell had been a friend of Bess's for some time, so it would be natural for him to be entertained by her; it is however generally assumed that Bess took the opportunity to discuss with him the prospects of her forthcoming legal battle with Gilbert Talbot.

She was anxious to ensure that the case, when it came to be heard, would be held in Derbyshire (where she could be more certain of a favourable outcome) rather than in London, and Pusey and Whalley were kept busy over those winter months engaging the services of as many lawyers in London as possible to prevent Gilbert bringing his case before the London courts. This was a tactic which Shrewsbury had used in 1586 when he was in the midst of his harassment campaign against Bess; he had sought to bring spurious claims for defamation against one of her Somerset tenants and had arranged for the case to be heard in York. Not only had the jury been handpicked by the Sherriff of York (who just happened to be related to Shrewsbury) but he had also engaged every lawyer in the vicinity and the tenant was unable to find one willing to act for him. Unsurprisingly, Shrewsbury had won the case and Bess had learned a useful lesson which she now intended to apply against Gilbert Talbot.[6] Bess's tactics paid off (though in order to win, she had to pay £430 in various legal fees); the case was ultimately heard in Derbyshire before a Sheriff's court, which found in favour of Bess. Relations between Bess and her daughter and son-in-law worsened even more. Bess's victory in court on this occasion did not mean the end of legal disputes between herself and Gilbert, which were to continue for most of the rest of Bess's life.

---

[6] The poor tenant was fined £1000; in the event, the Master of the Rolls of the day intervened and ordered a stay of execution of the judgement and the fine ultimately was never paid.

Chapter 18

Return to Derbyshire

Over the next few months, when not attending the Court or entertaining at Shrewsbury House, Bess kept herself busy by indulging in what was probably the greatest shopping spree of her life. Clothing was a high priority for her and in addition to purchasing copious amounts of yet more cloth of various types, she also purchased items such as furs, gloves and shoes made of Spanish leather. She ultimately spent over £300 on clothes during that visit to London. She also purchased jewellery, including two bracelets "set with diamonds, pearls and rubies" – they cost her £20 – and five little "jewels" (another 70 shillings), a small broach in the shape of a bee (probably for Arbella, it cost 6 shillings and eight pennies), a ruby, an opal and pearls. In total, she spent nearly £200 on jewellery. She also did not forget Hardwick, neither the Old Hall nor the New. Over £1200 (equal to more than £490,000 today) was spent on gold and silver plate. She bought a significant number of tapestries intended for Hardwick New Hall, including (late in the visit) thirteen tapestries from Sir William Hatton (who had inherited Holdenby House in Northamptonshire from his uncle Sir Christopher Hatton but also a significant amount of debt). The thirteen tapestries, made in 1578, depict the biblical story of Gideon and now hang in the Long Gallery of Hardwick New Hall. They cost Bess £321 and 6 shillings (she negotiated £5 off the original price to cover the cost of replacing the Hatton arms on the tapestries with her own.)

One important purchase for Bess was a new horse-litter, modelled on one made for Queen Elizabeth. As might be expected, it was costly (£30 and 16 shillings) and sumptuous, upholstered in tawny velvet with a silk fringe, windows of tawny and gold parchment and a felt-covered footstool.

Arbella was not forgotten (some of the clothing purchased would have been for her) but a key consideration for Bess was still Arbella's finances.

We may assume that Bess might yet again have tried to persuade Queen Elizabeth to increase Arbella's pension though probably by now with little expectation that the Queen would show more generosity than she had in the past. Bess may have been more hopeful about the proposal that Arbella be wed to Rainutio Farnese; that proposal was still on the table during the first six months or so of 1592, and if it had proceeded, Arbella's financial future would have been secure. The Duke of Parma (and presumably, his son) were now showing sufficient interest in the matter to request that they be sent a picture of Arbella, and the painter Nicholas Hilliard was commissioned to produce a miniature of Arbella in the mid-summer of 1592. Bess must have liked what she saw for in addition to Hilliard's fee of 40 shillings, she gave him a 20 shilling tip. She gave another 20 shillings to Rowland Lockey, Hilliard's apprentice, who produced a copy of the miniature.[1] Unfortunately, we do not know the reactions of Parma or his son when they received the original miniature, and in any event, Parma himself died on 3rd December 1592, which led to the idea of a possible marriage between Rainutio and Arbella being permanently abandoned.

The Court moved from Whitehall to Greenwich in May, and Bess and Arbella travelled there for a three week visit by means of three boats hired for the occasion (one of them was used to transport Bess's new horse-litter), with the servants following on horseback. Greenwich Palace was less formal than Whitehall, and there was generally a more relaxed atmosphere, something Bess seems to have enjoyed. She certainly seems to have been impressed by the Palace gardens at Greenwich, for records show that she gave generous tips to the gardeners (Bess, at least in this stage of her life, was generous with the tips she doled out to those who had pleased her). Bess paid a second visit to Greenwich in June, retuning to Chelsea on 19th July.

---

[1] Lockey would produce a famous picture of Bess around this time which now hangs in Hardwick New Hall; indeed, he may already have done so, for it is thought to have been painted some time shortly after 1590. A replica is in the National Portrait Gallery.

She may have intended to stay in Chelsea for several more months, but there was an outbreak of plague in London, and the decision was taken to return to Derbyshire (Arbella stayed behind in London for a little while longer). Bess set off northwards on 31st July 1592, travelling in some style on her new litter, followed by carriages carrying others of her party, ten baggage wagons and a number of servants on horseback. In total, her visit to London had cost her £6360 (about £2.6 million today), but Bess seems to have thought the money well spent; the visit would be the last she would make to the Court.

Bess was in no particular rush to return to Derbyshire, and her return trip took nine days. Once again, the passage of Bess and her retinue would have resembled a Royal Progress to observers; again, church bells were rung to signify her passing and each night there would have been fine food and music by way of entertainment. This time, her route took her and her party first to Dunstable, and then to Northampton. While at Northampton, Bess parted temporarily from most of her retinue (who continued on towards Derbyshire) and indulged herself with a spot of sightseeing. She headed for Holdenby House, from whence the Gideon tapestries, as well as some of the gold and silver plate she had purchased in London, had come. Holdenby was empty save for a few servants when Bess arrived and the housekeeper and gardener showed her around and were each tipped 20 shillings for their troubles. It seems likely that Bess was eager to see the splendours of Holdenby so she could compare them to her plans for Hardwick New Hall.

After leaving Holdenby, she hastened to catch up with the main body of her party and did so at Leicester. The next day they set off for Nottingham; just before reaching the town, Bess took herself off to Holme Pierrepont, to spend a night with her daughter Frances and her husband Sir Henry Pierrepont. They had family matters to discuss; Frances' and Sir Henry's daughter Grace was due the following year to marry George Manners of Haddon Hall (the son of Bess's old friend Sir John Manners), and the prospective marriage (which would in due course take place at Chatsworth) may well have been another example of Bess's matchmaking. In any event, she was clearly in favour of the match, and would provide the betrothed couple with a dowry of £700 (and a further £100 to buy plate).[2]

After Holme Pierrepont, Bess travelled to Wollaton Hall, the newly completed home of Sir Francis Willoughby and another of Robert Smythson's masterpieces of design. The purpose of the visit was two-fold; not only did Bess want to see Wollaton Hall for herself but Willoughby was an old friend and moreover had been a member of the commission set up in Ashford in 1586 to investigate the state of Bess's marriage to Shrewsbury. Unfortunately, the cost of building Wollaton Hall had led him into debt (and in fact the Willoughby family never would really recover from the financial burden of first building, and then maintaining Wollaton Hall). Sir Francis had to ask Bess for a loan of £3050, and she duly obliged, though not until May 1594, for she and Willoughby took some time to agree the terms of the loan. Under the agreement they finally struck, Sir Francis received his loan, with Bess receiving annual interest payments of £300, payable until the loan was repaid. Moreover, Bess insisted that the loan was secured on five manor estates owned by the Willoughbys, and the mortgagee was Arbella. The wisdom of this manifested itself in 1596 when Sir Francis died. Sir Francis' heir was encumbered with debts and unable to redeem the loan as required under the loan contract, with the result that Bess (acting in Arbella's name) was able to seize the mortgaged properties in full. The heir complained to Robert Cecil, arguing that the five manors now had an aggregate value of £15,000, far in excess of the money loaned but a contract was and is a contract, and it was held that Bess (or rather

---

[2] The marriage is referred to in a letter dated 2nd August 1593 from Roger Manners (Sir John's younger brother, who had visited Bess at Chelsea whilst Bess was attending Court the previous year) to Robert Cecil in which he said: "Yesterday, as I am informed, was appointed the day for a marriage betwixt my nephew George Manners and Mrs [sic – he meant Mistress] Grace Perpoynt at Chatchworth, effected by the old Countess …" The "old Countess" was presumably Bess. Lord Burghley also wrote to congratulate Bess on the marriage on 9th August 1593.

Arbella) was legally entitled to the lands. Thus, in due course, Arbella would have the definite promise of access to significant financial resources of her own, something Bess had been fighting for one way or another since Arbella was born. The key words here though are "in due course"; whilst she remained alive, Bess retained a lifetime interest in the income generated by those five manor houses.

But that is to anticipate. After departing Wollaton Hall, Bess headed back to Hardwick, arriving back on 5th August 1592. She moved into the Old Hall, and was no doubt pleased to note that from her windows there she could see the progress being made on the New Hall; by the end of August, work had already commenced on constructing the top floor. Arbella had now re-joined her, but on this occasion, she and Arbella only stayed at Hardwick for a few weeks; in early October they moved back to Chatsworth, the first time that Bess had stayed there for any length of time since her flight from it in 1584.

There may have been several reasons for this move. To begin with, with the construction work on Hardwick New Hall continuing apace, and finishing touches still being made to the Old Hall, daily life at Hardwick at that time was probably noisy and dusty. Then too, with William Cavendish and his wife Anne and their family (by now William and Anne had two surviving children and would have more) also in residence, the Old Hall must have seemed crowded at times even with the extensions ordered by Bess over the last few years. Furthermore, given the importance of Chatsworth to Bess, she probably simply wished to move back to her old house for a time.

There was a possible fourth reason. In September 1592, Lord Burghley wrote to Bess warning her that Queen Elizabeth's secret service had uncovered another Catholic plot aimed at ousting the monarch from her throne; this time the plotters had intended to kidnap Arbella and make her sovereign in Elizabeth's place.[3] The plot had been dealt with fairly easily but Burghley stressed the need to keep Arbella safe. With all the building work being carried out at Hardwick (at this time Bess was employing 375 workmen in the construction work at Hardwick), the view may well have been taken that for the time being at least, Arbella's safety might be better secured at Chatsworth than at Hardwick. Bess (using William as a scribe as her head hurt) wrote to Burghley on 21st September 1592 to say:

> *"I was at first much troubled to think that so wicked and mischievous practices should be devised to entrap my poor Arbell[4] and me ..."*

and she assured Burghley:

> *"I will not have any unknown or suspected person come to my house ... my house is furnished with sufficient company, Arbell walks not late, at such time as she shall take the air, it shall be near the house and well attended on ..."*

The letter was written from Hardwick, before the move to Chatsworth.

Lord Burghley had also asked Bess to keep an eye out for possible Jesuits and other suspicious Catholics. In her letter of 21st September, she told Burghley that she had had her suspicions about one of Arbella's tutors, a man called Morley, not least because he had seemed discontented and had told Arbella he wished to leave Cavendish employment. After failing to persuade Bess to give him a gift of money, he had left abruptly but then reappeared the following day stating he was willing to work for free. Bess had dismissed him, though she did admit to Burghley that she did not have actual evidence to enable her to "... charge him with

---

[3] Presumably they also assumed that Arbella would either be willing to convert to Catholicism or could be married to some suitable Catholic husband who could then rule the country in her name.

[4] Which was how Bess often referred to Arbella when using her name.

papistry ..." In any event, it seems that Morley's services as a tutor were not missed.

Bess and Arbella returned to Hardwick from Chatsworth in early December 1592 and remained there over the Christmas period. In addition to the usual Christmas festivities (which Bess always enjoyed, and insisted on keeping in the traditional fashion), Bess was also kept busy contemplating further land purchases. Part of the impetus for this may have been the overcrowding in Hardwick Old Hall; coupled with this was Bess's desire to acquire more land in the vicinity of Hardwick. She had the opportunity to do so in January 1593. On 17th January, Bess agreed to buy the manors of Heath, Rawthorne, Stainsby and Owlcotes (or Oldcotes) from the Savage family of Stainsby, Derbyshire for £3,416. The Hardwick family had links to the Stainsby estate; both Bess's father and grandfather had leased farmland there from the Savages. Now the Cavendishes would own the land outright.

The village of Owlcotes is about four and a half miles from Hardwick. Bess decided that she would build yet another house there for the use of William and his family. Again, Robert Smythson was involved in the design; Owlcotes was to be built according to the same general design as Hardwick New Hall, but on a smaller scale, possessing only two turrets. It was finally completed around 1600.[5]

May 1593 saw Bess moving back once again to Chatsworth, and this time she would stay for over a year whilst construction work continued at Hardwick. It was to be a busy summer for her; in addition to the marriage of Grace Pierrepont to George Manners in early August 1593, Bess was occupied in harmonising and expanding her various business interests. It has been estimated that about this time, her personal annual income (including that arising under her marriage settlement with Shrewsbury but excluding the income from lands she had passed to

---

[5] Bess purchased the land but much of the costs of construction of Owlcotes were met by William Cavendish. Owlcotes eventually became the property of the Pierrepont family in the mid-seventeenth century but now no longer exists.

William and Charles) was around £8300 (around £3.2 million today) and would rise to more than £10,000 by 1600.[6] To put that figure in context, it has been estimated that the total cost of the various building works at Hardwick during the period of 1584 to 1598 was approximately £5000. Bess clearly had surplus funds to invest during the 1590s, and invest them she did, primarily of course, in land, much of it situated around Hardwick, but she also bought properties throughout the Midlands including in Leicestershire, Lincolnshire, Nottinghamshire and Yorkshire. Many of those properties she would settle on William, who was still busy acting essentially as her second-in-command in relation to her business ventures.

Bess's income streams could take various forms. There were the simple rents she received from the tenants of her lands, and of course the income generated from activities such as raising and selling livestock and the sale of agricultural and other farming produce. In addition, she derived considerable income from the sale of iron, coal, lead and other minerals mined on her lands (though she usually leased mining rights to others and took a portion of the resulting profits rather than operate her own mines), and she was instrumental in setting up various glass manufactories; glass was an increasingly important product in late Tudor times. She also was not averse to indulging in money-landing; she was after all cash rich unlike most of the other noble and gentry families of the time, and as noted in the case of Sir Francis Willoughby, usually insisted that her loans be secured by mortgages on properties that she could seize if a borrower defaulted.

---

[6] It should be noted that during the years 1594, 1595, 1596 and 1597, the country suffered atrocious harvests due to heavy rain and as a result, famine and social unrest generally throughout the land was a very real problem. This did not directly affect Bess of course, but her income from her lands (like that of other wealthy landowners) fell as a result, by as much as 25 percent according to one estimate. This did not however interfere with her building works at Hardwick. Her income recovered in the late 1590s as weather conditions returned to normal.

Bess did not rely solely on her son William to assist her in these ventures. She had various servants who helped to make sure her business interests ran smoothly, including seventeen bailiffs who were primarily responsible for collecting rents and other payments due to her and making sure the sums so collected were delivered to her receiver, William Reason. Reason in turn was responsible for passing the monies to Timothy Pusey. Pusey technically was still Bess's steward, but his responsibilities were far greater than the name of his office suggests; he was in some ways Bess's third-in-command; it no doubt helped that he had received legal training (he was more than capable of drafting legal indentures and deeds when these were required by Bess) and could prepare accounts. Bess also had the services of various lawyers (as a substantial landowner she inevitably became entangled in a series of lawsuits of various kinds over the years and had need of those services); as the 1590s progressed, she increasingly tended to deal with her lawyers through Pusey. Pusey was highly valued by Bess. She invariably referred to him as "Tymothy" in her letters and her accounts, and she paid him an annual salary of £10 (and eventually he would lease a farm and a mill from her).[7] Another important assistant was Rowland Harrison, a gentleman servant who reported to Pusey and seems largely to have worked on Bess's money-lending ventures and helped to prepare her accounts.

In the meantime, Gilbert Talbot was still capable of causing trouble. His volatile nature had not been tempered over the years, rather, while he had been made Lord Lieutenant of Derbyshire following his father's death (and a Knight of Garter), he had not automatically assumed the office of Earl Marshal of England as he had expected and nor had he

---

[7] After Bess's death, he would continue to work for William Cavendish. In due course (after leaving William's service), he would marry, buy Selston Old Hall in Nottinghamshire, serve as a justice of the peace for the county and as Sherriff of Nottingham in 1625. Clearly working for the Cavendishes could be a way of substantially improving one's own fortune, at least for some of their servants. Another who did so was John Clay of Crich, the father of Pusey's wife Maria, who also worked for Bess for a time and became wealthy.

been made Lord Lieutenant of Nottinghamshire in succession to his father, and these failures made him even more aggressive, unpleasant and unreasonable. By 1592 he was looking around for someone to blame.[8] His attention fell on the Stanhope family of Shelford in Nottinghamshire, who had been friends with the Talbots for many years; indeed John Stanhope, a courtier and political ally of Robert Cecil had offered to assist Gilbert in his attempts to gain political offices to the extent that he could. Unfortunately, John Stanhope's brother, Sir Thomas Stanhope, was announced as a candidate for the Lord Lieutenancy of Nottinghamshire and Gilbert immediately decided he must have been betrayed by the Stanhopes (it isn't clear whether he was). This was the start of a long feud between Gilbert and the Stanhopes, encouraged it must be said by Mary Talbot, who was vocal in her dislike of Sir Thomas Stanhope in particular, declaring that his "wickedness" would turn him into the "vilest toad" in the world.

Gilbert's opening move in the feud was to raise the matter of an old dispute which had broken out 20 or so years before between the Stanhopes and the la Zouche family. Back in the 1570s, in order to improve his fishing, Thomas Stanhope had (quite legally) instructed that a weir be built across the River Trent near the family home at Shelford. The la Zouches had objected but eventually the matter had died down. Now Gilbert revived the argument once more, though it had nothing to do with him, and argued that the weir was depriving local people of fish. His servants attacked and damaged the weir several times, insults were exchanged and before long, violence was breaking out between the Stanhope servants and those of Gilbert.

---

[8] It was precisely because he was considered too aggressive and argumentative that he was not appointed Earl Marshal or Lord Lieutenant of Nottinghamshire. As far as the office of Earl Marshal was concerned, the office remained vacant until 1592 when it was put "in commission", that is essentially shared by members of a special commission comprised of Lord Burghley, Lord Howard of Effingham, the Lord High Admiral and Henry, Lord Hundson, the Lord Chamberlain. The office would be given to the Earl of Essex on 28th December 1597, though he wouldn't hold it for very long.

This in turn brought Charles Cavendish into the fray.[9] Still on very close terms with Gilbert, he felt obliged to intervene in the dispute on Gilbert's side and on 15th March 1593, he challenged John Stanhope to a duel at Lambeth Bridge. After some quibbling, it was agreed the duel should take place at five o'clock in the evening of the following day, the chosen weapons being rapiers. The duel however did not happen. When Stanhope appeared at the appointed hour, he was wearing a thick doublet, so thick it was later declared, that when inspected by "Mr Nowell" (Charles' second for the duel), Nowell "could hardly thrust a knife through it". Charles suggested they fight in shirt sleeves, but Stanhope demurred, saying it was too cold. Charles offered him the use of his waistcoat but that too was refused. Charles asked the views of the two seconds (Nowell and Stanhope's second, a man named Townsend); they took the view that a duel where one duellist was in shirt sleeves and the other was clothed in a thick doublet was unfair, and the whole matter was called off (though not forgotten).[10]

Eventually, the Stanhopes took the dispute about the weir to the Star Chamber, which found in their favour. This did not however, end the vendetta between Gilbert and the Stanhopes which was destined to continue for several more years, and moreover now involved Charles. Matters worsened when some Talbot and Cavendish retainers ambushed John Stanhope and a small party of his men in Fleet Street in London which led to one of Stanhope's servants being injured. News of

---

[9] He had only recently become a husband once again, having married Catherine Ogle, the daughter of Baron Ogle the previous year. Their eldest son William (not to be confused with Charles' son William by Margaret Kitson, who by now had died) would be born in December 1593 and in time be created the First Duke of Newcastle-upon-Tyne. Catherine's sister Jane was married to Gilbert Talbot's brother Edward, who would eventually succeed him as the Eighth Earl of Shrewsbury.

[10] Stanhope's behaviour may seem to some to have been unsporting, but it should be remembered that Charles (who was after all the challenger) by this time had a reputation of being a very fine swordsman indeed, almost certainly much better than Stanhope. Perhaps Stanhope thought wearing a thick doublet would even up the odds a little.

this eventually reached the ears of the Queen, who let it be known she strongly disapproved of the feud, though she seems to have been more in sympathy with the Stanhopes than the Talbots. Bess too must have had concerns, not only because Charles was involved and there was a danger of the Cavendishes generally being pulled into the dispute, which was the last thing she wanted (and she had been warning Charles of the dangers of duelling for several years now), but also because of the possibility that the dispute might somehow damage the prospects of Arbella achieving the throne.

Not content just with feuding with the Stanhopes, Gilbert continued to display animosity to other family members, a trait which became even more pronounced when the court found in favour of Bess in the matter of her rights under her marriage settlement. In 1594, a dispute arose between himself and his brother Edward when Gilbert claimed that Edward had accused him of granting a fraudulent lease. On 22nd June 1594, he wrote to his brother effectively saying that he would be willing to fight a duel over the matter. The letter was delivered to Edward by two servants, who appear to have thought a duel had definitely been proposed and that they were under instructions to agree the time, place and weapons of choice. Certainly, that appears to have been the impression they gave Edward and it says something of Gilbert's character that his own brother seems to have thought it quite believable that Gilbert had in fact actually challenged him. The next day, Edward replied to Gilbert in moderate tone, sensibly declining a duel and seeking to clarify that he had merely said that *if* Gilbert had granted a lease that jeopardised the underlying (entailed) freehold, and *if* the terms of the transaction undervalued the freehold (which was a concern to Edward as he was at that time the heir to the entailed Talbot family lands), then his counsel thought such a lease *if* designed to have such a purpose would be found by the courts to be fraudulent. Gilbert's reply the same day was not reciprocal in moderation and he accused Edward, first, of lying about having been challenged –

"… you write that I have given you a challenge to fight with you, I answer that you therein lie, for I only gave you the lie in your throat …"

- and to be fair to Gilbert, in his letter he did not actually issue a challenge, but merely said he would be willing to fight a duel. On the other hand, especially if the servants delivering the letter had spoken as if a challenge had been issued, it is easy to see why Edward might well have thought that one had been.

Gilbert then went on to accuse his brother of being afraid, and of hiding "… under the opinion of his counsel …" Edward replied as moderately as before, essentially stating that it seemed as though his brother was determined to quarrel with him, and that he himself had no wish to enter into hostilities with Gilbert. This whole affair became public knowledge; certainly, the Queen came to hear of it, and she told Essex to write to Gilbert, to warn him that such behaviour could be used by enemies to discredit him. Lord Howard of Effingham also wrote to him, deploring arguments between brothers. Gilbert's reply to Essex in particular is fascinating; he listed a long litany of complaints against his brother Edward and their younger brother Henry, stating that in their father's lifetime, both brothers had "by most vile means" not only procured "a greater portion" of their father's lands that he had intended should pass to Gilbert but had also caused most of the lands that Gilbert had in fact inherited to be subject to entails to his disadvantage. And there were other wild accusations. There is no evidence that any of these allegations were true, and it must have seemed to many (especially perhaps the Queen) that there were distinct similarities between the wild statements now being issued by Gilbert and those the Sixth Earl of Shrewsbury had been in the habit of making in the years before his death.

In 1595, the saga of Gilbert's dispute with Edward once again erupted. This time, the dispute related to an allegation that Edward had sought to entice Gilbert's own physician (or possibly his apothecary), a man named Wood, into murdering Gilbert, using poisoned gloves. Wood

233

appears to have made various statements to this effect, alleging that he had been offered an annuity of £100 to carry out the deed, and the result was that Edward accused him of slander. Wood was hauled in front of the Star Chamber, which found him guilty and he was sentenced to have an ear cut off and three letters branded onto his forehead. Wood himself sought to implicate Mary Talbot in the matter, possibly in the hope (vain as it transpired to be) that in doing so he might lessen his own sentence. As a result, Mary Talbot was called before the Master of the Rolls but no charges were brought against her. Gilbert for his part appears to have believed that there had been a plot to poison him, and he said so volubly, so much so that eventually the Queen banished him (and Mary Talbot) from the Court for a time, something which did nothing to raise his social standing (which was already pretty low).

Chapter 19

Hardwick New Hall

The spring of 1595 saw Bess and Arbella back at Hardwick once more. The construction work on Hardwick New Hall by and large was proceeding well, though Bess could be demanding if she was dissatisfied with the quality of the work carried out by her craftsmen, taking issue that year for instance with the quality of some plastering and whitewashing work (the plasterer was obliged to redo it at his own cost). In another instance, she complained about some panelling work that had been carried out in the Great Chamber of Hardwick Old Hall, and again, the joiner was required to correct it at his own cost.

But if she could be demanding, she could also be generous. One name that frequently appears in the accounts of the building works at Hardwick is that of Thomas Accres (or Acres), a stonemason particularly skilled at carving architraves and overmantels, and who would have a long association with Bess. He had worked at Chatsworth for Bess when she was making the final polishes to the building in anticipation of Leicester's visit in 1577, had probably worked for Shrewsbury when he was constructing Worksop Manor, had been "lent" by Bess to Sir Francis Willoughby to assist in the construction of Wollaton Hall and now was working hard for Bess at Hardwick. He must have been, for in 1595, she rewarded him with a tip of 10 shillings for helping to construct a water wheel. A year later, she gave his wife Grace 20 shillings "... in respect of her husband's device ...", that is, the waterwheel. And Bess rewarded other workers (and members of their families) when she thought it appropriate to do so. Accres in fact would work for Bess for the rest of his life, essentially on her payroll as her permanent master mason. She leased a farm to him and he died there in 1607.

Bess, as previously noted, as a significant landowner was usually involved one way or another in various legal disputes. Many of these were relatively minor matters, but in the spring of 1595, she was to become involved in one of greater significance than usual. Its origin lay back in the late 1560s when Bess acquired some lands at Edensor in Derbyshire, not far from Chatsworth. The lands had originally belonged to Sir Ingram Clifford, the younger brother of Henry Clifford, the Second Earl of Cumberland, but Sir Ingram was childless and he decided to transfer his land at Edensor to his elder brother. It is thought that the Second Earl used them as security for a loan made to him by Bess, but when he died (in January 1570), the loan was not repaid, and Bess seized the land. The Earl's successor was his son George; he in turn had a younger brother Francis, who for reasons of his own, in 1595, decided to attempt to get the Edensor lands back.

His opening gambit was to sponsor a challenge brought by two of his supporters as regards the legality of a lease at Edensor which had been granted years before. The tenant in question had long since moved away, but was summoned before the Court of Common Pleas in London during the Easter Term of 1595 to answer a charge that he had improperly acquired the lease, specifically because he had married the illegitimate daughter of an earlier tenant who had originally leased the land from Sir Ingram himself. This of course was no proof that the lease had been acquired improperly (in fact, it had no bearing on the matter at all), and the court had no problem in finding in favour of the tenant.

At this point, Francis Clifford himself intervened in the matter. After visiting Bess at Chatsworth in June 1595 (whether she had permanently moved back there once more from Hardwick at that time or whether she had gone there for the purpose of the meeting is unclear), and having failed to persuade Bess simply to surrender the Edensor lands to him, he lodged a complaint before the Star Chamber alleging that Bess and William Cavendish had bribed the jury who had heard the case against the tenant in the Court of Common Pleas.

Clifford claimed that he had a witness who could prove that his allegations were true. That witness was John Bamforth, who had worked for Bess for a number of years before being dismissed, in June

1595, seemingly in some disgrace, and seemingly without being paid his accrued wages. He therefore had grounds to dislike the Cavendishes and the motive to seek to do them injury.

The jury had been selected by John Rodes, then the High Sheriff of Derbyshire. William Cavendish would succeed him in that post in November 1595, but before this had happened, Rodes had met Bess at Hardwick. There may have been many reasons for such a meeting, but according to Bamforth, Bess had provided Rodes with a list of 24 possible jurymen, and some of them subsequently sat on the jury. To make matters worse, Rodes himself (according to Bamforth) apparently owed Bess £500, and the inference was that the loan would be waived if the jury selection was to Bess's liking. Several of the jurymen also owed money to Bess one way or another, and she allegedly also had paid some of their expenses in connection with the trial. If all this was true, it would not have been surprising if the Star Chamber had concluded that Bess and William had indeed been involved in jury bribery.

The trouble is that it isn't clear whether the allegations were true. The bribing of juries was fairly common in Tudor times, and it is by no means impossible to imagine that Bess and William might have indulged in it; many of their rich contemporaries would not have hesitated to do so if they felt the situation warranted it. Bess and William of course vehemently denied any impropriety as regards the jury selection, and unfortunately the records of the Star Chamber which might shed light on the court's conclusions have been lost. We do know that the case continued to rumble on for a number of years, until seemingly Francis Clifford grew tired of the whole matter and disappeared out of Bess's life for good. Bess retained the lands at Edensor, and they are still owned by her descendants to this day.

In the meantime, international events were occurring that would impinge on Gilbert Talbot's life. The war with Spain was continuing, and despite occasional tentative peace overtures from one side or the other, there was no sign that it would end soon (it would in fact continue until August 1604 when a peace treaty was finally signed at Somerset

House in London). In 1596 however, while the Spanish had failed in their attempts to subdue the Dutch or invade England, they remained a significant threat to both countries. France too had become embroiled in the war, partly as a consequence of its own wars of religion which had been raging on one way or another since 1562.

France's religious wars at this time essentially involved a struggle between French Catholics and Huguenots. In 1596, the French King was Henry IV; originally a Protestant but with links to the French royal family, he had initially fought on the side of the Huguenots and had declared himself king in 1589 following the death of Henry III. Phillip II of Spain had been providing considerable support to the French Catholics, and continued to do so to a Catholic faction opposed to Henry IV even after Henry agreed to convert to Catholicism as the price of securing his coronation as king.[1] This ongoing support of Catholics opposed to him eventually led Henry IV to declare war against Spain in January 1595.

France was keen to find allies to assist in its struggles with Spain. One obvious ally (despite the religious differences) was the Dutch Republic, which was allied with England. Although the Dutch were enthusiastic that England should be brought into the alliance they themselves had with France, the French (and especially Henry IV) were less so, partly for reasons of national prestige.

This reluctance on the part of the French was initially shared by Queen Elizabeth and the Council, partly because she was anxious, as were some members of the Council, such as Lord Burghley, to pursue peace (no matter how improbable the chances) and partly because there were concerns about potentially increasing the power of France.[2] What

---

[1] Henry IV was crowned as the French King on 27th February 1593. He is said to have declared that "Paris is well worth a mass".
[2] The Earl of Essex was very much in favour of continuing the war, principally because he hoped that he would have an opportunity of distinguishing himself

changed Queen Elizabeth's mind about an alliance with France was the Spanish conquest of Calais, which happened in April 1596, and gave the Spanish a seaport uncomfortably close to England. At around the same time, the Spanish made peace overtures to the French. The fall of Calais also focussed the mind of Henry IV as to the threat of Spain, and he was now more eager to ally with England but told Queen Elizabeth that if an alliance could not be concluded, he would have no choice but to accept the Spanish peace offer. This in turn would allow the Spanish to deploy the troops they currently had in France against the English and Dutch.

Seen in that light, Queen Elizabeth agreed to open discussions about an alliance with the French (the Dutch were kept out of the initial discussions), and in the early summer of 1596, it was agreed that a delegation should be despatched to Paris to discuss terms. The question arose as to who should lead the English delegation. Queen Elizabeth had initially been in favour of appointing the Earl of Essex as the leader, but he was eager to take part in an Anglo-Dutch assault which was planned to be made on Cadiz at the end of June of that year and was unavailable.[3] With Essex therefore engaged elsewhere, the Queen and

---

as a soldier. This attitude offended Burghley's deeply held religious principles; at one meeting of the Council, a fierce argument broke out between the two men on the topic. Eventually, Burghley, almost speechless with anger, stood up, pulled out a prayer book from his pocket and pointed to a passage in the Psalms - "bloody and deceitful men shall not live out half their days" it said. In the case of Essex, that turned out to be true.

[3] The assault took place, and the port of Cadiz was (temporarily) captured; however, one of the factors which had persuaded Queen Elizabeth to approve the raid in the first place was the prospect suggested by Essex (and others) that Spanish treasure ships might be captured (Cadiz was one of the principal ports used as a point of arrival for the treasure fleets bringing back gold, silver and other valuables from the Spanish possessions in the Americas). Unfortunately, the Spanish succeeded in sinking most of the treasure ships in Cadiz harbour before the treasures on board could be seized, and from a financial perspective, the raid was a failure, something which did nothing to enhance Essex's reputation in the eyes of his sovereign. (One of the other leaders of the raid,

Council decided that leadership of the delegation should be offered to Gilbert Talbot (possibly by way of compensation for the denial of the post of Earl Marshal and Lord Lieutenancy of Nottinghamshire). Gilbert, eager perhaps to redeem himself after his dismissal from Court the previous year, accepted and hastened off to Paris. Negotiation of the Anglo-French alliance was not to be his only task in Paris; he was also to confer the Order of the Garter on Henry IV and present the new English ambassador to France, Sir Anthony Mildmay, who was the son of Sir Walter Mildmay, the former Chancellor of the Exchequer. It was soon apparent that Sir Anthony Mildmay did not get on well with Henry IV, and he left the French court the following year, refusing to return.

Gilbert appears to have handled his responsibilities as leader of the English delegation to Paris well, and a treaty of alliance with France (and eventually with the Dutch) against Spain was signed in October 1596. He returned to London rather pleased with himself, though he may have been somewhat dismayed to learn on his return that in his absence, his enemy John Stanhope (Thomas Stanhope's brother) had been knighted and had received a promotion at Court, having been appointed Treasurer of the Chamber, the same post that Sir William Cavendish had "bought" from King Henry VIII for £1000 back in 1546. Nevertheless, he and Mary Talbot were welcomed back at Court once more, or rather they were until Mary asked the Queen for permission for two of her daughters to be appointed as maids of honour to Arbella. The Queen was not in the best of moods, having recently learned of the failure to seize the treasure ships at Cadiz, and abruptly refused, and dismissed Gilbert and Mary Talbot from the Court once more for impertinence.

1597 was a significant year for Bess as it was on 4th of October of that year (the day that may have been Bess's seventieth birthday) that Bess

---

incidentally, was Sir Walter Raleigh, by now at least partially rehabilitated in the eyes of the Queen after his marriage to Elizabeth Throckmorton.)

and Arbella were able to move into Hardwick New Hall, though as in the case of the Old Hall, further work on the hall would be carried out over the next few years, with the interior only being finished in 1601. Bess moved in with some style, her entrance being accompanied by music played by four of her servants, James Starkey (her chaplain), John Dodderidge (sometimes known as John Good), Francis Parker and Richard Abrahall.

Hardwick New Hall was very different from Hardwick Old Hall and Chatsworth. To begin with, though imposing from the outside, it was (and of course, still is) relatively small, having only 46 rooms (excluding service rooms) compared with 55 in Hardwick Old Hall and 97 rooms at Chatsworth. The house had a small base plan meaning that it had to be relatively tall to accommodate all the various rooms; Smythson (and Bess) took advantage of this by ensuring an unusual number of great windows were incorporated into the building plans; these are constructed in order of escalating height, with the windows on each floor being smaller than the ones on the floor above it, until the second floor which has the largest great windows of all.[4] The house itself is two rooms thick, with a two-storey transverse hall (as in the case of Hardwick Old Hall) that runs through the house from front to back, rather than at right angles to the entrance. Six towers rise above the main top floor, from which Bess and her guests could look down over the surrounding countryside; each tower is adorned with the initials "ES" carved in stone.

As the great windows suggest, the floors at Hardwick New Hall reflect the social hierarchy of the rooms they contain. The kitchens, servant rooms and a nursery (which functioned as a schoolroom for William Cavendish's children) were all situated on the ground floor. The first floor contained the lesser great chamber, Bess's rooms (including her withdrawing chamber), a chapel and Arbella's bedroom – she now had

---

[4] Hence the famous expression coined by Robert Cecil that Hardwick New Hall "is more glass than wall". A major disadvantage of this was that the New Hall could be very cold indeed in winter.

use of her own bedroom, but close to her grandmother's rooms so Bess could keep an eye on her, which would cause problems in years to come. The principal ceremonial rooms – the high great chamber, the gallery and the best lodgings of all were placed on the second floor. One advantage of this arrangement was that the design allowed for a grand ceremonial processional route from the kitchens, through the hall and up a magnificent stone staircase leading to the high great chamber. As might be expected, the high great chamber was great indeed; the royal arms of Queen Elizabeth were carved into the overmantel above the mantelpiece as an expression of loyalty and a coloured plaster frieze running around the room depicted the goddess Diana with nymphs and animals (real and imaginary) in a forest setting, intended as a symbol of peace and prosperity enjoyed under the reign of the Queen and contrasting it with the bloody and difficult reigns of earlier monarchs. The gallery too contained symbols praising the Queen, with statues depicting justice and mercy built into the overmantels, and other symbols depicting the Queen's virtues were to be found in other rooms. In 1597, Bess may well still have been hopeful that Queen Elizabeth might one day pay a visit to Derbyshire and stay with her, though this would never happen.

One surprising aspect of Hardwick New Hall is that there were only fourteen bedrooms, but should more accommodation be required, rooms could be made available in the nearby Old Hall. Nor was there a library when the house was first built. This in itself was not very unusual; many of the great houses of the time lacked libraries, which really only began to become common in the second half of the seventeenth century. Indeed, illiteracy amongst the leading gentry, at least those in more remote parts of the country was surprisingly high in the mid-Tudor period; it has been reported for example that in Northumberland, in the 1560s, 92 out of 146 members of the gentry were unable to sign their names. Bess was certainly not illiterate, but even she had relatively few books (reputedly six, which she kept in her bedchamber, though this figure is simply that recorded in an inventory made at Hardwick in 1601 and is almost certainly an underestimate. But she didn't have very many).[5]

Not content with her building activities at Hardwick, Chatsworth and Owlcotes, the spring of 1598 saw Bess commence yet another building project, almost certainly her last. Whereas her building works to date had been largely focussed on providing herself and her family with fine, comfortable, even glorious, accommodation in a fashion that proclaimed Cavendish status and power to the world, her last project was charitable in nature, and may have been prompted by the knowledge that her time in this world had to be coming to an end, and it might do no harm to perform a few acts which might reflect well on her in the next. She commissioned and endowed twelve alms houses in Derby and by 1600 they were completed and the first twelve residents (eight men and four women, one of whom was Isabell Heyward, who had been one of Bess's servants) were installed. They were given Cavendish livery when they first arrived, and then each year three yards of light blue cloth with which to make new clothes; they also each received a silver badge depicting Bess's initials and a weekly stipend of 2 and a half shillings.

There was also sadness for the Cavendishes in 1597 and 1598, and especially for William. First, in the autumn of 1597, around the time Bess moved into Hardwick New Hall, William Cavendish's son Gilbert, then aged around six, died. Then, a few months later, in February 1598, Anne, William's wife, died after giving birth to a son named James. Two of William's daughters also died shortly thereafter, meaning that by the end of the century, of all William's children, only his son William (who was known as "Wylkyn" in the family), his daughter Frances and James

---

[5] Lord Burghley and John, Lord Lumley (one of the judges at the trial of Mary, Queen of Scots), are each reported to have possessed over a thousand books, but this was regarded as very unusual. A library would finally be created at Hardwick New Hall in the early 1600s under the supervision of the philosopher Thomas Hobbes, who came to Hardwick in 1608 to act as tutor to William Cavendish's son William (and later Hobbes would act as tutor to *his* son).

were alive (and James himself would die in infancy). For Bess too, this no doubt would have been painful enough, but she also learned of the death of Burghley in August of 1598, and sincerely mourned his passing. Lord Burghley after all had proven himself a stout friend to Bess over the years. There was also the simple fact that Bess was of an age when one by one, the friends of her youth were beginning to die, and the knowledge that one day it must happen to her no doubt was beginning to impinge on her consciousness as the years passed.

The following year, 1599, saw the feud between Gilbert Talbot and the Stanhopes flare up again, and once more Charles Cavendish was involved. Indeed, this time, he was centre stage. In 1597, Bess had provided Charles with money to build himself a new house at Kirkby-in-Ashby in Nottinghamshire. Bess, no doubt distracted by the move to Hardwick New Hall and the construction of her alms houses had relatively little to do with the planning of the new house, but Charles initially entered into the new project with enthusiasm. By the early summer of 1599, it was well underway, and in June of that year, as he was staying in a house only half a mile or so away with his wife Catherine, he decided to pay a visit to see how the building work was coming along. He set off just before ten o'clock in the morning, accompanied only by Henry Ogle (a relative of his wife), Launcelot Ogle (his page) and a groom; as they were approaching the building site, they saw 20 men on horseback approaching down the nearby hill. They thought at first it was Sir John Byron (a local landowner) with a party out hunting, but it was in fact John Stanhope[6] with supporters. Charles and his party were attacked, they tried to ride to the (relative) safety of the partially constructed new buildings, but Charles' horse stumbled over and Charles was thrown to the ground, his foot still in the stirrups. Someone in Stanhope's party shot him, and he was struck on the inside of his thigh. Notwithstanding this, and even though outnumbered, Charles and his three companions seem to have managed to fight off

---

[6] Almost certainly John Stanhope, son of Sir Thomas Stanhope, rather than Sir John Stanhope, the Treasurer of the Chamber.

their attackers, killing two of them, and holding the others off long enough for the builders working on Charles' new house to come and investigate. According to later reports, Stanhope and his party then fled the scene, with Stanhope (who had been "hindmost" in the fight) being the foremost in "running away".

Charles survived his injuries, though they took a long time to heal (they were still troubling him a year later, and the Queen sent her own doctor to "meddle with his probe"). Stanhope seems to have suffered no sanction for the attack; the principal legacy of the whole affair was that the attack was that it soured Charles on the whole notion of building a new house at Kirkby-in-Ashby. The construction work was halted and never resumed.

Chapter 20

The Fall of Essex

Although Bess no longer visited the Court, she still took some trouble to monitor events there from afar, exchanging letters regularly with prominent courtiers such as Robert Cecil, who seems to have been fond of Bess, and willing to do her favours from time to time. She had been a good friend of his father and would have seen him grow up. She kept an eye on the affairs of Court for several reasons, not least because it was in her interest to do so from a political and financial perspective, and also because there was still the issue of Arbella's potential claim to the throne and what her future might be. There was also an element of wishing to be kept informed of the latest social aspects of Court life; Bess was as interested in gossip, and even scandal, as anyone, provided of course that such gossip and scandal involved someone other than herself.

In the late 1590s, one of the principal subjects of gossip, certainly as far as Bess and Arbella were concerned, was the Earl of Essex. The failure of the Cadiz raid in 1596 had made him more temperamental than ever, and this was compounded by another military failure in the summer of the following year, when he led an Anglo-Dutch naval expedition tasked with the destruction of Spanish warships and Spanish settlements on the Azores, and the capture of the Spanish treasure fleet. Essex, in defiance of orders from the Queen, led the Anglo-Dutch fleet in an attempt to capture the treasure fleet without first attacking the Azores or searching out the Spanish warships, which unbeknownst to him (at that time) had orders to proceed to England with the intention of capturing either the port of Falmouth or of Milford Haven, as a prelude to invasion.[1] Although the Third Armada ultimately failed

---

[1] The Spanish fleet became known as the Third Armada. There had been a similar invasion attempt by an armada (the Second Armada) the year before which had failed as a result of storms.

thanks partly to bad weather, the Spanish did succeed in landing a few hundred troops near Falmouth and in the Dyfi Estuary in Wales for a few days; more importantly though, thanks largely due to Essex's actions, the coast of England had been left virtually unprotected by English ships for a time, which infuriated both the Queen and many on her Council. Essex's standing in the eyes of the Queen dipped even further, and Essex grew even more desperate to find a way of claiming a glorious triumph which he now sincerely believed he deserved.

An opportunity (the last one as it transpired) then arose, beginning in 1598. There was growing unrest in Ireland, where a new chieftain named Hugh O'Neill, the Earl of Tyrone had managed to assemble a coalition of various Irish clans under his leadership and effectively rebelled (with considerable success) against English rule. In order to reimpose order and quell the rebellion, it was decided in 1598 that a new Lord Deputy of Ireland should be appointed and a number of members of the Council (including Essex) met with the Queen to decide who that should be. The Queen favoured Sir William Knollys (incidentally, Essex's uncle); Essex countered by proposing Sir George Carew, largely because Carew was a political ally of Robert Cecil and Essex wanted him despatched away from the Court. The Queen overruled Essex, and he lost his temper and turned his back on the Queen. Infuriated, she boxed his ears and he turned in rage, reached for his sword and was only prevented from drawing it by having his arms seized by other Council members.

Essex hurriedly left the Court and refused to apologise when advised to do so by a friend. "I have been content to do Her Majesty the service of a clerk but can never serve her as a villein or a slave" he is reputed to have said. Perhaps for the sake of her memories of Leicester, perhaps because she still cherished at least a little affection for Essex, Queen Elizabeth was willing to forgive Essex once again, but she did not forget the incident and Essex was now on very thin ice so far as royal approval was concerned.

There was a brief interlude of a few months, and then Irish affairs once again became the topic of intense debate in the Council. By the spring of 1599, the Earl of Tyrone's rebellion had become so serious that the Queen and Council decided they had no choice but to despatch a military force consisting of some 16,000 men with instructions to restore order and engage with Tyrone's forces, then largely situated in Ulster. This, Essex thought, was his best chance to win glory (and possibly regain the affections and support of Queen Elizabeth), and he persuaded the Queen and Council to appoint him as leader of the expedition. He duly landed in southern Ireland, but despite very firm instructions to march north and engage with Tyrone as soon as possible, he wasted several months in the south, fighting inconclusive (and largely pointless) campaigns, setting up garrison bases and generally wasting money and supplies.

He received messages from London urging him to march north, but it took six months before he did so. When he finally did, instead of engaging with Tyrone's forces, he met with Tyrone alone, both of them on horses in the middle of a river. It was later claimed that Essex eventually conceded most of Tyrone's demands in exchange for a promise that Tyrone would assist Essex in gaining control of the Queen and England, and despatching his enemies there.

Did he truly intend to return to England in an attempt to seize the Queen by force? He almost certainly wouldn't have succeeded had he tried, but in the event, he didn't. Instead, towards the end of September 1599, despite being ordered to stay in Ireland until he was formally recalled, he abandoned his army there and hurried back to Nonsuch Palace, in Surrey, where the Queen was then in residence. He reached there early in the morning of 28th September, and forcing himself past Queen Elizabeth's guards, he burst into the Queen's private apartments without first announcing himself, to find her surrounded by some of her ladies-in-waiting, and in the process of dressing and preparing herself for the rigours of the forthcoming day.

The Queen naturally was startled (and no doubt later had some choice words to express to those who had been guarding her) but by all accounts, greeted Essex pleasantly and assured him that they could talk later once she was fully dressed and had attended first to some urgent business which awaited her. Essex withdrew, seemingly reassured that he still ranked high in her favour. After he had left, the Queen sent for Sir Robert Cecil, and a meeting of the Council was summoned urgently. The next day, Essex was called before the Queen and her Council, and he soon found out that the Queen took a very dim view indeed of his behaviour. After coldly questioning him as to his activities in Ireland, he was dismissed from her presence and soon placed under house arrest, under the custody of Sir Richard Berkeley. Queen Elizabeth and Essex would never meet again.

Essex was still popular with many of the general public, and even now, the Queen and Council were cautious about being seen to deal harshly with him, though in June of 1600, he was brought before a special commission and charged (amongst other matters) with disobedience to orders and abandoning his post in Ireland. He was convicted, but in the circumstances, his punishment was light enough – he was stripped of the right to serve in any public office and ordered to continue to be held under house arrest, though in August, his personal freedom was restored to him. By now though, his personal finances were in disarray; he was almost entirely financially dependent on the right to claim royalties on the sale of sweet wines. This right however was due to expire in October 1600, and the Queen refused to renew it.

The prospect of financial ruin seems to have been the final catalyst which drove him into open treason. By early February 1601, he had gathered around him some supporters, who probably had as much to lose as Essex if his state of disgrace continued, and he and they contrived a plot whereby they would seize the Queen, remove the Council (and particularly Waler Raleigh and Robert Cecil, who Essex now bitterly asserted had principally been responsible for his fall), and take control of the City of London. Unfortunately for Essex (and by now he probably wasn't thinking very clearly, if at all), Robert Cecil had made sure that all of Essex's activities were being carefully monitored, and Cecil had a full report of Essex's plans for treason before even a first step had been taken. Security measures at the Court were enhanced, and Robert's half-brother Thomas Cecil (by now of course, the Second Lord Burghley) was despatched to alert the authorities of the City of London.

On 8th February, Essex and a band of around 200 supporters marched out of his house, Essex House, on The Strand and tried to enter the City of London; failing to rouse ordinary Londoners to join them, they were intercepted at Ludgate Hill and forced to retreat back to Essex House once more. There, they were surrounded by forces loyal to the government and within a few short hours, Essex found himself in the Tower charged with treason.

He was put on trial in Westminster Hall on the 19th February 1601 before a court of his peers. Essex claimed the charges against him were false, and that witnesses against him were in the pay of papist forces, and particularly that Robert Cecil, not he, was a traitor. Cecil, he claimed, had declared that the rightful heir to the English throne was the Infanta of Spain.

Cecil himself had been monitoring events at the trial from a doorway concealed by a curtain; when Essex made his allegations against him, he dramatically stepped into view of the court and in a powerful speech, demanded Essex tell the court who had claimed he supported the Infanta. Essex named Henry Wriothesley, the Third Earl Southampton (who was also on trial);[2] Southampton in turn said he had heard it from Sir William Knollys. Cecil demanded that Knollys be summoned to the court, but wisely asked that the messenger sent to collect Knollys should not tell him why he had been summoned. In the event, Knollys

---

[2] He was found guilty and sentenced to death, but at the urging of Robert Cecil, Queen Elizabeth commuted the punishment to life imprisonment. Southampton was released in 1603. Robert Cecil incidentally, was not the only person Essex claimed was a traitor. He also denounced his own sister Penelope, Lady Rich but no one took any notice of this.

completed exonerated Cecil, and Essex's last hopes of escaping his fate evaporated.

He was sentenced to death (along with four other conspirators), and on 25th February, was beheaded on Tower Green, out of the public gaze within the walls of the Tower, the last person to be beheaded on the Green itself. As in the case of Mary, Queen of Scots, it took three strokes of the executioner's axe to remove his head from his shoulders. (His executioner was a man called Thomas Derrick; several years before, he had been found guilty of rape and sentenced to death but Essex himself had pardoned him on condition that he became an executioner.)

Essex's execution signalled the end of his attempted coup, but it was very unpopular with ordinary people, who still saw him as a hero; they blamed Cecil for Essex's death. Back in Derbyshire, Bess and Arbella had been following the events through letters from correspondents in London, as well as occasional visitors. It isn't entirely clear what Bess felt about Essex's downfall and execution. She had made a point of staying in touch with him over recent years, as he had with her; after all, they both in their own ways were favourites of the Queen, at least (in the case of Essex) in earlier happier days, and Essex certainly visited Bess at Hardwick at least once, so it is probable that she felt moderately well-disposed to him. On the other hand, she was careful to be seen as remaining scrupulously loyal to the Queen (and indeed, generally was), and would never have approved of Essex's attempt to seize control of the Queen and her government by force, even if she had thought he had the slightest chance of succeeding, which seems very doubtful indeed. At the end of the day, she probably concluded that he had ultimately sought too much power for vainglorious reasons, and that his downfall was inevitable.

As for Arbella, we know that she was upset by Essex's death, partly because of the historic fondness which she had borne for him ever since their attendance together at Court in 1588, but also because it helped to emphasise the difficulties of her own position. Arbella was in her 26th year when Essex was executed, and over recent years she had felt increasingly frustrated over the extremely circumscribed life which by order of the Queen, she was now being forced to live much of the time at Hardwick under her grandmother's watchful eye, not exactly treated as a child anymore, but denied the freedoms open to other aristocratic females of her age. Still unmarried, she was now aware that Queen Elizabeth still essentially regarded her as a potentially useful political pawn, whose hand the Queen would not hesitate to offer in marriage to a foreign prince at any time it seemed expedient to do so. But she also must have wondered if she would marry at all. After all, all previous explorations of possible marriage opportunities had come to nothing, and she might well have feared that she would, for political reasons, remain unwed at least for the best years of her young adult life, and possibly even forever.[3] Arbella increasingly saw herself a kind of prisoner at Hardwick, and as she passed through her early and mid-twenties, tensions steadily mounted between herself and Bess.

They were fundamentally different characters. Bess, through long experience, was controlled and measured in her mannerisms, not inclined to act impulsively, at least not to her own detriment, and could generally anticipate the long-term consequences of any particular course of action. She was also by now used to being obeyed as the family matriarch (except of course, by Gilbert Talbot, who was still feuding with her about her marriage settlement rights). Arbella, by contrast, was young and impatient, still haughty, arrogant and moody, yet also with a romantic side to her personality which Bess may not have fully appreciated. Bess could still be generous towards Arbella, as witnessed for instance by Bess settling on Arbella the five manor houses acquired from Sir Francis Willoughby, but she could also speak sharply to Arbella, even on occasions administering a slap or tweaking her nose if she thought the occasion warranted it. It is not surprising therefore that

---

[3] Arbella's feelings of frustration concerning the apparent lack of desirable marriage opportunities may well have been exacerbated by the marriage in November 1601 of her cousin, Elizabeth Talbot, to Henry Grey, nephew of the Sixth Earl of Kent. She was seven years younger than Arbella.

Arbella increasingly yearned to escape from Hardwick, preferably to a household of her own where she could be her own mistress.

In the meantime, quite apart from domestic dramas at Hardwick, and events at Court, there were the routine matters of life for Bess to attend to. In early 1601, she gave instructions that inventories be taken of the contents of both her halls at Hardwick (something for which subsequent historians have blessed her memory ever since), and in April she prepared a new will (though she would amend its provisions in the years to come). While the will made some sort of provision for most of her children and their spouses, even Henry, who was to be left the contents of Chatsworth, Bess pointedly excluded the making of any kind of gift to Gilbert and Mary Talbot, or to Charles, because of the "unkindness" they had offered to her (in the case of Charles, presumably the unkindness was associating too closely with Gilbert whilst he was arguing with Bess about her settlement rights).

She also gave thought to her own funeral arrangements. Perhaps understandably, she had no wish to be buried in the Shrewsbury family vault in Sheffield, nor next to any of her earlier husbands. Burial with her Hardwick ancestors also appears not have appealed to her. Instead, she decided that when the time came, she wished to be buried in Derby in All Hallows' Church (later known as All Saints' Church and now Derby Cathedral), and she commissioned Robert Smythson to design an imposing tomb for her, made principally of blackstone and marble. By April 1601, it was said to be "be finished and wanting nothing but setting up". The tomb was to be set up over vaults which took some time to construct; they were ready three years later. It was in time to be surmounted with an effigy of Bess wearing a countess' coronet. (It should, incidentally, be noted that the current epitaph on her tomb is not contemporary, but added some time after the Restoration, probably in 1677).

Bess was still having problems with Gilbert and Mary Talbot, but there was the occasional attempt at reconciliation. Sometime in 1600, probably late spring or early summer, Charles Cavendish wrote from Leicester to his mother warning her that Gilbert and Mary would be travelling by close to Hardwick, and proposed to stop off and see her, and hoped to stay "one day at least with your ladyship". Presumably they did so, but it seems that the visit was not a success. Gilbert and Bess quarrelled over some lands which (at least according to Bess) should have been treated as hers, and which she had passed to her children. Gilbert however had included them in a package with other lands which he owned and had then conveyed them to two of his servants. On 2nd June 1600, Bess wrote to Robert Cecil to complain about Gilbert's behaviour, but on this occasion, there was little Robert Cecil could (or would) do about this. On 6th October, she was writing to Cecil once more about Gilbert, this time complaining that he was continuing to hold onto lands that according to Bess had been passed to her son Henry. Bess raised the matter in the Star Chamber, sending William down to London to represent her in the court, but the matter was put on hold and it is not clear whether or how it was ever resolved. Gilbert was also writing to Robert Cecil, essentially arguing he had acquired the disputed lands legally, but admitting that his "… dear good mother-in-law (dear I may justly term her) …" meant to overthrow him but that he intended to resist, and asking that Cecil keep an open mind with regard to the argument, at least until he had heard both sides. Presumably he did, and that probably explains why he was unable or unwilling to intervene in the matter when Bess first wrote to him in June.

Chapter 21

"I think she hath some vapours on her brain."

By the early spring of 1602, Arbella had decided she could endure her unmarried state, and life with her grandmother, no longer, and concluded that the solution to both problems would be for her to marry. Her proposed solution however raised problems of its own. First, the question of who she should marry and secondly, the issue of the Royal Marriage Act. She gave some thought to the first issue and appears to have given absolutely no consideration to the second, which is odd indeed, considering the identity of the person she concluded she should marry.

That person was none other than Edward Seymour, the grandson of Lady Katherine Grey (long since dead) and the Earl of Hertford (very much alive). Given the fact that Edward Seymour was a descendant of King Henry VII (and considered to have a claim to the throne notwithstanding that his father had been declared illegitimate), and bearing in mind Arbella's own royal links, it is difficult to think of a more dangerous choice she could have made. Making her choice seem even more peculiar were the facts that Arbella had never even met Edward Seymour and that Seymour was ten years or so younger than herself.

Nevertheless, she was determined to proceed. She realised she would need assistance to carry out her plan, and in March 1602, she approached James Starkey, Bess's chaplain and tutor to William Cavendish's children, telling him (he later claimed) that "... she would use all the means she could to get from thence ..." By now, Starkey nursed a grievance of his own against the Cavendishes - he believed he had been promised a church living by William which had not materialised – and he agreed to deliver letters for her. That summer, however, Starkey left the employment of the Cavendishes and moved to London, and several months went by without Arbella receiving any communications from him.[1] By December 1602, Arbella decided she would have to rely on someone else, and she approached John Dodderidge, one of Bess's most trusted servants.

Somehow, Arbella managed to cajole Dodderidge into agreeing to go to London to deliver a message to the Earl of Hertford. Specifically, he was to say he was delivering the message on behalf of two of Arbella's uncles, namely Henry and William Cavendish, who (Dodderidge was to tell Hertford) wished to propose a marriage between Arbella and Edward Seymour and that as a first step, Seymour, accompanied by either his father or grandfather, should come to Hardwick to discuss the matter. This visit would have to be made secretly however, and to this end, Arbella's message specified that Edward Seymour and whoever accompanied him should come to Hardwick in disguise, claiming that they wished to sell some land. They were also to bring with them some form of identification; Arbella suggested a picture or specimen of handwriting of Lady Jane Grey, or of Lady Katherine Grey or of Queen Jane Seymour, since she claimed she could recognise any of these. Dodderidge was initially very reluctant to carry out Arbella's instructions, very much doubting that Bess had approved all this (and she hadn't and at this point knew nothing of Arbella's intentions and nor did William Cavendish) but eventually he agreed. On Christmas Day of 1602, he set off for London on a horse supplied by Henry Cavendish, who clearly was involved in Arbella's intrigues one way or another.

He arrived at Hertford's house in London on the evening of 30th December 1602. Hertford, who in December 1600 had married his third wife, was no doubt anxious not to incur any more royal disfavour, particularly regarding marriage proposals, and was suspicious when Dodderidge began to recite the memorized message. Hertford made Dodderidge repeat his message in front of witnesses, following which

---

[1] That summer, Arbella also sent some of her jewels and money to a friend in Yorkshire for safe keeping after Bess threatened to confiscate them during one of their arguments.

he immediately sent word to Sir Robert Cecil advising him what had happened. As for Dodderidge (who by now must have been wishing he had never agreed to deliver Arbella's message in the first place), he was locked away pending interrogation.

Arbella's plan was clearly such nonsense that had Robert Cecil simply heard of it by way of rumour, it is likely that he would have dismissed it as romantic dreamings on Arbella's part. The fact that Dodderidge had actually come to London to deliver the message to Hertford made the whole affair appear far more ominous. On 2nd January 1603, Dodderidge was brought before the Privy Council, before whom he made a full confession of what he knew. The Queen and her Council concluded immediately that further investigation was warranted, and it was decided to send a royal commissioner, Sir Henry Brounker, to Hardwick as soon as possible. After being briefed on the matter personally by Queen Elizabeth, Brounker set off for Hardwick, where he arrived, without advance warning on 7th January.

Sir Henry Brounker was a member of Parliament and courtier known to be fiercely loyal to Queen Elizabeth; he was also seemingly a man of considerable tact and discretion, which is probably the reason why he was selected to go to Hardwick. Dodderidge had sworn repeatedly that Bess had known nothing of Arbella's plans, and the Queen and Council believed him. The matter had to be investigated thoroughly, but the Queen in particular must have been anxious not to upset Bess more than was absolutely necessary, hence the selection of Brounker as her commissioner.[2]

Brounker's unexpected arrival must have caused consternation at Hardwick New Hall, especially for Arbella, who had been expecting very different visitors. Upon Brounker's arrival being announced, Bess ordered that he be brought up to the long gallery at Hardwick New Hall,

---

[2] He seems to have been a kind man too. He went out of his way to ensure that Essex had at least some comfortable furniture in his cell in the Tower for his use during the last few days before his execution.

where she had been walking with Arbella and Sir William Cavendish. Brounker later recounted that upon meeting Bess, he had first stressed to her that he brought friendly greetings to her from the Queen, which seems to have been a great relief to the Dowager Countess of Shrewsbury. "The old lady took such comfort from this message" he later reported to Queen Elizabeth, "that I could hardly keep her from kneeling …" He then led Bess towards the far end of the gallery, away from Arbella and William, where they could speak privately, and handed her a letter from the Queen, which basically said she wished Brounker to have a private word with Arbella. By now, Bess must have been suspecting that Arbella had been up to some mischief, and apparently it was serious enough to warrant the despatch to Hardwick of a royal commissioner. Brounker would later report:

> *"In the reading thereof, I observed some change of countenance which gave me occasion again to comfort her with the assurance of your Majesty's good opinion and favour …".*

Arbella, when interviewed by Brounker, initially denied any wrongdoing; the problem was that she wasn't a very good liar, and she changed her story several times. Eventually, Brounker produced from his pocket Dodderidge's written confession, and Arbella, by now crying and terrified, while still trying to deny any improper involvement in a marriage proposal to Edward Seymour, eventually agreed to write down an account of what she claimed to know. Unfortunately, her account, when she finally produced it, was rambling, incoherent, and nonsensical in parts. Moreover, it contradicted elements of Dodderidge's confession which Arbella had not read in detail. Brounker began to wonder about her mental state, later reporting:

> *"… her wits were somewhat distracted either through fear of her own grandmother or conceit of her own folly".*

Eventually, Brounker himself wrote down a confession for Arbella to sign which she duly did.

As for Bess, Brounker took the decision that she should be told all that was known about the matter; when she heard, she was, according to Brounker:

> *"… wonderfully afflicted with the matter and much discomforted … that she took it so ill as with much ado she refrained her hands …"*

– that is to say, she was sorely tempted to strike Arbella. She was clearly very upset, and furious with her granddaughter.

Brounker departed shortly thereafter, carrying not only Arbella's confession, but also a letter from Arbella to the Queen apologising for her behaviour and "… craving pardon for what has passed …". Brounker also carried a letter from Bess addressed to the Queen and written on 9th January in which she stressed that she herself had known nothing of Arbella's scheming and asked whether Arbella might be

> *"… placed elsewhere, to learn to be more considerate, and after it may please your Majesty either to accept of her service about your royal person, or to bestow her in marriage …"*

Bess, it seems, had finally run out of patience so far as Arbella was concerned. As for Arbella, perhaps the only point on which she now agreed with her grandmother was the desirability of her leaving Hardwick as soon as possible, and both women must have waited anxiously for the Queen's answer to Bess's request.

Brounker's return journey to London took him a little longer than he expected, as he had a fall from his horse and damaged his back, but he was back on 13th January and reported to the Queen and Robert Cecil. His interviews with Arbella at Hardwick, and his discussions with Bess had led him to believe that the whole matter looked worse than it actually was and that Arbella had not really intended to challenge the Queen's position but had simply not thought through the likely consequences of her actions. He did concede that perhaps Arbella was being kept in too close a confinement at Hardwick, and admitted the possibility that "base companions" may have encouraged Arbella to act foolishly. He went out of his way to stress that Edward Seymour was not involved in the matter at all. This was accepted, and Cecil and the Queen were also inclined to agree with his assessment of Arbella's actions.

As regards the request that Arbella be moved elsewhere, the answer to that was a firm no, delivered in a letter written by Sir John Stanhope and Sir Robert Cecil on the Queen's behalf, the reason given being that the Queen could think of no better place for Arbella to be than Hardwick. The letter also repeated the suggestion that base companions may have led Arbella astray, and indicated that the Queen herself was inclined to take this view. It also included a recommendation that Arbella be permitted more freedom in the future. It was not the answer that either Bess or Arbella had been hoping for, and relations between the two of them worsened even more until they reached a point where they could communicate with each other only by written notes.

Despite Cecil and Stanhope recommending a relaxation of the regime at Hardwick under which Arbella was living, Bess took few or no steps to follow this advice. In fact, in some ways the regime was tightened; Arbella's letters to friends and indeed family were routinely intercepted, usually by Timothy Pusey, and when thought advisable, forwarded to Robert Cecil. This happened for example to a letter Arbella sent to John Hacker, who was a servant of Mary Talbot. In the letter, Arbella (who after all, knew Mary well and thought of her as an ally) beseeched Hacker to pass on a message to Mary begging her to come to Hardwick as soon as possible. The letter was intercepted and sent to Robert Cecil. Whether Mary ever received the letter is doubtful but she certainly didn't go to Hardwick in February 1603 in response to Arbella's request.

To her own eyes, Arbella's situation was becoming desperate, and it is difficult not to feel some sympathy for her plight. On the other hand, one can also feel sympathy for Bess, who was trying to carry out the Queen's instructions that she keep Arbella at Hardwick and safe from undesirable influences. Moreover, even after Brounker's visit in January 1603, Arbella did not always act in her own best interests. Around the end of that January, Arbella sent Bess a long and rambling letter in which she purportedly apologised for her behaviour and (incoherently) explained her supposed reasons for her dealings with Edward Seymour. She also discoursed at some length about an imaginary lover, a "noble gentleman" whose name she would not reveal; it was a complete fabrication, probably designed to taunt Bess, but Arbella also hinted that the imaginary gentleman would free her from Bess's custody. Bess almost certainly knew that this was all fictional, but taking no chances, she wrote to Stanhope and Cecil again, sending them a copy of Arbella's letter and essentially stating that Arbella's past history of lying and poor judgement made it very difficult to assess whether or not there was any truth in what Arbella had claimed. Bess asked again that consideration be given to moving Arbella elsewhere.

There were also developments in London. Dodderidge had been kept imprisoned after his appearance before the Privy Council and ultimately lost his position at Hardwick. Worse was to befall James Starkey; once his involvement in Arbella's scheming came to light (as it did), he was vigorously interrogated by agents working for Cecil. The experience broke him; on 1st February, after leaving a note of apology to Arbella, he hanged himself.

In the meantime, Arbella was writing long and often incomprehensible letters to Cecil, Stanhope and Brounker demanding that she be allowed to select her own servants and companions, not in itself perhaps an unreasonable request, and begging to speak with the Queen. Back in London, the frantic tone of the letters was causing some, including Robert Cecil, to begin to wonder whether Arbella was succumbing to madness. It was around this time that Cecil would write on the back of one of her letters: "I think that she hath some vapours on her brain". It has been suggested that she may actually have been suffering from porphyria, some of the symptoms of which can include hysterical behaviour. Mary, Queen of Scots may too have suffered from it (which would explain many of her bouts of illness), as did King George III.

On 21st February, Bess wrote a letter to Cecil reporting that Arbella was complaining that she had a pain in her side though Bess thought it was all in her mind – interestingly, another symptom of porphyria can be abdominal pains - and that Arbella was demanding to see Brounker once again. Bess beseeched Cecil to send Brounker as soon as he could, adding in a postscript that Arbella had declared that she would not eat or drink at Hardwick or wherever Bess was until she heard from Queen Elizabeth. For the preservation of Arbella's life, said Bess, she had been forced to send Arbella to Owlcotes for a time.

Arbella had returned to Hardwick by the time Brounker arrived for his second visit on 2nd March. He again interviewed Arbella, this time focussing on her supposed secret lover but as before, he found her replies to his questions evasive and at times self-contradictory. She refused to identify the mysterious lover[3] and Brounker had no choice but to return to London no wiser in this regard than when he arrived. Bess by now (by her standards at least) was almost frantic in her eagerness for Stanhope and Cecil to persuade the Queen to agree to move Arbella somewhere else, and when he left on 3rd March, Brounker carried a letter from Bess once more making this request. Bess added words to the effect that if she had to live through many more weeks like the last few she had endured, it would be the end of her – those were emotional and no doubt heart-felt words for Bess, but once again, they fell on deaf ears. On 14th March, the Council wrote to Bess reiterating that Arbella was to stay with Bess, but suggesting that some of the burdens of dealing with her might be shared with her son William. The Council also evidently had not yet finished making its enquiries into the

---

[3] Some biographers assert that Arbella eventually named King James VI as the imaginary lover, but it seems more likely that if she did mention him, it probably was a comment made sarcastically rather than sincerely, and it certainly wasn't taken seriously by Brounker or anyone else. This is unsurprising since by now King James was married to Anne of Denmark and had yet to set foot in England. Moreover, he and Arbella had never even met, though to be fair, that hadn't been an impediment to Arbella when she had been seeking to make a proposal to Edward Seymour.

matter of the supposed Seymour marriage proposal. In that same letter, the Council reminded Bess that they were expecting a response from Henry Cavendish explaining his part in the matter.

As a matter of fact, Henry had been becoming more and more involved in his dealings with Arbella. He had somehow managed to get in touch with her once again without Bess's knowledge (it may have happened during Arbella's short stay at Owlcotes) and seemingly, together with a Catholic called Henry Stapleton, they put together a plan to help Arbella "escape" from Bess. The plan, initially scheduled for the morning of 10th March, required Henry, Stapleton and a band of eight men, with another 32 (or more) in reserve, to ride to Ault Hucknall Church and from the church tower there to wait and look out for Arbella, who was sometimes in the habit of walking to the church. The intention was that they would then spirit Arbella away on horseback. Unfortunately for Henry and Stapleton, they were unable to persuade the local vicar to provide them with the key to the church (it seems the vicar was suspicious of their intentions). In any event, while they were there, two of Arbella's servants arrived to inform them that Arbella had been unable to leave Hardwick.

Dispersing most of their men, Henry and Stapleton decided to ride to Hardwick New Hall, and they arrived at the porter's lodge by the hall's main gates at two o'clock. Henry explained he wished to visit Arbella, and Bess sent word that he was to be permitted entry. Stapleton however was not, Bess had encountered him before, and disliked and mistrusted him. By now she had also been made aware that Henry and Stapleton had been seen in the company of a band of armed men and had made sure the gates to Hardwick New Hall were locked and that the hall itself was guarded by some of her retainers.

Henry entered and spoke briefly and in private with Arbella, and they then announced that they wished to go through the gates to speak with Stapleton. When Bess heard of that, she forbade Arbella to leave the grounds of the hall, giving later (in a letter to Brounker) the explanation that she did not think it advisable for Arbella to meet Stapleton. Arbella asked if she was now a "true prisoner" of Bess, and declared that she would soon see if that was so. She then tried to open and go through the gates, but on Bess's instructions, the gates remained locked. At that moment at least, it transpired that she was a true prisoner of Bess. Arbella briefly spoke through the gates to Stapleton, asking him to hold himself in readiness to come back another day, but there was little that he or Henry could do, so they departed. Before they left, Arbella asked that Henry come to visit her the following day, but Bess forbade that too.

That evening, Bess wrote an account of what happened in a letter to Brounker.[4] Inevitably Cecil was informed. In London, Bess's account seemed even more serious than it might have seemed to her; before receiving Brounker's report of his first visit to Hardwick in January, Cecil in particular had been worried that Arbella might have become a secret Catholic. In fact she hadn't, and Brounker had been able to reassure Cecil and the rest of the Council of this. Now though, the actions of Henry and Stapleton had all the appearance of an attempt to seize Arbella (possibly with her willing assistance), as part of one more plot by Catholic sympathisers to oust Queen Elizabeth from her throne. Brounker rushed up to Hardwick once again, but Arbella would not see him, refusing, as she declared, to leave her room until she regained her freedom. Temporarily frustrated by Arbella's intransigence, Brounker interviewed Arbella's servants, Henry Cavendish,[5] villagers in Ault Hucknall, and in fact just about everyone in the vicinity of Hardwick with even the slightest connection with the matter. The one person who wasn't interviewed was Stapleton; he had fled to London by the time Brounker arrived at Hardwick on 17th March.

During this third visit to Hardwick, Brounker learned little more than he had known before setting off from London. His report back to the

---

[4] It was in that letter of 10th March that Bess referred to Henry as being her "bad son".

[5] He ultimately seems to have escaped any form of sanction for his part in attempting to help Arbella escape from Hardwick.

Council in London did have one positive result, however. It was decided that Arbella should be removed from Hardwick without delay, partly because it was now felt it was dangerous for her to remain in an area where there was still a considerable degree of sympathy for the Catholic cause, and partly to relieve the burden on Bess. It was decided Arbella should move to and remain at Wrest Park in Bedfordshire, home of Henry Grey, the Earl of Kent, whose nephew had married Elizabeth Talbot, and she finally left Hardwick towards the end of March. As for Bess, she presumably was happy to see the back of Arbella, and of Henry too for that matter. To emphasise the point, on 20th March, she summoned her lawyer to amend the will she had made back in April 1601 to disinherit Arbella, who under the original version of the will had been left various jewels and pearls and £1000 in cash. Henry too was disinherited. Bess couldn't prevent him from being heir to Chatsworth as this property had been entailed to him under his father's will, but her original will had specified that he was to receive all that house's contents. This gift was now revoked.

It is doubtful (but not impossible) that Henry and Stapleton really intended to kidnap Arbella as part of a plot to remove Queen Elizabeth, though there is also no doubt that Henry Cavendish was at the very least being reckless in associating with Stapleton, whose Catholic sympathies by now were notorious. It is more likely that Henry simply wanted to create mischief for his mother. If, however, he and Stapleton had seriously been planning to kidnap Arbella with a view to treason, and assuming they could have succeeded, the timing would have been very interesting, because whilst Henry and Stapleton were concocting and then failing to implement their plans successfully, Queen Elizabeth back in London was very ill. Actually, she was dying, though very few people knew that in early March 1603. Even Bess probably wasn't aware of it.

The Queen's health had been failing for several months; her condition noticeably worsened after the death of her cousin, friend and lady-in-waiting Katherine Howard, the Countess of Nottingham on 25th February 1603. Exactly what the Queen was suffering from is unknown; some have suggested food poisoning, others have suggested poisoning due to her use of lead-based makeup, still others have suggested bronchitis or pneumonia. What is known is that after the Countess of Nottingham's death, the Queen began to refuse to eat and drink, sitting motionless on cushions in Richmond Palace and displaying a "settled and unremovable melancholia", falling prey at last to advancing age.

She began to speak only rarely, despite the cautious efforts of those around her to engage her interests and raise her spirits. When her godson Sir John Harington[6] tried to cheer her up by telling her a joke, she said:

> *"When thou dost feel creeping time at thy gate, these fooleries will please thee less – I am past my relish for such matters"*

and fell silent once more. But even now she was still capable of showing an occasional spark of Elizabethan wit and determination. When Robert Cecil told her that she must go to bed, she responded as she might have done in years gone by:

> *"Must is not a word to be used to princes! Little man, little man, if your father had lived, you durst not hath said so, but ye know I must die and it makes ye so presumptuous!"*

But she suffered her attendants to move her to her bed.

By this time, Sir Robert Cecil had been in secret communication with King James about his likely succession to the throne for nearly two

---

[6] Incidentally an interesting man. Amongst his various achievements was the creation of the epigram: "Why does treason never prosper? Because if it does prosper, why, none dare call it treason." He was something of a favourite with Queen Elizabeth – she called him her "saucy godson" - but his writings could sometimes be too risqué for the Queen's tastes and periodically they got him into trouble. More prosaically, he is often credited with the creation of England's first flush toilet, though it wasn't perfect, partly due to the materials he was forced to work with and partly because the concept of the "S bend" pipe designed to prevent the leakage of noxious odours from the sewers up through the toilet itself had yet to be invented.

years,[7] but in the interests of ensuring a smooth succession, there still remained the task of gaining the Queen's agreement, and preferably in front of witnesses. On 22nd March 1603, he, together with the Earl of Nottingham and Sir Thomas Egerton, the Lord Keeper of the Great Seal[8] assembled around the Queen's bed and asked Elizabeth to name her successor. That was when the Queen referred to her throne as a seat of kings and asked who could succeed her other than a king. Cecil thought a little more clarity was needed and asked her whom she meant. "Who but our cousin of Scotland" she replied, raising herself a little and then, settling back onto her bed again, asked them to trouble her no more.

Alas, it was felt they had to, as it was deemed advisable for the Queen to declare her wishes before a larger body of witnesses. Those witnesses assembled at Richmond Palace on the afternoon of 23rd March, but they found the Queen barely conscious and incapable of speech. Again, Cecil took the lead, and asked her to give a sign that she meant her throne to pass to King James. She slowly moved her hands above her head, and spread her fingers to imitate the shape of a crown. Her last task as England's monarch was done.

She died shortly after two o'clock in the morning of 24th March 1603. Sir Robert Cecil immediately despatched riders to notify King James in Scotland that he had acceded to the English throne. The Council was assembled and informed, and the next day, proclamations were issued all over the country announcing James as the new King of England. The news by and large seems to have been received without significant

---

[7] Cecil had long since secretly decided that it was in the country's interests for James to succeed Queen Elizabeth; if he ever had any lingering doubts as to whether Arbella might not prove the better choice, Arbella's recent behaviour at Hardwick must have promptly dispersed them.

[8] He was the friend of Essex who had tried to persuade him to apologise to the Queen after the incident in the Council meeting when he had begun to draw his sword on her. During Essex's rebellion, he had been sent to Essex House in attempt to gain Essex's surrender; instead, he had been seized and held hostage for a few hours until he was released by one of Essex's supporters. And he had been a judge at Essex's trial for treason and pronounced sentence on him.

opposition.[9] Sir Robert Cecil had cause to be pleased, "The King's ship", he said:

> *"has come into the right harbour without cross of wave or tide that could overturn a cock-boat."*

Nobody seemed to be concerned what Arbella might have thought.

---

[9] There were, it must be said, rumours that Edward, Lord Beauchamp had travelled to the West Country where he was planning to raise a force of several thousand men to challenge King James' accession (Frances Pierrepont mentioned those rumours in a letter she wrote to Bess in early April – she seems to have been unimpressed by what she had heard, for in the letter she referred to Beauchamp's "feeble assemblies"), but in the event, even if Beauchamp had been planning such a course of action, he presumably changed his mind because nothing came of it.

Chapter 22

The Final Days

Although we have no explicit record of Bess's reaction to the death of Queen Elizabeth, the news that the Queen had died, when it reached Hardwick, must have caused Bess considerable distress; after all, the two women had known each other since before the Queen's accession. Elizabeth's death (she had been 69 when she died, considerably younger than Bess was in 1603) would also have served as another reminder, if one was needed, of Bess's own mortality. Indeed, it may have had an even deeper and more profound effect than that. Already, many of the friends and acquaintances of Bess's youth and middle age had passed away, and though Bess's life still had a number of years to run, the Queen's death in particular must have made Bess acutely aware that the Tudor, and above all the Elizabethan era, the world she knew so well, was rapidly drawing to a close. There were some similarities between that era, and Jacobean one which was to follow it, of course, but there were also differences which began to manifest themselves swiftly once King James was on the throne. The Jacobean world, especially at Court, became coarser and darker than that of Elizabethan times, there was more extravagance, more greed, more corruption and, generally speaking, a worsening of morals. As she was now living permanently at Hardwick, Bess was perhaps somewhat insulated from the changes that were to come, but she wouldn't have been the woman she was if she hadn't sensed that those changes were coming.

Queen Elizabeth's funeral was scheduled to be held on 28th April 1603 at Westminster. Whilst the preparations were being finalised, King James was making his way to London, having departed Edinburgh on 5th April. As he and his party slowly moved south, the most powerful of his new subjects vied to meet him and to offer the hospitality of their houses, all eager to curry favour and establish good relations with their new sovereign. Some rode north to greet him; Robert Cecil did so for instance, joining the new King at York on 17th April. From Cecil's perspective, that meeting was a success. Though he would never feel fully at ease with King James (nor did King James with him), Cecil succeeded in establishing a sufficiently close relationship with James (or at least the simulation of one) for his position as Secretary of State, which he had held when Queen Elizabeth died, to be confirmed by the new sovereign. It was a position Cecil would hold for the rest of his life.

Another eager to establish good relations with King James was Gilbert Talbot. Upon hearing of James's accession, Gilbert had written to him offering to serve him and inviting the King to break his journey south for a few days at Worksop Manor, and James was pleased to accept. The fact that Gilbert's father had supervised the execution of James's mother seems not to have been a problem.

James and his party arrived at Worksop Manor on 20th April, where they stayed for several days being lavishly (and expensively) entertained by Gilbert and Mary. Gilbert in particular was very proud of this early sign of apparent royal approval and invited many of the local nobles and gentry to join the party, though perhaps mindful of his still parlous financial situation, he stressed that he would not be offended if they wished to bring fat capons, hens, partridges and the like with them. As for James and his fellow Scots, they seem to have been overawed by the various prodigy houses they visited on their journey south, especially Worksop;[1] the contrast between the beauties of Elizabethan prodigy houses and many of the grim and remote Scottish castles they were used to must have been stark indeed.

Mary Talbot too took pride in apparent royal favour, and shortly after the King's arrival at Worksop, she took advantage of it by asking the King to agree to allow Arbella the freedom to leave Wrest Park. Now

---

[1] James also is said to have been awed and dazzled by Cecil's palace at Theobalds, inherited from his father and which the King visited in May. He must indeed have liked it, for a few years later, he offered to exchange Hatfield Palace for it, and Cecil accepted the offer. Robert Cecil would go on to build a new and spectacular house at Hatfield, and his descendants have lived there ever since.

James had been proclaimed King, he could afford to be magnanimous to his cousin, and once established in London, in response to Mary's request, he invited Arbella to visit him at the Court then assembled at Greenwich.

King James did not attend Queen Elizabeth's funeral, but that would not have seemed unusual, given the length of his journey from Edinburgh to London. Nor did Bess, she no doubt considered she was now too old to journey to Westminster herself. James did ask Arbella (who appears to have accepted King James' accession to the throne of England with surprising equanimity) to be the Principal Mourner at the funeral, but she refused. Now at Wrest Park, she sent word essentially saying that as in recent years, she had not been permitted access to the Queen, she would not after the Queen's death "… be brought upon the stage for a public spectacle …" In the event, the Marchioness of Northampton assumed the role of Principal Mourner, and Arbella remained cloistered at Wrest Park until mid-May when she accepted the King's invitation to visit the Court at Greenwich. Mary Talbot accompanied her there.

Perhaps not unexpectedly, Henry Cavendish, who had been keeping a low profile following his dealings with Stapleton, re-appeared in Bess's life in April 1603 to bedevil her once more. By now Henry was again living unhappily at Tutbury with his wife Grace,[2] and very short of money. He seems to have contacted Sir Robert Cecil seeking assistance, possibly asking him to intercede with his mother in the hope that this might induce Bess to provide Henry with some financial aid. If this was indeed his hope, it was soon to be dashed, for on 13th April 1603, Bess wrote to Cecil in tones which, given their long-standing friendship, were surprisingly stern. She refused to assist her "unnatural son" and reminded Cecil (as if he needed reminding) of Henry's recent attempts to remove Arbella from Hardwick. She pointedly referred to Henry's part in the suborning of members of her household (she presumably

---

[2] A year or so later, Henry would spitefully declare that Grace was a harlot, and accuse her of sleeping with some of his servants.

was thinking of Dodderidge and possibly Starkey) and essentially declared that while she had no friend who stood a better chance of persuading her to relent than Cecil, she had been so hardly and unnaturally dealt with that she could not agree to do so even for him.[3]

A change of monarch did not mean an end to the incessant plots to oust the sovereign from the throne, and two plots in particular arose in that year of 1603. The two plots were linked and the first, the Bye Plot, the smaller of the two conspiracies, arose in June. The exact details of both plots are somewhat obscure since those involved subsequently gave wildly contradictory evidence, trying to implicate others to save their own skins. Nevertheless, it seems clear that the broad aims of the conspirators in the case of the Bye Plot, who were a strange mixture of Roman Catholics and Puritans, were first, the removal from power (and probably from life) of Robert Cecil, and secondly encouragement of the King to pass laws permitting religious tolerance, the encouragement to be rendered by the kidnapping of the King. In fact, the Bye Plot probably never got beyond the general discussion stage; it failed because some of the Catholic conspirators reported the matter to the government as they were worried about possible retribution against Catholics generally.

The Main Plot was a far more serious affair. Some of the conspirators in the Main Plot had links to those involved in the Bye Plot. The aims of this plot seem to have been drawn up in parallel with those of the Bye Plot, but this time they included not only the removal of various ministers (including, inevitably, Robert Cecil), but also the assassination of King James and his eldest son Henry, (later to become the Prince of Wales), and the placing of Arbella on the throne in James' stead.

---

[3] Bess was similarly cold in her refusal to help Arbella financially when Cecil raised this with Bess a few months later; Bess had ceased supporting Arbella when she left Hardwick. Eventually, the King agreed to provide her with £660 in cash, and a yearly pension of £800 (about £276,000 today), which was raised to £1000 a few months later. Admittedly this was better than the £200 pension which was all that Queen Elizabeth had been prepared to provide Arbella, but on the other hand, now that she was free to attend King James' Court, Arbella's expenses had increased dramatically. She was still short of money.

Unfortunately for the Main Plot conspirators, details of that Plot's existence were revealed during the interrogation of some of the conspirators involved in the Bye Plot, and a series of arrests of those involved were made during the summer months of 1603. Amongst those arrested were Sir George Brooke and his brother Henry Brooke, the Eleventh Lord Cobham (incidentally both George and Henry Brooke were brothers-in-law to Robert Cecil and Cobham was one of Bess's godsons) and Sir Walter Raleigh. The two sets of conspirators were tried in November 1603 in Winchester and all but one found guilty of treason. Some (like Sir George Brooke) were executed, others (like Cobham, who lost his titles, and Sir Walter Raleigh) were imprisoned.

It was accepted that Arbella had no knowledge of the Plots. During the trials however, some of those charged had alleged that Henry Cavendish had been involved. He was summoned to London for examination; it must have been a worrying Christmas for him. He was eventually exonerated but appears to have returned to Tutbury depressed. His money problems continued to weigh down upon him and Bess showed no sign of being willing to relent sufficiently to provide him with some financial assistance. Nor had she shown him any support when he was being examined for possible involvement in the Main Plot. As far as Bess was concerned, Henry would have to address his problems, financial or otherwise, on his own. This stony refusal to help also extended to Grace, notwithstanding that Bess was fond of her daughter-in-law.

By April 1604, Henry's financial woes had reached such a state that he was beginning to think that he would have no choice but to sell his reversionary interest in Chatsworth (Bess still had her life interest of course which would expire when she died). Edward Talbot heard rumours to this effect around this time and wrote to Grace to ask if it was true that Henry was contemplating selling Chatsworth to Gilbert. Grace wrote back on Henry's behalf essentially confirming that "great and extreme necessity" would make a sale necessary in due course. Gilbert however was then in no position to buy Chatsworth even if he had wanted to, and had declined to do so. In her letter to Edward, Grace added: "… we are hardly dealt with by my old Lady and my Lord …" (meaning both Bess and Gilbert). Whether Henry at this time looked for another potential buyer elsewhere is unclear, but if he did, he failed to find one, as he retained his reversionary ownership of Chatsworth until 1609, when (after Bess's death), he sold it to his brother William Cavendish for £8000.[4]

As for William, in 1604, he married again. His second wife had been born Elizabeth Boughton, and was the widow of Sir Richard Wortley, a Yorkshire landowner. Together, she and William would have a son, John, who would be knighted in 1616. Elizabeth seems to have been a woman of strong character, and occasionally clashed with Bess. Bess moreover did not always win these engagements; on at least one occasion, one of their arguments was only resolved when Bess apologised to Elizabeth for her behaviour, which was not exactly an everyday occurrence. Perhaps wisely, if only from the perspective of seeking to maintain domestic harmony, William and Elizabeth moved to Owlcotes, though William seems to have continued to operate out of Hardwick Old Hall when engaged on his mother's business interests.

In the meantime, Arbella had been enjoying herself mixing in royal circles. Anne of Denmark, King James' Queen, had followed her husband to England (like her husband, paying a visit to Gilbert and Mary Talbot at Worksop Manor along the way), arriving in London in early July. King James' English coronation was held at Westminster Abbey on 25th July; it isn't clear whether Arbella was present but she may well have been. In any event, at this time, she was being treated with some distinction at Court,[5] as a close relative of the King, and she appears to have soon become a favourite of Queen Anne and was given the honour of carrying the Queen's train when she went to Chapel, as

---

[4] Just before Bess's death, there had been some discussion between William and Henry about William buying Chatsworth, but they had been unable then to agree a price.

[5] At this time, when not at Court, she based herself at the home of the Marchioness of Northampton in Sheen.

well as being seated close to the Royal Family at feasts and other public spectacles.

Notwithstanding her disagreements with Bess, Arbella had contrived to remain on good terms with Gilbert and Mary Talbot (indeed, when they were not at Court, she wrote to them endlessly keeping them informed of the latest developments). At this time of her life, now that she had achieved her wish of escaping from Hardwick, she seems to have settled down, and there was no more talk about the possibility of her being "hysterical" or otherwise mad. Indeed, her letters from this time seem rational and balanced. She may have been missing her family more than she liked to admit however; certainly, when William Cavendish paid a visit to Court in the summer of 1604, she seems to have been pleased to see him (and he to see her). Indeed, she was so pleased that by July, she had commenced a campaign to persuade King James to grant William a barony. Her campaign would not generate immediate results, but the seed for William's elevation into the peerage had been sown.

She even seems to have begun to think more fondly of Bess once more, and arranged for a relative (William Kniveton, the son of Bess's half-sister Jane who was still at Hardwick) not only to deliver a verbal greeting to Bess but also a brief note. Bess's reaction to this is not known, but she must have at least suspected that part of Arbella's motivation for seeking to re-establish reasonable relations with her grandmother was financial self-interest. Nevertheless, there does also seem to have been a genuine desire on Arbella's part to heal the rift between herself and Bess, at least to some extent.

In February 1605, Bess was taken ill with what one of her neighbours described in a letter to Gilbert as her "old infirmity". Exactly what the infirmity was is not clear, but it was sufficiently serious for rumours to begin to spread that it was possibly fatal. The news reached Arbella at Court, and she asked permission of the King to leave the Court to visit Bess. The King agreed, and also wrote a letter to Bess urging her to treat Arbella kindly. Bess appears to have reacted cautiously to this latest overture from Arbella, writing to her friend James Montague, the Dean of the Chapel Royal (and probably anticipating that the King would see her letter) that she found it strange that Arbella should be so eager to visit Hardwick when only recently, she had been so eager to leave it. She also made the point that she believed she had treated Arbella kindly and with generosity in the past and that while Arbella was welcome to visit her at Hardwick, she had "… divers grandchildren that stood more in need [of financial support] than she". Nevertheless, Arbella's visit to her grandmother appears to have gone as well as might have been hoped, given the history of Arbella and Bess, and there does seem to have been at least a degree of reconciliation between the two of them. When Arbella departed from Hardwick to return to the Court, she brought back with her a gift of £300 and a gold cup worth £100.

Back at Court, preparations were being made for the christening of a new royal baby, the Princess Mary, and Arbella was asked to be a godmother. The ceremony was held on 19th April, and was the cause of considerable celebration, not least because the baby was the first child of the King and Queen to be born on English soil. The King took the opportunity to announce the creation of several new peers and the promotion of others; Robert Cecil for instance (who had been created Baron Cecil of Essendon in May 1603 and Viscount Cranborne the year after that) was raised another rank in the peerage to become the Earl of Salisbury though his actual elevation would not happen until 4th May 1605. His brother Thomas would be created the Earl of Exeter on the same day. As for Arbella, she had not abandoned her efforts to encourage the King to make William a peer, and now the King was willing to indulge her. He gave her a blank patent for the creation of a barony and told her she could insert the name of any recipient she chose. She chose William, of course, and he became Baron Cavendish of Hardwick, a title which must have delighted Bess when she heard of it.[6] The King's indulgence of Arbella had a price however, specifically

---

[6] William was one of eight peers who held a canopy over Princess Mary as she was carried to the font for her christening. Sadly, Princess Mary died from pneumonia seventeen months later.

£2000, a payment (presumably made to the King although this isn't entirely clear – it may have been paid to Arbella) which was duly recorded in William Cavendish's accounts book. It seems likely that Bess provided the money.

Arbella may have remained on good terms with Gilbert and Mary Talbot, but the financial wranglings between Gilbert and Bess were still ongoing. In June 1605, Bess received a letter from Thomas, Lord Ellesmere, the Lord Chancellor, asking her formally to respond to a bill which Gilbert had filed against her. Gilbert was now alleging that Bess had improperly spoiled and laid waste lands which he claimed rightfully were his, and had done so specifically by chopping down trees and sinking coal mines. Bess countered that on the contrary, the lands were hers for her lifetime (they were lands over which Shrewsbury had granted her a life interest) and in any event, Gilbert still owed her £4000 in respect of her marriage settlement rights. Bess won the case, but was very angry with Gilbert.

November 1605 brought the news of the thwarting of the Gunpowder Plot, the attempt by Catholic conspirators to blow up the King and Parliament, and ultimately those of the conspirators who had not died in the course of the Plot were executed.[7] There were however suggestions that Gilbert had been somehow associated with the conspirators (Mary Talbot had known one of them and Gilbert's cousin had been approached by another seeking asylum as he tried to evade arrest) and as in the case of Henry in relation to the Main Plot, Gilbert too was interrogated (in the Tower). Luckily (for him), Gilbert managed to convince the authorities of his innocence, but again as in the case of

---

[7] James Montague kept Bess informed by letter about developments in relation to the Plot and its aftermath, especially the trials of the surviving conspirators. They were all sentenced to hanging, drawing and quartering. Guy Fawkes managed to avoid this fate (though he had been horrendously tortured during the course of his interrogations after being arrested) by falling (or jumping) off the scaffold and breaking his neck.

Henry in relation to the Main Plot, it must have been a worrying time for him and Mary.

By early 1606, Bess was noticeably beginning to succumb to the problems of old age. She was ill once again at the beginning of the year, confined to her bedchamber for several weeks, and by June she was having some difficulty walking due to her arthritis. Ill-health made her tetchy, and her mood was not helped by the continuing legal disputes with Gilbert. There were however still some good times; Gilbert and Mary's daughter, Alethea, married Thomas Howard, Earl of Arundel in September 1606 and this was a match supported strongly not only by her parents but also by Bess. Arundel had only recently been allowed the opportunity of enjoying being an earl, his earldom having been attainted during the life of his father and it had only been restored to the Howards in 1604.

The marriage helped to pave the way for something of a reconciliation between Bess and the Talbots. Within a year, Alethea was pregnant and gave birth to a son John, who took the courtesy title of Lord Maltravers. Alethea and the Earl had originally intended to ask Bess to be his godmother, but Queen Anne decided she wanted this role and Arundel had to write a letter to Bess on 27th June 1607 explaining what had happened. He prudently added that if for whatever reason the Queen changed her mind, he and Alethea would once again be asking Bess to assume the role of godmother. Bess does not seem to have been noticeably distressed by this, and the christening proceeded at Whitehall in July. Bess took the opportunity of sending Mary Talbot a "fair and well wrought ermine" to celebrate the event. Mary in turn responded with a letter of thanks on 8th July, saying that she was glad the pain in Bess's hip had improved (presumably the warm weather was helping to ease Bess's arthritis) but added that she herself had been suffering from headaches. It was the start of a genuine rapprochement. By the end of November, Bess was feeling sufficiently friendly to the Talbots for her to write to Mary asking for news of themselves and "little sweet Lord Maltravers".

The winter of 1607 and early 1608 was bitterly cold in England.[8] Unsurprisingly, the cold weather affected Bess's health, and this prompted a visit from Gilbert and Mary, together with Charles Cavendish, in early December. The visit appears to have gone well, though it was the first time Bess and Gilbert had been in the same room together for several years. Gilbert later reported back to Robert Cecil that he and Mary had found Bess "... a great lady, of great wealth and great wit ...", adding that there had been no mention of the legal disputes he and Bess had been engaged in ever since Shrewsbury's death, but rather only "compliments, courtesy and kindness". In a separate letter to Henry Cavendish however, Gilbert commented that Bess was barely eating and no longer able to walk the length of her great gallery even with the assistance of two people.

On 30th December 1607, Mary Talbot had sent her mother a cushion for her to use during her daily prayers. By now though Bess's health was beginning to fail fast. In early January 1608, Gilbert wrote to inform Henry that Mrs Digby had sent the Talbots a secret message that Bess was now so ill that she "... could not be from her day or night ..." Bess was now largely confined to her bed, probably suffering from some form of bronchial infection or pneumonia.

As her condition worsened, Henry, Gilbert (and Mary) and William were watching each other carefully, all anxious to make sure none of the others took unfair advantage of Bess's ill-health to improve their likely inheritances. Henry and Gilbert were particularly worried about William; they had long since realised that in many ways, William was her favourite son[9] and he had the advantage not only of being constantly at Hardwick but also of being so intimately involved in Bess's business affairs. Gilbert told Henry that he had heard that William had given an

---

[8] So cold in fact that the River Thames in London froze. It was cold across the Northern Hemisphere generally. In England, it became known as the "Great Freeze".

[9] Though she did once tell Mrs Digby that she had a greater liking for Charles and Frances than she had for William.

order to the effect that as soon as Bess died, all the cattle and sheep on the lands at Ewden in Yorkshire were to be driven elsewhere; these were lands that would revert back to Gilbert when Bess died. William could not prevent that from happening, but he took the view that the cattle and sheep belonged to Bess outright (and he was probably right about that).

In early January 1608, William and Wylkyn were at Court for the Christmas celebrations when word was sent to him to return to Hardwick at once. He hastened back and found his mother still alive. She was pleased to see him, though she told him she thought she was dying. Over the next few days, William spent much time with Bess, who was anxious to give him details of her last wishes as regards her business interests and advice of how best to protect the family fortune. Her mind sometimes began to wander; she became very concerned that her will be honoured, and ordered that William inform the Chancellor of Lichfield that she had made a will and that it was not to be interfered with. William for once disobeyed his mother; he knew the will was safe and that her lawyers were aware of it and so he did nothing. A day or so later, Bess asked him if he had yet contacted the Chancellor and was noticeably annoyed when he said he had not.

Bess spent much of her last few days making minor alterations to her will, recorded as a codicil by her faithful Timothy Pusey. She left as a last-minute bequest to Mary Talbot her "pearl bed", that is the marriage bed she had shared with William Cavendish, though Mary was to be denied the hangings that went with it. She wanted to leave £100 to Mrs Digby and a gold cup valued at £100 to Robert Cecil, and £100 to her alms houses in Derby. £20 was left to each of her other ladies-in-waiting. Charles too was not forgotten; he had long since been excluded from his mother's will, but as he was independently wealthy, this mattered little to him. Nevertheless, Bess clearly wanted to make some sort of gesture to him and so she left him 4000 marks so he could buy lands for his two sons. None of these last-minute alterations were significant and William raised no objection to them.

Her family doctor, Doctor Hunton, moved into Hardwick on 2nd February but Bess by now was beyond the help of Jacobean medicine. On 13th February, Charles, Gilbert and Mary arrived, and together with William, they gathered in a small room next to Bess's bedchamber. Late in the afternoon, Mary was summoned to see her mother privately. Mrs Digby later noted that William became extremely concerned about this, and she concluded that William was worried that Mary might make a last-minute attempt to persuade Bess to make a dramatic alteration to her will. In fact, it seems that Bess simply wanted to say farewell to Mary without the others being present. Gilbert later reported to Robert Cecil that Mary had told him that Bess had had the great blessing of sense and memory to the end.

Bess died around five o'clock in the afternoon of 13th February 1608.

Chapter 23

Legacy

Bess was to be buried as a Countess, which meant that her funeral arrangements would be prepared under the guidance of the Garter King of Arms. These arrangements inevitably took some time to be put in place, and in the meantime, her body had to be readied for burial in a manner that minimised putrefaction. An embalmer was summoned, her body was drained of blood and disembowelled, she was embalmed and her body then sealed in wax. It then lay for four days in Hardwick New Hall, draped in a black cloth, before it was transported to All Hallows Church in Derby, where it was placed in a lead coffin in the vault Bess had ordered be constructed back in 1601, pending her funeral service.

Arbella came to visit and pay her respects; she stayed with the Talbots at Sheffield Castle but travelled to Hardwick while Bess's body was still there. She is reported to have sat silently next to it for some time.

William, as his mother's sole executor, took charge of the task of beginning the administration of Bess's estate, whilst awaiting finalisation of the funeral arrangements. One of the first things he did was to pay Doctor Hutton 40 marks for his services. Then he turned his attention to Bess's will. Her will was relatively simple given the size of her estate. She left £2000 to cover her funeral expenses. In her will, she had specified that her funeral should not be "… over sumptuous, or otherwise performed with too much vain or idle charge …", a request one would think impossible to discharge given that she was to be buried as a Countess. In fact, her funeral costs ultimately amounted to £3257, which was more than each of the funerals of Lord Burghley and Leicester had cost. Other bequests included £1000 to be shared amongst her servants, and £100 to each of the Lord Chancellor and the Archbishop of Canterbury. King James received a gold cup worth £200. And Arbella received £1000, perhaps as thanks for her help in obtaining a peerage for William. William's two surviving children, Wylkyn and

Frances, each also received £1000. She left 20 shillings to each of the residents in her alms houses.

As for her children, she had already during her lifetime given significant amounts of land to both Charles and William (especially to the latter).[1] Under her will, she now gave William the contents of both Hardwick Old Hall and Hardwick New Hall, as well of those of Owlcotes and Chatsworth. Her daughter Frances was provided with a costly book of gold and inset with rubies and a diamond which her father had given to Bess and which Bess had cherished. Mary simply received the pearl bed Bess had included in her last codicil. Henry Cavendish received nothing, as did Gilbert Talbot. Bess had stayed true to her word of ensuring they were excluded as beneficiaries.

Not unnaturally, the provisions of Bess's will were the cause a great deal of mutual resentment between her children. All of them (except William) thought that the will was too generous to him, but some were more angered than others. Mary, though she genuinely grieved her mother's death, was bitter about only having received the pearl bed; she had hoped that her reconciliation with her mother in the last year or so of her life might have led to Bess increasing the size of *her* bequest. As for Henry, he tried to challenge the codicil which denied him the contents of Chatsworth but failed. Frances may have been disappointed that she received no more than a book, but perhaps took comfort from knowing that it had been commissioned by her father and was a treasured heirloom – it contained a picture of both Sir William Cavendish and Bess. Charles, as previously noted, by this time was independently wealthy, and so was perhaps less troubled by Bess's will than some of his siblings, but was no doubt happy to accept Bess's gift of 4000 marks intended for his sons. And as for Gilbert, as soon as Bess

---

[1] Shortly after Bess's death, both William and Charles commissioned surveys of their respective estates. They took nineteen years to complete, and when finished (after both William and Charles themselves had died), they revealed that both families possessed 100,000 or more acres of land.

had died, he began the process of reclaiming the Talbot lands over which Bess had enjoyed life interests.

Bess's funeral was eventually scheduled for 4th May 1608 (there had been a memorial service a little while earlier), but before that happened, there was another family event, namely the wedding of William's eighteen-year-old son Wylkyn to Christian Bruce, the twelve year old daughter of Lord Kinross, which was held in London on 10th April. Both families approved of the match (it may in fact have been the last example of Bess's matchmaking). The problem was that Wylkyn didn't want to marry Christian as he was in love with someone else, namely Margaret Chatterton, who had been one of the ladies of Bess's household. Nevertheless, he had to go through with it and it is perhaps just as well that he did, for he was to die relatively young and in considerable debt, and it was Christian who managed to salvage the situation so that her son William, who became the Third Earl of Devonshire, had a family fortune to inherit.

There are no contemporary accounts of Bess's funeral, but based on guidance issued by the College of Arms from around this time which set out the procedures to be expected at the funeral of such a high-ranking person, together with details of payments that were made as recorded in William's account books, it may be possible for us to gain at least a general picture of how her funeral would have proceeded. All those attending would have entered All Hallows Church slowly in a solemn procession, led by a knight carrying a banner displaying Bess's coat of arms. He would have been followed by heralds from the College of Arms, and then Bess's coffin (temporarily removed from the vault for the purposes of the service), carried by six gentlemen. Two ushers carrying white rods would be behind them, and then Mary Talbot would have followed as the lady chief mourner, with the long train of her mourning dress carried by one of her ladies-in-waiting. Mary would have been supported by two hooded barons, and followed by the rest of Bess's family (excluding Gilbert Talbot and Henry Cavendish, who seem have chosen not to attend). They in turn would have been followed by the wives of Mary's supporting barons and lastly Bess's servants, the servants of the barons and baronesses in attendance, the residents of her alms houses and a number of "poor women" who had been hired for the occasion.

The funeral sermon itself was delivered by Tobias Matthew, the Archbishop of York, who based it on the description of a virtuous woman to be found in Proverbs. The service concluded with Bess being laid to rest in the vault, and was followed by a funeral feast. And with that, Bess's funeral was over.

There remain the issues of considering Bess's legacy to posterity, and how she has been viewed by subsequent generations. Taking the latter question first, many of her earlier biographers were less than kind to her memory, seeming to echo some of the criticisms made of her by Shrewsbury at the height of their discord. Some of them called her shamelessly greedy, callous, calculating, shrewish, a termagant of a woman. This is far too harsh, and indeed inaccurate; more recently biographers have generally been inclined to adopt a more balanced view of her character. She certainly could be angry at times, but usually only after much provocation, and demanding, but such surviving evidence as there is suggests that as a general rule, she was adept at maintaining a good temperament. That evidence also suggests that she was usually generous and kind-hearted, at least to an extent, particularly with members of her family, who were very important to her. We know nothing of her relationship with Robert Barlow, of course, but there is no reason to think it was anything other than amicable, and she certainly enjoyed close and happy relationships with her second and third husbands (to the extent that when they died, they left her life interests over virtually all of their estates, which they were under no legal obligation to do). Even the first half of her marriage to Shrewsbury seems to have been successful, and happy, and under very difficult conditions thanks to the need to incarcerate Queen Mary of Scotland. As for the difficulties she encountered with Gilbert, and to an extent, Mary Talbot, Henry Cavendish and Arbella, it took a long time and much provocation before her relationships with each of them broke down, and when that happened, it was not generally actions on the part of Bess which triggered the estrangements. And even then, at the end, there was a measure of rapprochement, at least with Mary and Arbella.

Bess was also of course strong-minded and determined to succeed; she must have been else she would not have survived and thrived in the way that she did. Money certainly was important to her, as it was to most of her contemporaries, and it is true she liked to live well, but by and large she used the money she acquired one way or another to provide security for herself and her family, as well as to create a financial foundation upon which subsequent generations could build.

Which brings us to the first issue of describing her legacy. The financial fortune she accumulated was certainly part of this, and in many ways continues to be to this day, especially of course in the case of Chatsworth and the Devonshires. In physical terms, her principal legacy must be the prodigy houses she built and inspired. In genetic terms too, over the centuries which have followed her death, many of the members of the great aristocratic families (and some of the lesser ones as well), including royalty, have been able to claim descent from her. Many of those descendants would in the fullness of time play significant roles in history. To give just some examples, the Third Earl of Devonshire's son (yet another William) would play a central role in the Glorious Revolution (the ousting of King James II from the throne and the elevation of William and Mary in his place), and gain his dukedom as a result. The Fourth Duke of Devonshire would become Prime Minister, as would another of Bess's descendants, the Third Duke of Portland, and many others would hold high political office, both in Britain and overseas. And a grandson of the Second Duke of Devonshire, Henry Cavendish, would prove to be one of the greatest (and eccentric) scientists of the eighteenth century. Bess no doubt would be proud.

Lastly, in many ways much as Queen Elizabeth herself, her memory is a symbol and a reminder of the glories and dangers, strifes and passions, prejudices and achievements of the vanished world of Elizabethan England. And that is her legacy to us all.

Appendices

1. In which year was Bess born?

As previously noted, most biographers reach the conclusion that Bess was born sometime in 1527, probably sometime between June and November of that year. Some however have argued that her birth year was as early as 1521.

1521

The evidence supporting a birth year of 1521 comes primarily from two sources.

1. In 1604, Gilbert Talbot wrote to Robert Cecil and mentioned that Bess was in her eighty-fourth year. It is however likely that Gilbert was not truly aware of Bess's actual date of birth. Furthermore, it is no means impossible that he was being malicious in depicting his mother-in-law to be older than she actually was (and of course, it is possible that he simply made a mistake).
2. The epitaph on Bess's grave refers to her as being eighty-seven. The epitaph was only erected after the Restoration however, by which time no one was truly sure how old Bess was when she died.

1527

The following points support the argument that her birth year was 1527:

1. In sworn court testimony given during the time when Bess was fighting Sir Peter Frencheville for her dower rights, Bess is stated to have married Robert Barlow whilst she was of tender years, a phrase typically used to refer to someone under the age of sixteen. We know that Bess married Barlow a short time before Barlow's father died, and that he died on 28th May 1543.

2. If Bess had been born in 1521, she would have been around 22 years old when she first married. Not only does it seem very unlikely (though not impossible) that a woman of that age would have married a boy aged thirteen and a half, but it is very likely that by the age of 22, she would already have been married to someone else.

3. Assuming Bess did spend several years in the la Zouche household prior to her first marriage, if she had been born in 1521, she would have entered the la Zouche household in her late teens, say eighteen. This would have been late to join a noble household as a "guest member" (as opposed to simply to going as a servant, but there is no evidence that Bess went as such). On the other hand, if she was born in 1527, she would have been twelve when she joined the household, which would have been far more typical.

At the end of the day, there is no conclusive evidence for either argument, but on balance, a birth year of 1527 seems the more plausible of the two possibilities.

2. The Scandal Letter

The letter, which ultimately found its way into Lord Burghley's collection of papers, is undated but it is generally accepted it was written sometime in 1584; some have suggested it might date from as late as November 1584, but if this is so, it could not have been referred to in a letter dating from 5th January 1584. In any event, the letter, which is addressed to Queen Elizabeth, demonstrates extreme animosity on the part of Queen Mary towards Bess and sets out (amongst other matters) a long list of scandalous stories which Bess is supposed to have circulated concerning Queen Elizabeth. These include allegations that the Queen was exceptionally vain, that the Queen had enjoyed a long list of lovers (whose numbers included Leicester, Sir Christopher Hatton and Jean de Simier, an agent of the Duke d'Anjou who at one time was a potential suitor of Queen Elizabeth), that the Queen had some form of sexual malformation and that she was an object of derision at Court, not only to Bess but also the Queen's own waiting women, that Bess had sought Queen Mary's agreement to a proposal that Arbella should marry King James VI and more. There is no evidence that there is any truth at all to the allegations so far as Bess herself is concerned (though the Queen could appear vain at times and in 1585, Walsingham would indeed suggest that a marriage between Arbella and the Scottish King might have some advantages; in the event nothing came of this). Nevertheless, had Queen Elizabeth believed the allegations, Bess would have found herself in a very difficult situation. In fact, the Queen never believed the allegations for the simple reason that it would seem that she never received the letter (and no doubt we would have heard if she had). Rather, it seems either that the letter was never posted but later found in Queen Mary's correspondence after her execution, and that it subsequently made its way into Burghley's hands, or that the letter was sent but intercepted before the Queen could receive it.

3. What Happened to Bess's Immediate Family and Arbella?

Charles Cavendish

Charles remained happily married to his second wife Catherine, and remained lifelong friends with Gilbert Talbot (they died within a year of each other). Charles and Catherine eventually had two sons, William (known as "Will" in the family) and Charles. Will would become the First Duke of Newcastle-upon-Tyne.

Charles maintained his interest in building works; in 1613, he acquired Bolsover Castle and Welbeck Abbey from Gilbert Talbot, and during the last few years of his life devoted himself principally to various building projects. He died on 4th April 1617.

Henry Cavendish

After Henry sold Chatsworth to his brother William, he moved to a small estate at Doveridge in Derbyshire, and lived there unhappily with Grace until he died in 1616. Grace died sometime after 1625. He and Grace had no children, but ultimately a descendant of one of Henry's illegitimate children would found the line of the Barons Waterpark, whose family seat was at Doveridge.

William Cavendish

William Cavendish would continue to administer the estates he inherited from Bess and though he perhaps lacked Bess's financial flair, he ensured they stayed safe and well-administered during his lifetime. Indeed, he was prepared to venture into business areas that Bess had by and large avoided; he invested in the East India Company (founded in 1600) and involved himself in the slowly burgeoning trade with Russia. His interests also extended to the Americas, he was a supporter of the English colonisation of Bermuda and Virginia.

He was advanced in the peerage, being created the Earl of Devonshire in August 1618, though he had to pay £10,000 for the privilege. He died on 3rd March 1626, and was the last of Bess's sons to die. He was buried in St Peter's Church, Edensor, on the Chatsworth estate.

Frances Pierrepont

Frances continued to live at Home Pierrepont; her husband Sir Henry Pierrepont died in 1615. Frances died in January 1632, in the same year as her sister Mary also died. She was the ancestress of the later Dukes of Rutland and Kingston-up-Hull and the Earls Manvers.

Arbella Stuart

After Bess's death, Arbella continued to attend at Court until 1610, when she fell from favour with the King and the Queen after accepting an offer of marriage from William Seymour, the younger brother of Edward Seymour, to whom Arbella had sought to propose in 1602. William Seymour was twelve years younger than Arbella. The King refused to give his permission for the union, due to the proximity of both Arbella and Seymour to the throne, but Arbella and Seymour married secretly in the early morning of 22nd June 1610 anyway. When news of the marriage reached the King, Seymour was sent to the Tower and Arbella was ordered into the custody of Sir Thomas Perry at Lambeth. Later, she was ordered into the custody of William James, the Bishop of Durham, but before she could be moved there, in June 1611, both she and Seymour contrived to escape from their respective captivities. They planned to escape by boat to France, but before they could meet, Arbella was recaptured and sent to the Tower. Seymour managed eventually to escape to Ostend but would never see Arbella again.

Arbella remained held in the Tower for the rest of her life. Eventually, despairing that she would never be released, she refused to eat and in September 1615, succumbed to a terminal illness triggered by her hunger strike. She was 39.

Gilbert Talbot

Following Bess's death, Gilbert assumed control of those Talbot lands over which she had enjoyed a life interest, and worked to rebuild the family fortune as best he could. He was damaged politically by Arbella's fall from grace, and lost his seat on the Privy Council. He died on 8th May 1616. Having no surviving sons, his brother Edward succeeded him as the Eighth Earl of Shrewsbury.

Mary Talbot

Mary Talbot too was damaged by Arbella's marriage to Seymour, not least because she had provided financial assistance to Arbella when she tried to escape to France, for which she was sent to the Tower and heavily fined. By now she had converted to Catholicism, which also did not endear her to the Protestant authorities. In 1615, by which time Gilbert's health was beginning to fail, she was released from the Tower, but in 1618, she refused to testify before a commission assembled to investigate rumours that Arbella had borne William Seymour a child before she died. The result was that Mary was despatched back to the Tower, where she remained until 1623. She died in April 1632, the last of Bess's children to die.

Bess of Hardwick Timeline

June – November 1527	Probable birth of Bess
6th January 1528	John, Bess's father, purports to set up a trust to protect his lands from the Office of Wards
24th January 1528	Death of John Hardwick
2nd October 1528	First Inquisition Post Mortem into the Hardwick estate
September 1530	Second Inquisition Post Mortem – wardship established
1539	Bess probably joins the la Zouche household
8th December 1542	Birth of Mary Stuart
14th December 1542	Death of King James V of Scotland; accession of Mary Stuart to the Scottish throne
Early (May?) 1543	Bess marries Robert Barlow
28th May 1543	Death of Robert Barlow's father
24th December 1544	Death of Robert Barlow
1545	Bess possibly joins the Grey household
October 1546	Bess wins her dower rights claim over the Barlow lands
28th January 1547	Death of King Henry VIII, accession of Edward VI
20th August 1547	Bess marries Sir William Cavendish
18th June 1548	Birth of Frances Cavendish
1549	Birth of Temperance Cavendish (died 1550)
17th December 1550	Birth of Henry Cavendish
31st December 1550	Sir William Cavendish buys Chatsworth

27th December 1551	Birth of Bess's son William Cavendish
6th July 1553	Death of King Edward VI, disputed accession of Lady Jane Grey, accession of Queen Mary Tudor
28th November 1553	Birth of Charles Cavendish
12th February 1554	Executions of Guildford Dudley and Lady Jane Grey
31st March 1555	Birth of Elizabeth Cavendish
2nd March 1557	Birth of Lucres Cavendish (died 1557)
August 1557	Sir William Cavendish ordered before the Star Chamber
25th October 1557	Death of Sir William Cavendish, Bess "inherits" his debts to the Crown and acquires a life interest in Chatsworth
24th April 1558	Marriage of Mary Stuart to Francis, Dauphin of France
17th November 1558	Death of Queen Mary Tudor, accession of Queen Elizabeth
15th January 1559	Coronation of Queen Elizabeth
10th July 1559	Death of King Henry II of France, accession of Francis II. Mary Stuart becomes Queen of France
27th August 1559	Bess marries Sir William St Loe
October (?) 1559	Bess appointed Lady of the Privy Chamber
20th November 1559	Death of Lady Frances Grey
February (?) 1560	Attempted poisoning of Bess
November 1560	Lady Katherine Grey secretly marries Edward Seymour

5th December 1560	Death of King Francis II, accession of Charles IX
August 1561	Grey/Seymour marriage scandal erupts
19th August 1561	Mary, Queen of Scots returns to Scotland
1562	Marriage of Frances Cavendish to Henry Pierrepont
Summer 1563	Bess's debt difficulties with the Crown resolved
Early February 1565	Death of Sir William St Loe, disputes with St Loe family members over will
19th July 1566	Birth of James Stuart
24th July 1567	Abdication of Mary Stuart as Scottish Queen
Late summer/autumn 1567	Probable date of marriage of Bess and Shrewsbury
9th February 1568	Marriages of Henry Cavendish and Grace Talbot, and Gilbert Talbot and Mary Cavendish
16th May 1568	Mary Stuart arrives in England after fleeing Scotland
December 1568	Shrewsbury appointed custodial guardian of Mary Stuart
4th February 1569	Mary Stuart arrives at Tutbury
22nd April 1572	Shrewsbury and Bess enter into a deed of gift
2nd June 1572	Execution of the Duke of Norfolk
22nd August 1573	Mary Stuart commences first visit to Buxton

Early November 1574	Charles Stuart, Earl of Lennox marries Elizabeth Cavendish
Early November 1575	Birth of Arbella Stuart
Early April 1576	Death of Charles Stuart, Earl of Lennox
1577	Shrewsbury orders the commencement of the construction of Worksop Manor
7th March 1578	Death of Margaret, Dowager Countess of Lennox
Spring 1580	Growing estrangement between Bess and Shrewsbury
April 1581	Death of James Hardwick; Bess buys Hardwick Old Hall in June 1583
21st January 1582	Death of Elizabeth Lennox, mother of Arbella
August 1582	Francis, heir to Shrewsbury's earldom dies; Gilbert Talbot becomes heir
July 1583	Parting of Bess and Shrewsbury
July 1584	Shrewsbury harasses Charles Cavendish and Bess; Bess flees Chatsworth
September 1584	Shrewsbury relieved as custodial guardian of Mary, Queen of Scots
23rd December 1584	First commission of enquiry into the Shrewsbury marriage
December 1585	Mary, Queen of Scots moved to Chartley Manor
12th January 1586	Second commission of enquiry into the Shrewsbury marriage
July 1596	Babington Plot

October 1586	Trial of Mary, Queen of Scots
8th February 1587	Execution of Mary, Queen of Scots
Summer 1587	Arbella's first visit to Court
July 1587	Work underway at Hardwick Old Hall
Summer 1588	Arbella's second visit to Court
November 1590	Work commences on the construction of Hardwick New Hall
18th November 1590	Death of George Talbot, Sixth Earl of Shrewsbury
13th January 1591	Funeral of Shrewsbury
Spring 1591	Beginning of estrangement of Bess and Gilbert Talbot
November 1591 – July 1592	Bess and Arbella visit Court
17th January 1593	Bess buys the manors of Heath, Rawthorne, Stainsby and Owlcotes
15th March 1593	Charles challenges John Stanhope to a duel
Summer 1595	Francis Clifford attempts to recover Edensor lands
4th October 1597	Bess moves into Hardwick New Hall
Spring 1598	Construction commenced of Bess's alms houses
June 1599	Charles Cavendish attacked at Kirkby-in-Ashby
Early 1601	Bess orders inventories taken at Hardwick Old Hall and Hardwick New Hall; commissions tomb at All Hallows' Church, Derby

April 1601	Bess prepares new will
December 1602	Arbella seeks to propose to Edward Seymour
7th January 1603	Sir Henry Brounker arrives at Hardwick to investigate Arbella
End of January 1603	Arbella claims to have an imaginary lover
2nd March 1603	Brounker returns to Hardwick to investigate Arbella a second time
10th March 1603	Brounker arrives at Hardwick to investigate kidnap attempt
10th March 1603	Bess amends her will to disinherit Arbella and Henry Cavendish
24th March 1603	Death of Queen Elizabeth; accession of King James
End of March 1603	Arbella leaves Hardwick and moves to Wrest Park in Bedfordshire
20th April 1603	Gilbert Talbot entertains King James and his party at Worksop Manor
Mid-May 1603	Arbella visits Court
June 1603	The Bye Plot
Summer 1603	The Main Plot
Summer 1604	Arbella sends friendly greetings to her grandmother
February 1605	Bess falls ill; Arbella visits Bess
April 1605	William Cavendish created Baron Cavendish of Hardwick
November 1605	Gunpowder Plot

September 1606	Alethea Talbot marries the Earl of Arundel, leading in time to a partial reconciliation between Bess and Gilbert and Mary Talbot
Winter 1607/early 1608	The Great Freeze in England; Bess taken seriously ill
13th February 1608	Death of Bess of Hardwick

Bess of Hardwick Family Tree

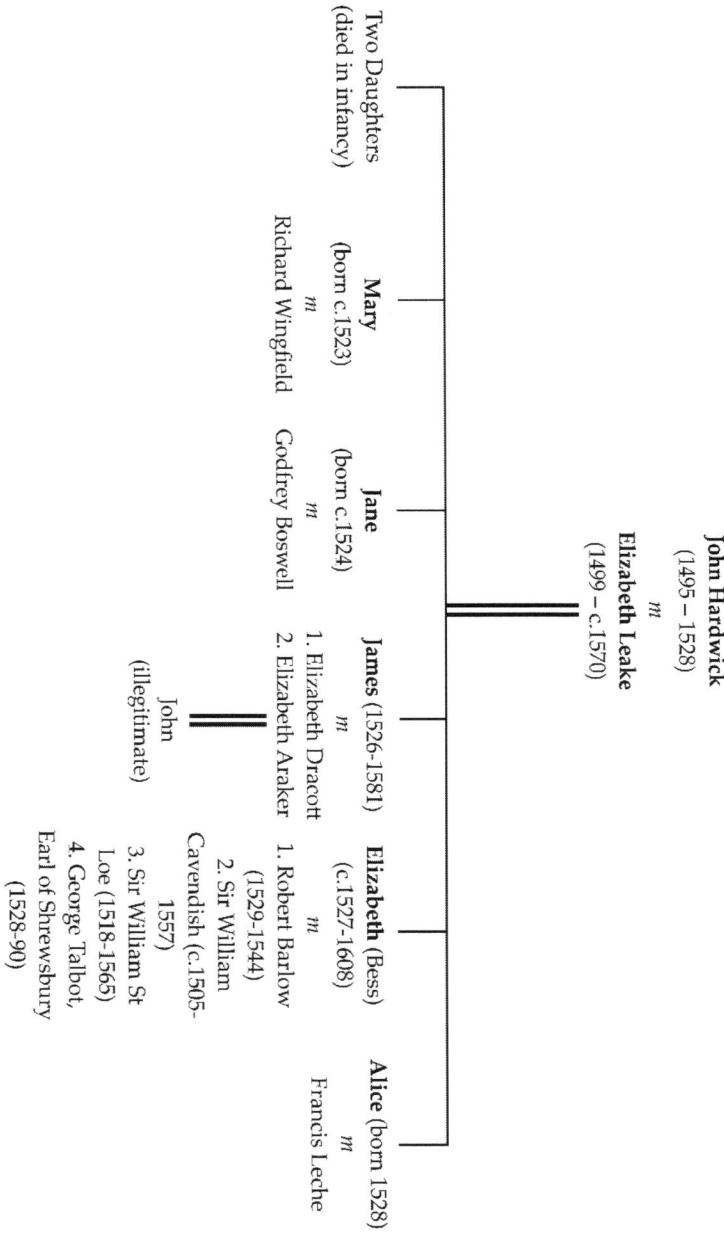

John Hardwick
(1495 – 1528)
m
Elizabeth Leake
(1499 – c.1570)

Two Daughters
(died in infancy)

Mary
(born c.1523)
m
Richard Wingfield

Jane
(born c.1524)
m
Godfrey Boswell

James (1526-1581)
m
1. Elizabeth Dracott
2. Elizabeth Araker

John
(illegitimate)

Elizabeth (Bess)
(c.1527-1608)
m
1. Robert Barlow
(1529-1544)
2. Sir William
Cavendish (c.1505-
1557)
3. Sir William St
Loe (1518-1565)
4. George Talbot,
Earl of Shrewsbury
(1528-90)

Alice (born 1528)
m
Francis Leche

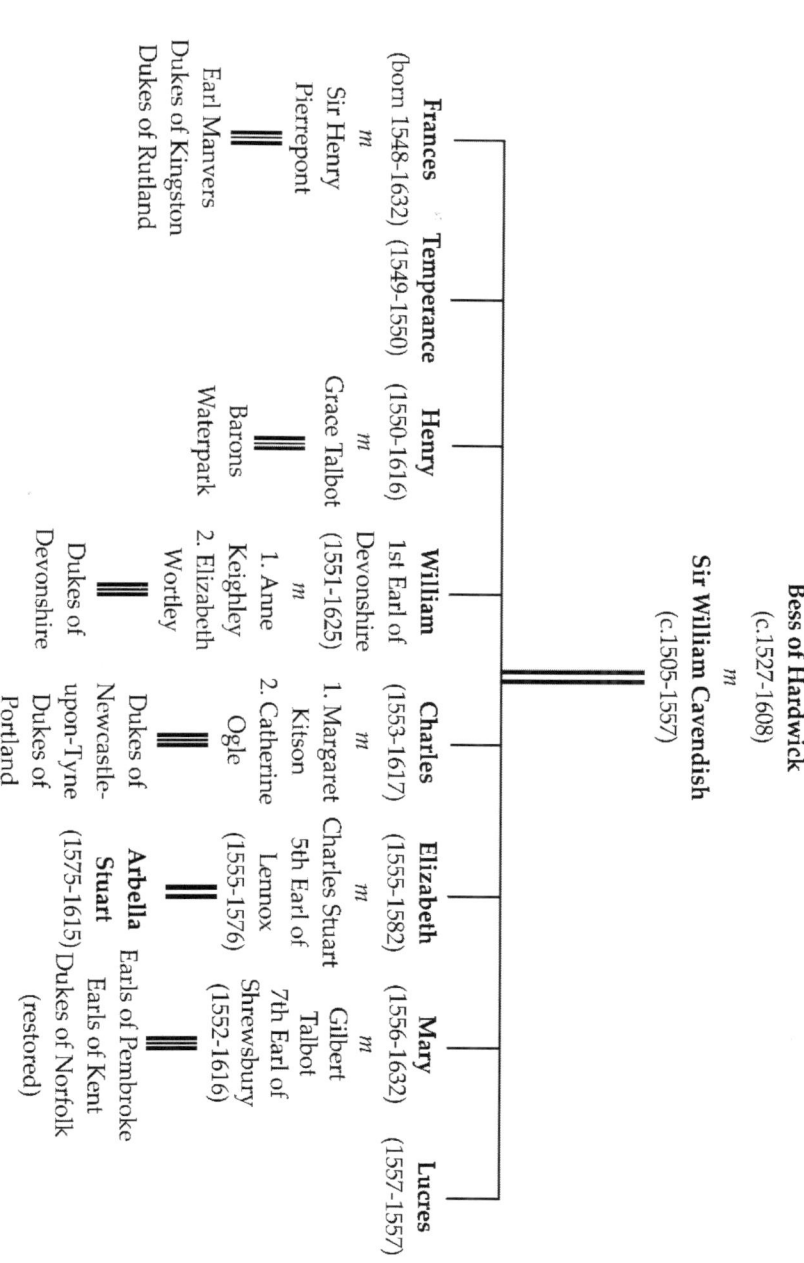

Bess of Hardwick
(c.1527-1608)

m

Sir William Cavendish
(c.1505-1557)

Frances
(born 1548-1632)

m

Sir Henry
Pierrepont

Earl Manvers
Dukes of Kingston
Dukes of Rutland

Temperance
(1549-1550)

Henry
(1550-1616)

m

Grace Talbot
(1551-1625)

Barons
Waterpark

William
1st Earl of
Devonshire
(1553-1617)

m

1. Anne
   Keighley
2. Elizabeth
   Wortley

Dukes of
Devonshire

Charles
(1553-1617)

m

1. Margaret
   Kitson
2. Catherine
   Ogle
   (1555-1576)

Dukes of
Newcastle-
upon-Tyne
Dukes of
Portland

Charles Stuart
5th Earl of
Lennox

Arbella
Stuart
(1575-1615)

Elizabeth
(1555-1582)

m

Gilbert
Talbot
7th Earl of
Shrewsbury
(1552-1616)

Earls of Pembroke
Earls of Kent
Dukes of Norfolk
(restored)

Mary
(1556-1632)

Lucres
(1557-1557)

Select Bibliography

Lord David Cecil – *The Cecils of Hatfield House* – Constable 1973

Jesse Childs – *God's Traitors: Terror and Faith in Elizabethan England* – Bodley Head 2014

Leanda de Lisle - *Tudor: The Family Story* – Vintage 2014

David N Durant: *Bess of Hardwick – Portrait of an Elizabethan Dynast* – Peter Owen Publishers 1999

Lady Antonia Fraser – *Mary, Queen of Scots* – W & N 2018

Mark Girouard – *A Life in the English Country House – A Social and Architectural History* – Penguin 1980

Sarah Gristwood – *Arbella: England's Lost Queen* – Bantam 2003

Kate Hubbard: *Devices and Desires – Bess of Hardwick and the Building of Elizabethan England* – Vintage 2018

Edmund Lodge – *Illustrations of British History, Biography and Manners volumes 1, 2 and 3* – John Chidley 1838

Mary S Lovell - *Bess of Hardwick – First Lady of Chatsworth* – Little, Brown 2005

John Pearson – *Stags and Serpents – A History of the Cavendish Family and the Dukes of Devonshire* – Country Books 2002

John Martin Robinson – *The Dukes of Norfolk* – Phillimore & Co Ltd - 1995

Agnes Strickland – *Letters of Mary, Queen of Scots, volumes 1, 2 and 3* – Henry Colburn Publisher 1842 – 1844

Alison Weir – *Elizabeth, the Queen* – Vintage 2009

Alison Wiggins - *Bess of Hardwick's Letters: Language, Materiality, and Early Modern Epistolary Culture* – Routledge 2019

Index

Author Biography

Wyn Derbyshire originally trained as a chemist before qualifying and practising as a lawyer. He is the author of various financial histories and biographies and currently lives in Hay on Wye in Powys, Wales.

Other Titles

Six Tycoons: The lives of John Jacob Astor, Cornelius Vanderbilt, Andrew Carnegie, John D. Rockefeller, Henry Ford and Joseph P. Kennedy

Dark Realities: America's Great Depression

Jean Paul Getty: "The meek shall inherit the Earth – but not its mineral rights"

Hetty Green: The First Lady of Wall Street